Returning home from Afghanistan with 70 pages of notes and no answers, the author embarks on a decade of citizen diplomacy to prove that ordinary people can impact world affairs.

Bold and brave. Connects readers to the other side of the world.
—Sana Momand, *The Wealthiest Woman in Afghanistan*

Abandoning narrow cultural fears and the comfort of familiar surroundings, the author launches herself into the unknown. After a decade of hard travel, she arrives at a point of calm and clarity.
—Duncan Lyon, *Sand Paper Stone*

To Mom

Afghanistan
and
Beyond

Confronting the War on Terror

Linda Sartor

Cune

Afghanistan and Beyond:
Confronting the War on Terror
by Linda Sartor
© 2022 Linda Sartor
Cune Press, Seattle 2022

Hardback	ISBN 9781951082574
Paperback	ISBN 9781951082314
EPUB	ISBN 9781614572626
Kindle	ISBN 9781614572633

Library of Congress Cataloging-in-Publication Data

Names: Sartor, Linda, author.
Title: Afghanistan and beyond : confronting the War on Terror / Linda Sartor.
Other titles: Turning fear into power
Description: Seattle : Cune Press, 2022. | Originally published as: Turning fear into power: how I confronted the War on Terror / by Linda Sartor. Mt. Shasta, Calif. : Psychosynthesis Press, 2014.
Identifiers: LCCN 2022013866 (print) | LCCN 2022013867 (ebook) | ISBN 9781951082314 (trade paperback) | ISBN 9781951082574 (hardback) | ISBN 9781614572626 (epub)
Subjects: LCSH: Sartor, Linda--Travel--Middle East. | Peace-building--Middle East. | War on Terrorism, 2001-2009--Social aspects. | Middle East--Description and travel. | Middle East--Social conditions--21st century.
Classification: LCC JZ5584.M628 S27 2022 (print) | LCC JZ5584.M628 (ebook) | DDC 303.6/60956--dc23/eng/20220416
LC record available at https://lccn.loc.gov/2022013866
LC ebook record available at https://lccn.loc.gov/2022013867
CPSNo: 07242022(11)

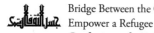 Bridge Between the Cultures (a series from Cune Press)

Empower a Refugee	Patricia Martin Holt
Confessions of a Knight Errant	Gretchen McCullough
Nietzsche Awakens!	Farid Younes
Muslims, Arabs & Arab Americans	Nawar Shora
Apartheid Is a Crime	Mats Svensson
Kivu: Journeys in Eastern Congo	Frederic Hunter
Arab Boy Delivered	Paul A. Zarou
The Wealthiest Woman in Afghanistan	Sana Momand
Music Has No Boundaries	Raf Gangat

Cune Cune Press: www.cunepress.com

Acronyms

AYPV – Afghan Youth Peace Volunteers
CD – Civil Disobedience
CPT – Christian Peacemaker Teams
IDP – Internally Displaced Person
IPT – Iraq Peace Team
IGC – International Governing Council (of NP)
INGO – International Non Governmental Organization
ISM – International Solidarity Movement
LTTE – Tamil Tigers
NATO – North Atlantic Treaty Organization
NGO – Non Governmental Organization
NP – Nonviolent Peaceforce
NPSL – Nonviolent Peaceforce Sri Lanka
PAFFREL – NP's local partner in Sri Lanka, an election monitoring NGO
RDF – Rural Development Foundation
SAVAK – Iranian Secret Police
TPNI – Third Party Nonviolent Intervention
TJCG – Transitional Justice Coordinating Group
UNICEF – United Nations Children's Fund
USAID – US Agency for Internal Development
Voices – Voices for Creative Nonviolence
US – United States
UN – United Nations

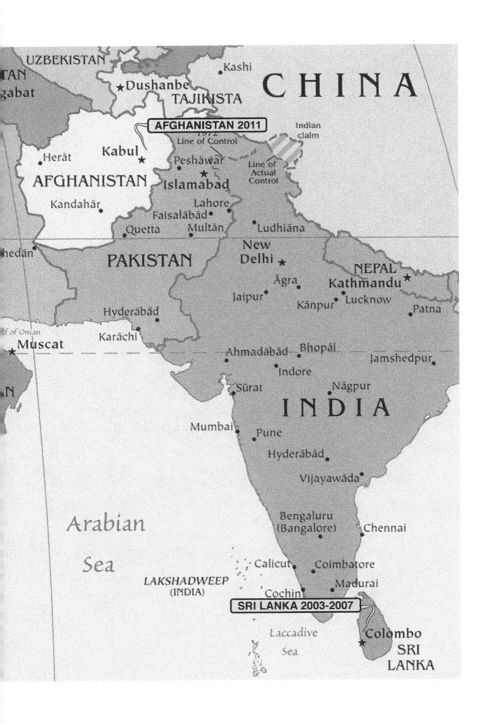

Contents

Photos

Introduction

IT IS LATE AFTERNOON WHEN ELEVEN internationals are walking together into Balata Camp from Nablus. As we get close to the village, a Palestinian ambulance passes us. Ambulances are the only Palestinian vehicles allowed out on the street during curfew. Suddenly, an Israeli tank further ahead fires a line of machine gun fire at the ground in front of the ambulance and us—a scary warning not to proceed further. At first, we are jolted and swerve to the side in unison. Someone reminds us what Starhawk told us at the beginning of our brief training—to "ground." We turn to walk the other direction.

The driver of the ambulance stops and lets all eleven of us climb aboard. The two Palestinians in the vehicle are grim as they take us around to another entrance into Balata Camp. It is growing dark and we know it is dangerous to be out after dark because soldiers can't see who we are. To get into the neighborhood, we have to walk past another tank. We clump closely together and put our hands up as we pass the tank. I reassure myself with the idea that it would be bad public relations for an Israeli soldier to hurt a US citizen, since their operations would not be possible without US funding.

This self-reassurance supports me in my two-week visit to Israel/Palestine in 2002 where I participate in peace activism with an organization called the International Solidarity Movement (ISM).[1] I describe my experiences in Israel/Palestine in Chapter 2. This book brings to life my peacekeeping and citizen diplomacy work during a decade, when I travel with several different peace and justice organizations to six war-torn countries.

Let me begin by revealing a little about myself. I don't particularly like traveling to other countries. The few times I traveled in Mexico, both as a child and again as a young adult, I felt uncomfortable on the streets among the poor local people—like I was flaunting my class privilege just by being there. I have found discomfort even traveling into more prosperous countries. In my thirties I took a trip with a friend to Scotland and Holland; I found that I was on edge, easily irritated, and not a pleasant traveling companion. Most importantly, I don't like traveling alone. Therefore, traveling alone into a war zone is essentially an outrageous idea for me.

I have always been an environmentalist and a peace and justice activist. When I was a middle school teacher in my forties, I went to the Nevada Test Site for a weekend every spring to engage in civil disobedience, protesting that the USA continued to test nuclear weapons using our tax dollars. Near the same time in the school year, I assigned my sixth-grade students to read a biography of Martin Luther King. While discussing the important contribution that civil disobedience provides to democracy in the USA, I could share a little about my personal experience.

Through telling my story, I hope to inspire readers to get more in touch with their own inner wisdom and to follow their hearts' longings even when it is scary. My belief is that our fears keep us small and prevent us from actualizing our full contributions, and that the powers of domination in our world create and perpetuate cultures of fear in order to stay in control. I hope that the more we all learn to accept fear and follow our hearts anyway (no matter how big or small are the tasks we are called to do), the more likely we as a global society will find our way out of the bad times in which we find ourselves now—times of war, torture, intolerance, economic crises, poverty, injustice, degradation of natural systems, global warming, and other environmental and cultural catastrophes.

In the face of these crises, it is easy to get caught in a sense of hopelessness that there is nothing one individual can do to make any significant difference and so do nothing. We need to find the courage to take the actions that our hearts are longing to take even when the odds seem hopeless and overwhelming and we know we may not see the results within our lifetimes.

My belief that fear is a powerful limiting force and distracts people from following their hearts' longings comes out of another involvement of mine; I guide wilderness trips called "vision quests." At the core of these nine-day experiences, participants spend three days and nights alone fasting in the desert (ritesofpassagevisionquest.org). While preparing to go out to be alone in the desert, participants often confront fears. During the time out when all distractions are removed from their lives for three full days and nights, they usually learn to listen better to their hearts' longings. Then upon their return from this solo time, they are confronted with the challenges and fears of bringing the guidance of their hearts back into their everyday lives.

Fears that emerge in preparation for the solo experience are of mountain lions, rattlesnakes, or being alone in the dark, for some examples. When initially facing such fears, it seems from a participant's perspective that his/her life is truly in danger. Yet I am familiar enough with mountain lions, rattlesnakes, and being alone in the dark to know that visitors to the desert can learn enough to be reasonably safe. Through this experience of guiding participants through confronting fears, I have witnessed how important it is to acknowledge and then to actually embrace the fears in order to learn from them. Yes, mountain lions and rattlesnakes are potential threats, but we can learn to be safer around them, and we can learn something about our relationship with fear itself in the process. I work with participants to better understand mountain lions and rattlesnakes so that they know how to respond if they should encounter one. We also work with the less concrete fears like fear of the dark. I encourage them to acknowledge and accept the fear (whatever the source) and then to get in relationship with it—to even have a dialogue with it—in order to learn the lesson(s) that the fear has to teach.

The experience of guiding these trips is critical in inspiring me to face my own fears and to not let them stop me from following my heart's longings. My heart leads me to make the decision to go to Israel/Palestine and beyond. The life threatening fears experienced by participants on vision quests are parallel to my fear that traveling into a war zone is life threatening. I use the same strategies in taking care of my fears as I suggest when guiding vision questers to work with theirs; I acknowledge and accept the fears and then learn as much as I can about the dangers I might face. Furthermore, I recognize that the thought of the risks can easily grow out of proportion when considered from a distance, and that experiencing the situation first hand is really not so scary when I am actually there.

© Asif

Linda in Afghanistan

When fear is denied and not faced, it has more power over us and prevents us from following our hearts' desires. I have seen that when vision quest participants learn to be with their fears in a new way, the limiting power of those fears decreases significantly. Witnessing the vision quest process many times has led me to hear my own heart's longings more clearly and thus face my own fears. My heart's longing is to change my country's commitment to military dominance in the world and stop the atrocities that accompany that military dominance. I feel called to respond in a way that is bigger than I have ever before imagined.

My intention in this book is to share some of my inner and outer journey during the ten years beginning on September 11, 2001, the day of the attack on the World Trade Center in New York City. My response to the way many US citizens and our government reacted to that attack is that I cannot sit still as if life is "business as usual." Protesting and educating aren't enough anymore, I need to take a stand with my body that as a US citizen my life is not any more precious than anyone else's life.

More About Myself

I'm single and live alone in my house as part of a rural intentional community. The community currently consists of sixteen adults and four children living in ten households. We share a sense of extended family and attempt to steward responsibly the land where we live. I love the natural world and have been devoted to taking care of the environment since I learned about the balance of nature in a fifth grade science lesson. I attempt to live my life in integrity with my values.

I have a PhD in integral studies and a master's degree in environmental education. As a young adult I was a naturalist in environmental education programs. Later I taught in middle school for eight years and then second grade for two. Since then, I have been adjunct faculty in a number of graduate programs, often working with students at a distance through the Internet. The vision quests I lead require a time commitment of ten days. I can get away for international work in between the vision quest trips as long as I have access to the Internet so I can continue my work with students. I've always enjoyed working and I live simply, so I have saved enough money to afford travel expenses.

My spiritual path has emerged over time and it is connected to the natural world. I have participated in my own vision quests several times and I spend much of my time outdoors. I meditate sporadically, do free-writing several times a week, and during the early years of this story I follow a regular practice of shamanic journeying in which I connect with a number of spirit guides who play a significant role in my ability to hear and follow my heart. The spirit guides in these shamanic journeys give me access to knowledge and wisdom that I have inside that may otherwise be difficult to access.

I'm an introvert and my usual tendency when I am with others is to hide out in silence as opposed to speaking up and being seen. One of the fears I face in this ten-year journey is a fear of being seen and not understood.

Chapter Summary

The book is written from personal journal entries, transcripts of my shamanic journeys, and e-mails written and received during those years (2001-2011).

In the first chapter, I tell the story of my tormented heart following the terrorist attack of 9/11, deeply troubled as I am by the way that leaders and others in my country are responding to that attack. I depict internal struggles along with the encouragement I find within as I discover and learn to accept my heart's longings. Despite the appearance of many good reasons to talk myself out of going, my inner voice relentlessly drives me to face my fears and to travel alone into Israel to join the International Solidarity Movement (ISM) in Palestine.

I cover my two weeks in Israel/Palestine in Chapter 2. I begin with four days in Balata Camp witnessing Israeli soldiers ransacking Palestinian homes and bashing holes in the walls to create passages for soldiers to use so that they won't have to walk on the streets, where they would be vulnerable to snipers. I also visit Jenin City, Jenin Camp, Ramallah, and Bethlehem, where I see and hear citizens' accounts of recent devastation in each of those places.

Although one of my fears while preparing to go to Israel/Palestine is that I might return with post-traumatic stress, I actually find after I've been home for a while that I am feeling more alive than ever (Chapter 3). Yet, President Bush continues to promote his "war on terror" and plans to bomb Iraq. I struggle now to discern what my inner voice is telling me to do next. My decision to go to Iraq to join the Iraq Peace Team (IPT) finally comes clear.

In Chapter 4, I join the IPT just a month before President Bush begins bombing Baghdad in 2003. This chapter covers my two-week experience in Iraq and also portrays life in Baghdad once the bombing begins through the eyes of the IPT folks who remain there after I return home.

Later in 2003, I am hired to be a field team member in the pilot project of a new international non-governmental organization (INGO) called the Nonviolent Peaceforce. We attempt to learn what it means to bring Gandhi's vision of a peace army of unarmed civilians into a real situation of violent conflict in Sri Lanka (Chapters 5 and 6). I go for multiple short-term (one to two month) sojourns during the first three years and then I stay for a final fifteen months during 2006 and 2007. Through vignettes of my time in three different field sites in the volatile North and East of Sri Lanka, I bring to life the beginning stages of the project.

Home from Sri Lanka in the final year of George W. Bush's presidency, I am concerned that he is talking about invading Iran next. I join a citizen diplomacy tour to Iran (Chapter 7). In keeping with the purpose of citizen diplomacy, I create and give presentations designed to introduce other US citizens to a different perspective of Iran and Iranians than the one our media provides.

Finally, in Chapter 8, I bring to life my experience with Voices for Creative Nonviolence in a delegation to Afghanistan in 2011. We spend time with the Afghan Youth Peace Volunteers and other "ordinary people" of Afghanistan getting to know how they feel about the presence of the US forces in their country.

The book concludes with my reflections on this journey as a whole, and what it means to be with fear while following my heart. As part of these Final Thoughts, I include a summary of four days in Bahrain that took place after I completed the first draft of this book.

1

My Tormented Heart

September 11, 2001

ITHOUGHT WE WERE TRULY GETTING BEYOND WAR. There had been the end of the Cold War between the USA and the Soviet Union, the tearing down of the Iron Curtain, and a ten year moratorium on testing nuclear weapons to name a few of the indications that contributed to that hope. I hear about the terrorist attack on the Twin Towers in New York this morning and driving through town this afternoon, I see a billboard that reads: "They attacked the wrong country." My heart sinks.

September 13, 2001

I am attempting to continue functioning as normal. After stretching, meditating, and having breakfast this morning, I go through a pile of unread mail, and I speak with my mother on the phone. She smokes heavily and is beginning to have difficulty climbing the stairs in her house. My brother Dale and I have begun talking to her about what she will do when she can no longer live there alone, but I don't think she is yet ready to accept a move.

I'm thinking about the class of first year teacher interns I have yet to meet, and whether or not the Cultural Consciousness Project (a project for which I am the lead faculty) will survive because the enrollment is poor. Molly Brown and I expect to have a draft of the *Consensus in the Classroom* book ready for readers soon. I met with my colleague Scout yesterday to discuss the vision quest that we are co-leading in November.

My life continues fairly normally while this major crisis lurks in the background—the US response to the terrorist attack on the World Trade Center and the Pentagon. I am extremely disturbed by President George W. Bush's reaction, as well as what I'm hearing about a backlash of hate messages towards Arabs and Muslims. Even if we in the USA knew who was behind the attack, I couldn't justify these responses, and we don't even know.

September 14, 2001

I engage in a shamanic journey today with a tape recording of shamanic drumming. The drum beat takes me into a trance state in which I meet various spirit guides. I provide excerpts from my trance journeys in several chapters to give readers a sense of the inner story that accompanies and supports my decisions and actions in the world. The italicized passages are the voices of the spirit guides who give me advice and encouragement.

Today, I ask for support in doing my part in bringing forth good relations among people all over the world.

Power dynamics are gradually shifting from the media holding the power to individual citizens finding your participatory power. As you each learn your own power as participants in society, you come more into creating the participatory reality that can actually change the power dynamics that are in place. So your work right now is learning how to come into your own power and how to inspire others to do the same.

That power is the love energy that wants to flow through everyone.

So how do we participate? How can I make a difference? Perhaps it is because I haven't had full access to my personal power that I haven't discovered those answers yet. I ask for support in letting things look chaotic and unclear. I'm learning to be with ambiguity and uncertainty.

I receive an e-mail about a call for silence at noon today for "American solidarity." I'm not interested in nationalistic solidarity. The overall response of US citizens as portrayed in the media seems to be that of concern over people in the USA who were injured or lost loved ones, but what about the rest of the world? At noon, I enter a moment of silent meditation in which I send my prayers to everyone, including Arabs and Muslims all over the world, and also even to President Bush and people who commit hate crimes.

September 16, 2001

It is difficult to function these days with the terrorist attack and the nation's response in the background of everything. I'm feeling more and more sad and frightened. With that underneath, when the usual everyday ups and downs come, the ups are shaded and the downs can get really low.

September 17, 2001

I'm heavy hearted to know that in the whole House of Representatives, only one congressional representative voted against providing the funds President Bush requested for military action.

September 19, 2001

Brace yourself. You're prepared and you're capable. You've got all that you need. You know what you need to know. You've got the skills and you've had the experiences that you need. That is all accessible. So it's up to you to trust yourself and trust that you'll go just where you're supposed to be, you'll know what to do, and you'll do it well as long as you stay centered, grounded, and present.

Being true to your heart provides protection. Just like what you teach people to do with fears out on vision quests. Prepare the best you can and know that you're safe from anything that isn't going to support you in carrying out your heart's work. You've got to stay true to your heart.

I don't know what to do in this world right now.

Yes, you do. You can't cop out like that. You can't shrivel. You can't hide out.

I don't know what to do to show up.

Yes, you do.

I yawn.

Just sit here. Just be.

I sit here in this very foreign place [in my mind] so far away from all that's familiar. The uncertainty, the ambiguity, the unknown—this is where I have to be present.

I don't know that I know.

That's my whole point. You know and you don't know that you know.

I'm still thinking that I don't know how to do this, but I'm not going to say that. I'm just going to pretend like I know.

My guide hears my thought even though I don't speak it out loud to her. *That's a good strategy,* she says.

September 22, 2001

What about the state of the nation and the world? My heart is heavy when I ask that.

Your intention is a good one—to find a way to be with integrity in this situation the way it is—and that will guide you in a good direction. Stay open to possibilities. This is your work. You don't know how it's going to manifest, but it will. There's no other more important work for you to be doing right now, because out of this place, your heart will open more and more and you'll find that your love is able to flow more and more—both in and out. You'll see what you need to see, you'll know what you need to do, and you'll do it without hesitation even when it's difficult, even when it's scary. What will sustain you is the passion that comes from your heart as it beats out the love that's there. Hearts circulate the love that flows through the world while also circulating the blood that flows through your veins.

You can't play small. You can't let your fears hold you back. You've got to stay full out visible even when you're scared—especially when you're scared. There's scary stuff out there, but there's also love wanting to flow, wanting to find its way through all human beings, wanting to clear the blocks that have created what looks like evil. You have to show up and be willing to not be understood, even though it's scary.

I keep my attention on being grounded, centered, and present even though I'm scared about what's next.

This is what it is to be alive. This is love. Keep your heart open, let the passion show, and let yourself show up fully as the loving entity that you are, without holding back. Remember that the best defense is an open heart. That's how you'll be safe. Keep all of your channels open. Bring your gifts forth.

September 23, 2001

I am attending a conference about shamanism this weekend. I participate in a ceremony during which a medicine man hands me a little bundle that he says contains "wolf medicine."

September 26, 2001

That wolf medicine bundle was handed specifically to you for a reason. Take on that responsibility with loving hands, open heart, and conscious attention. Let it be your guide, especially with regard to the world situation right now.

I look up Wolf in Ted Andrews' (1997) book *Animal Speak* that tells the symbolic meanings various peoples have given to different animals:

> Wolves are probably the most misunderstood of the wild

mammals. Tales of terror and their cold-bloodedness abound. Although many stories tell otherwise, there has never been a confirmed attack and killing of a human by a healthy wolf. In spite of the negative press, wolves are almost the exact opposite of how they are portrayed. They are friendly, social, and highly intelligent (p. 323).

. . . The wolf teaches you to know who you are and to develop strength, confidence and surety in that, so that you do not have to demonstrate and prove yourself to all.

. . . For those who have a wolf come to them, look for its energies and influence in your life to take twenty-two to twenty-four months (p. 324).

. . . Wolves show up as a totem to remind us to keep our spirits alive. . . . to listen to [our] own inner thoughts and words. The intuition will be strong.

. . . [The wolf] will guard you as it teaches you—sometimes strongly, sometimes gently—but always with love. When wolf shows up, it is time to . . . find a new path, take a new journey, take control of your life. You are the governor of your life. You create it and direct it. Do so with harmony and discipline, and then you will know the true spirit of freedom (p. 325).

October 4, 2001

It's hearts in collaboration that can change the world, can change the way things are, can do the healing job that needs to take place on the planet at this time, and then change the way humans relate to each other and to all beings forever. Here is where you reach that unreachable star. Here is where you find that for which you've been longing.

The more open you are to the infinite possibilities that exist, the more choice you have. So you can't be attached to the place where you live, you can't be attached to have things manifest in particular ways. You just have to be open to unknown possibilities, be comfortable with ambiguity, embrace uncertainty, know there are patterns, and expect the patterns to be bigger than you could ever grasp with anything other than the heart. The heart can expand large enough to be able to grasp the pattern that is behind what is. You just get to see glimpses—little pieces—in your everyday life.

October 8, 2001

How do we survive with intact integrity in this system the way it is?

We don't. We can't. We can't have integrity and survive in the system the way it is. We must change the system.

And where is a leverage point?

October 16, 2001

Since the USA started bombing Afghanistan this week, we had an unusual meeting Friday night at the intentional community where I live. We didn't do any business, but just talked about the war. I realized that I want to start a Living with War Support Group here in order for us to continue the conversation, to support each other to stay present to the fact that the USA is engaging in war, and to do whatever makes sense for us to do in the face of that.

The bombing in Afghanistan, how are we going to stop it?

You're being called forth right now by the scene in the world the way it is. Go forward with the intention of developing relationships fully, completely, and deeply— every one of them. The more you avoid coming fully into yourself and being fully in relationship with others, the more you are complacent and contributing to the state of the world as it is.

Sigh. I don't want to. I sort of enjoy playing small, sleeping, not opening my eyes completely, not opening my ears completely, not opening my heart completely, hiding out, hiding from myself, sticking my head in the sand—all of those ways of not being fully present, not fully paying attention, not being fully in relationship with myself and the other people in my life, not thriving.

I'm here to be alive.

October 20, 2001

The war in Afghanistan is in the background of everything. I don't see or antici-pate immediate resolution. I ask for the confidence and guidance I need in order to carry on with my life in a loving life-enhancing way.

November 13, 2001

I groan. I'm working on belonging again.

Remember unconditional love. It will help you feel like you belong wherever you are and by the way, you do belong where you are. Otherwise you wouldn't be there.

You need to learn about being in constant motion and in constant change and being fully present anyway. Learn to relax no matter where you are or what you're doing.

November 15, 2001

I'm still looking for right action. I'm finally starting the Living with War Support Group here in my community. I want to prevent us from going into denial about what's happening in the world and the responsibility that we as US citizens have in that. In support of that purpose, members of the group will meet to share what we know about the world situation, how we feel about it, and what we might do individually and/or collectively in response to it.

March 4, 2002

Three and a half months have passed, during which President Bush's ongoing war on terror slipped further out of my consciousness. There was no significant mention of the war in Afghanistan or my relationship to it in my personal writings and journeys.

The four members in the Living with War Support Group met again last night. We haven't been finding the time to meet much at all. I still don't see a clear right action for myself for now. Just being present to the reality of the situation, I am trusting that my right action will emerge in its own timing. At least, the group helps me stay awake to what is going on. Having the group is in alignment with Joanna Macy's (1983) work—being with the difficult feelings with each other and getting out of isolation. In isolation, we tend to spiral down into powerlessness. Together, we might bring a glimmer of hope to each other, which can help in keeping us ready for worthwhile action. I think that full presence with myself, with others, and with the situation is required for the right action to come through—the leverage point. That thought gives me hope anyway.

Eagle is sitting on my shoulder, working with me on expanding more fully into all of who I am. We are on the Sacred Mountain walking around the lake where Jumping Mouse met her doom by becoming prey to Eagle (Storm, 1972). *Another perspective according to Eagle is that it wasn't Jumping Mouse's day of doom; it was her day of glory, because she became Eagle that day. She became more fully who she was meant to be in the world—powerful, far-sighted, visionary, teacher Eagle. Jumping Mouse heard the call, faced her fears, followed the longing in her heart, and learned about her contribution in a big way.* Maybe Eagle will teach me more about what I have to give and how to give it.

March 11, 2002

I reflect upon some of my limited travels in the past—one time with a friend in Holland and Scotland, and another time with a boyfriend in Hawaii. Both times, I proved to be a difficult traveling companion due to my insecurity about traveling. I don't like being in unfamiliar places. I don't like not knowing the language and culture. I don't like the feeling of flaunting privilege that I get in some places like Mexico. Furthermore, I love being home. I love my house, the land where I live, and my community. I have no desire to travel.

March 14, 2002

Eagle says, *Just remember that I'm here coaching you in this task of expanding more fully into who you are at any time in any place. It's time for you to be doing that.*

My understanding is that expanding should feel comfortable—I'm supposed to relax into it.

It could feel comfortable and yet, you will be pushing an edge, so you won't always feel absolutely secure. In fact, you'll always feel just a little bit insecure, so feeling a little bit outside of your comfort zone is quite all right. There is a difference between feeling off center and feeling like you're pushing an edge in order to expand more and more fully into all of who you are. The idea is to stay centered even though you're pushing an edge. Push the edge from a centered place and you expand from that center out. The more you do that, the more gifts you give to all those around you without even trying.

March 20, 2002

I've registered for a women's retreat in May on the island of Iona in Scotland. I have to get there on my own and as I reflected just last week, I don't like traveling alone, so deciding to do this is a big deal for me.

April 2, 2002

A member of my community Michelle told me about the work the International Solidarity Movement (ISM) is doing in Israel/Palestine. ISM is a peacekeeping group that is attempting non-violently to get in the way of violence there. Here is an opportunity for protesting the violence perpetrated by the US government's war on terror. Using our tax dollars and calling it foreign aid, the United States is essentially financially supporting the Israeli soldiers in their abusive treatment of Palestinians in Palestine. Joining ISM would be action that demonstrates that my life as a US citizen is not any more precious than lives of other people in the world. The idea is pretty exciting and it feels pretty right to me.

There's a part of me that acknowledges the danger yet feels strong and certain. I'll work out whatever I need to work out in order to be there. I'll say my good-byes just in case and ask for blessings, and then take off. I've been waiting for this ever since September 11. It's so great to finally have a possibility for action that feels so right.

April 3, 2002

I send an e-mail to Thom in Ann Arbor, Michigan; he works with ISM in Israel/Palestine. I express my interest in joining and request more information. Before I go, I need to organize my living trust to help my brother Dale take care of my finances just in case I should not return. It is good to have something meaningful to be thinking about doing.

April 4, 2002

I get an e-mail back from Thom telling me about ISM:

> Our campaign, which started in August 2001, is based on the philosophy and commitment to militant nonviolent action exemplified in the Civil Rights campaigns of Dr King, particularly in Birmingham and Selma. ISM is led by a *tremendous* group of people. You will not find a more disciplined, committed, brave, and loving group of people who are committed to meaningful peace and justice. We are international citizens in partnership with Palestinians and Israelis. We are Jews, Christians, Muslims, adherents of other religions and none. We are not siding with Palestinians against Israelis, but siding against violence and for a

peace based on justice that will allow Israelis and Palestinians to live in mutual security.

Obviously, this is dangerous work, and some of the volunteers have been injured and wounded, but if you decide to go, please accept my assurance that you will be among people who have experience in facing danger, and in taking proper precautions. If you join us, I can promise that you will have a life-changing experience that will radicalize you.

On Monday, I spoke with Adam Shapiro of ISM. He was weary from a sleepless night of shelling. Obviously it is very, very dangerous right now, and there are indications that the Israeli authorities may be prohibiting groups they think might join ISM from entering.

Thom follows with the specific information ISM wants me to include in a letter introducing myself. He is leading a group in two to three weeks (April), and he invites me to come in May, June, or July if I can't make it for his April trip.

As part of my response, I tell him I was ready to go to Afghanistan to do this sort of thing had I heard of anyone who was organizing something. I think it is atrocious what our government is doing, and believe that marching in various protests isn't enough to change things; educating people about the atrocities isn't empowering anyone to really make a difference; and to sit back and do nothing is comparable to people who didn't do anything to change what was occurring in Nazi Germany.

I also tell him that because of other commitments, May, June, or July would be easier for me than his trip in April, and I respond to questions he sent to further introduce myself. One question was about my spirituality; I say that I meditate regularly, I follow an earth-centered spiritual path, most of my guidance comes from within, and I am committed to words and actions that are for the good of all beings.

April 6, 2002

I dreamed a lot last night. I don't remember any of the specifics, but I do remember that my dreams were intense and I attribute the intensity to this plan to go to Israel/ Palestine.

I attend an event in Berkeley at which a man named Rob speaks about his experience with ISM in Israel/Palestine. He says that an increasing number of ISM folks are in the West Bank and they are mostly Europeans. ISM is an organization that is one year old and was started by Palestinians and Israelis. Rob participated in a two-week program of non-violent civil disobedience, "But," he says, "the civil disobedience evolved into human shield work that was terrifying."

Rob gives a bit of history of the conflict. In 1948, other countries in the world without consulting Palestine gave 55% of the land and water to Israelis, who are 35% of the population. The West Bank of the Palestinian Territories is now completely surrounded by Israel. Gaza is a separated section of the Palestinian Territories and shares one border with Egypt. Israel taxes Palestine and uses that money for occupation. Israeli settlements in the already-small Palestinian Territories are inhabited by ultra right-wing religious settlers. Many of these settlers are from the USA. Israeli control of all the water resources is also an issue.

Rob says that internationals who go there have a hugely potent effect relative to their numbers.

April 7, 2002

I'm wondering about my Israel/Palestine trip—how it will work and how I can know that this is the right group. I will check with people I trust.

April 18, 2002

The decision to go to Israel/Palestine has gotten more real and my resistances are showing up now. I learned from the people at ISM that I could go any time and so I'm trying to figure out when to actually do it and how to tell Mom and Dale. My fears about traveling alone are looming. I wish there was a group scheduled or that at least one other person would join me. I am not looking forward to contacting the people in my life who are important to me to tell them what I am planning to do and why, but I want to do this because I think it is important to give each of us a chance to say anything that needs to be said between us and I want to ask for their blessings.

My friend Penny has been to Israel/Palestine. She knows many of the ISM people there and she knows Rob, the one who did the presentation in Berkeley. She expresses concern about my going to a war zone and she suggests that I talk to Rob. I feel a little foolish about the triviality of the questions I want to ask: how to prepare, what travel arrangements to make, what to pack, and such. I fear that asking such questions reveals my feelings of vulnerability about traveling alone when the more important concern is the violence that is occurring there.

Maybe I'm just really not ready to do it. I also wonder what I'm missing by not being part of a training here, which would be the experience if I were going as part of a group like the group that Thom is preparing to take soon. How do I best prepare myself psychologically? I wish I wasn't so alone with this. I need guidance and support. People in my life whom I have told just say something like, "That's not something I would do. I admire your courage."

I think I'll wait to call Mom until I've gotten a little clearer about my plans. I start a list of everything I need to do to prepare. It includes making contingency plans for any commitments I have scheduled following the trip just in case I don't return when planned. Michelle has volunteered to be my support person here. She will make media contacts, communicate with the others in my life, take care of my cat, and do anything else that I need done here so that I can be fully present while I'm there.

It's a big deal, a life shifting experience.

I pray for support and guidance, clarity, trust, surrender—whatever it is that I need in order to be able to do that which is calling to me. Help me to talk to my mother in a way that she understands, that she can live with and accept. I don't know how often I'll be able to call her to let her know I'm okay. She's got to know it's okay no matter what happens to me. It's as it should be, as it has to be.

Help me to know how to be safe, as safe as one can be. To be in a war zone is like the ultimate in what I've avoided all of my life—what I just can't understand. Help me to know whatever it is (if anything) that I can do to help heal the situation.

April 19, 2002

I hear back from Thom today. He says ISM is asking for a two-week commitment. He gives me an idea of the cost of housing, food, transportation, and logistics. He suggests entering Israel as an individual or couple because groups are getting turned away. I am to give him my travel information once I make my travel arrangements, and he will send that information on to George S. R., with ISM in Palestine.

Thom lists the kinds of tasks in which ISMers sometimes engage while in Palestine:
- Providing protection for civilians by staying with families in refugee camps, villages, and towns.
- Accompanying ambulances.
- Helping deliver food and aid to families, if needed.
- Being part of nonviolent protests, if organized.
- Documenting the facts, either through cameras or video or writing diaries to be published through e-mail and Internet.

Thom mentions that this summer is to be "Freedom Summer;" named after the Freedom Summer in Mississippi, which provided a turning point in the Civil Rights Movement.

I feel better tonight about going to Palestine, probably because I told Mom and Dale today. I feel more positive, less residue of depression than I have had since September 11, and the whole idea brings back memories of adolescence and teen years—those exciting righteously rebellious times in the 60's. I think about poor Mom and how she probably thought she was finished with needing to worry about me once I grew up. For me to follow my heart and spirit is to go ahead and do this, and I'm glad for the opportunity.

April 21, 2002

Following my friend Penny's advice, I speak with Rob today. Remembering in his presentation in Berkeley that he had described quite a fearful situation in Palestine, I ask how he is feeling now about his experience. He says that he is finding it difficult to process. He is busy with media and organizational stuff here, but he still cries a lot and feels impatient. He says he thinks he needs to go to therapy to take care of some post-traumatic stress. At the same time, he feels people should go if they want to. "Nothing is completely safe." He goes on to say that it is unclear just what is needed now in Palestine—there is a sort of chaos.

Rob suggests that I should get to know the area and have some good contacts. In contrast to what Thom said that I will be among people who have experience in facing danger and in taking proper precautions, Rob warns that in his experience the ISM people aren't necessarily wise about making decisions. "You must make your own decisions about what's right for you." He advises me that it is essential to have a mobile phone, which I can rent at the airport.

I ask questions about whether a credit card is useful, how drinkable the water is, and what to tell or not tell to the travel agent. He says I need a good story to get into the country because Israel is sending peace activists back home from the airport, and warned me not to say that I'm a tourist visiting the Holy Land.

April 22, 2002

I'm waiting for my friend Peter before I make my reservation to fly to Israel, because he is considering whether it's possible to go with me. I know I'll feel 100% better if he goes with me. I think about my other upcoming trip to Iona in Scotland—how simple that seems and feels in comparison now. I look forward to an enjoyable vacation there followed by a quick week at home with lots of busyness, and then I'll be on my way to Israel/Palestine.

Today's lesson has to do with the fears you are facing about the horrors and terrors that you might witness, and how you're going to cope with them and learn from them. You will find the gifts, the contributions that await you in that untapped resource of your fears. Humankind has suffered many thousands of years of abuse that humans have brought upon each other. It's not about understanding it; it's about being with it with your heart open. Great possibilities can emerge only through the process of accepting it all—that this is what is, not that it is okay.

It's about being with the fear and going ahead anyway. It's about inviting in the fear and talking to it, listening to it, dancing with it, embracing it, and then seeing the other possibilities; and also seeing that there are more possibilities still existing in the unknown, because we don't have labels or the mental constructs that help us to understand all that is there, and in that chaos is the magic that can heal. An open heart can synthesize and create that which has never been created before that you've dedicated your life to bring forth through the vessel that is you, contributing to the healing that you so profoundly desire.

April 24, 2002

I receive a long e-mail from George Q. (a Palestinian working with ISM) that provides much information about coming. He writes that the Israeli government has declared martial law in Ramallah and Bethlehem, making it illegal for foreign civilians (including press) to be there right now. He warns not to say anything about Palestinians at the airport. I will have to get to Jerusalem on my own and then they will put me in touch with people for training and escort to Ramallah. Further, he states: "Please be aware that our activists have come under Israeli fire. So your unarmed, foreign civilian nature is no longer a safety jacket. Israel wants us out."

George Q. includes some instructions (which he says are a bit out of date) about what to expect while coming into the airport. If authorities try to refuse me entry, I should demand to be allowed entry. There may be a few hours of waiting and psychological game playing before they'll let me in. He advises that I shouldn't undress naked or do anything that violates my personal integrity at the security check, and warns me not to accept an offer to have personal items taken away and sent later. Finally, he cautions that leaving Israel to come home could be even worse. It could take much longer and feel nastier. He recommends staying calm and cool, and reassures me that I will catch my flight.

George Q. also includes an outline of what to expect once I get there. It shows check-in, orientation, and non-violence training—all of which are supposed to be facilitated by one or two ISM people. I find that bit of structure to be reassuring.

April 25, 2002
Peter is unable to join me. Now there is a very slim possibility that another good friend named Doug, will. I doubt he will, but I would love it if he did. And I'm trying not to get too attached to that idea.

April 28, 2002
A Quaker peace activist couple who are friends of mine contacted the members of a family they know in Israel. I was hoping to ask the Israeli family if I could use their name at the airport as my reason for coming to Israel, but they told my friends that they are much too frightened themselves right now to be of any help to me.

April 29, 2002
An acquaintance gives me the phone number of her brother who lives in Israel and is an ex-Israeli soldier. When I call, he describes the situation as a "real war in the field supported by a propaganda war in the world" and he states that they are playing for high stakes. He warns that well-meaning peace activists get caught in unpleasant cross-fire, that we're being manipulated, and that I shouldn't count on Palestinians to have consideration for my welfare. He advises that I stay tuned in to where they're placing me and what I'm doing. He speaks of suicide bombers, shooters, and other bombers who target civilians, and believes that the Palestinians are building and hiding bomb factories.

I buy my ticket today. I will be traveling alone.

Now that I have my flight scheduled, I send e-mail messages to many of the people in my life and they respond with blessings and prayers. I'm feeling strong because I'm going to be carrying lots of people's prayers. The decision was difficult, and now that I've finally bought my ticket, I feel energized. At least I feel good right now.

The thing I need to trust is the intention, my reason for going and ISM's reason for existing and for supporting the actions that it supports. I stand for peace and justice. I want the people there to know that though I'm from the USA, George W. Bush does not represent me. I don't want to be blinded by illusions of smallness and separateness that are created in me by those in power who try to take the aliveness out of us by giving us false fears.

May 1, 2002

I receive an e-mail today from George Q. asking me to come in July for Freedom Summer instead of in June as I have planned. Ay yi yi! It's too late now to tell me that; I already have my ticket! Receiving this e-mail re-stimulates my feelings of insecurity.

May 6, 2002

I'm now in the women's retreat on the Isle of Iona in Scotland. I want to make the most of being here in terms of whatever it is that I need to do to further prepare my mind and spirit for my trip to Israel/Palestine. I have fears I must face, fears I must let live. I need to distinguish the fears that I really need to honor from those I do not need to allow to alter my path. I tell participants on vision quests that they will know the difference; I want them to trust that so they will stay on their path even when the unnecessary fears are present. I pray to trust my own discernment, so that I will know to keep going when it really is okay, and that I will know when it is not. I pray for good guidance in terms of all that I still need to do to prepare to go, both while I'm here on the Isle of Iona and once I'm back home. And I pray for guidance for making this time of preparation as stress-free as possible.

May 8, 2002

I am stressed, wanting to make the most of my time here on Iona as preparation for this all-important scary trip, and I don't feel like I've been getting any clear messages. I'm in a place of darkness and unknowing, the place of fear; but also the place of mystery and healing.

May 10, 2002

I'm feeling weighted down right now. I heard news about Palestine. There was another suicide bombing on Monday. Israeli President Sharon cut his meeting with George W. Bush short to go back to Israel and now tanks are lined up outside of Gaza, just waiting for the go-ahead to enter. I'd been hoping that the prayers people have been sending would have made a difference for the good there, but it is difficult to see anything good about this right now.

May 11, 2002

Today I get a good clear message that I just need to be fully present here and now on the Isle of Iona and that's the best preparation I can do. I see that I've been living too much in the future, thinking about my trip to Israel/Palestine. Being present takes lots of practice—at least for me.

I will go ahead, with all that is in me: fear, confidence, faith, trust, and openness to learning and contributing. I will listen well and seek openings, which I trust will lead to where I might make my best contribution(s). When I stay present, I find and stay on my path.

The fearful part of me is living in a cloud of dread. I'll be glad when it's June 11 at 9:20 pm.—when I arrive back in San Francisco Airport after flying home from Israel. I acknowledge that I am in the future; I just can't put it out of my head.

May 13, 2002

Still in Iona, I have a brief meeting with one of the leaders of this women's retreat, whom I have respected as a mentor since I met her a year ago. She reaffirms that from her perspective it is right for me to be going to Israel/Palestine and she gives me some advice: "Pay attention to where you need to be and what you need to be doing. Put a circle of protection around yourself and then let go of the fear; your spirit helpers will be with you and you can trust that." She confirms that if I get caught by fear, it could be more dangerous.

May 16, 2002

I'm back at home now. I receive a communication about the ISM Freedom Summer campaign, emphasizing the need for training before going. The trainings include: history, geography, and background of the conflict; media training; non-violence training and philosophy; first aid/street medic training; role plays for non-violent direct action as well as non-violent resistance to invasion; cultural sensitivity and orientation. But, alas, there is no such training available for me here at this time. Also the message says that each delegate should have a support team to be responsible for fundraising, media, legal support, contacting embassies and congress people, emotional support, and emergency contact. I'm thankful for Michelle, who is fulfilling many of those roles for me.

Mom sent me an article she found in her local newspaper about an ex-Berkeley man who got arrested in Israel while working with ISM. She underlined the part that says that ISM is a pro-Palestinian group. I think she thinks that I'm collaborating with the enemy. Up until now, Mom has been helping me with a big needlepoint project that I have undertaken (six chair cushions for a dining room set I inherited from her mother). She stops working on the needlepoint project at this time. She says that she doesn't want to work on it because she doesn't want to think about me right now.[2]

A community member gives me a copy of an e-mail dated May 12 that was forwarded to her from someone in Jerusalem. On the subject line it says: "Women in Black Israel Update." Women in Black is an organization of women all over the world who stand every Friday in silent vigil against war. The following excerpts give a glimpse of the way it is in Israel/Palestine right now from an Israeli peace activist's perspective.

> This week had its measure of horrors—Palestinian bombs in Rishon, Letsiyon, and Beersheba, the Israeli army re-invading Tulkarm and enforcing cruel curfews elsewhere. . . The ranks of the refuseniks—soldiers who refuse to serve the occupation— are growing. . . The Israeli media now refrain from giving this phenomenon any publicity, as part of its policy of acting as cheerleaders for the government, rather than reporters of Israeli current events. . . Several thousand Palestinians are being held in "administrative detention"—no trial, no due process, no exposure of the evidence—under the accusation of being terrorists. . . Elsewhere, a brave group of activists entered Ramallah to defend against attempts to expel Arafat, as rumors to that effect reached the public. . . Peace Now held a rally last night in Tel-Aviv, as some 100,000 Israelis turned out to demand, "Get Out of the Territories Now!" This was the largest rally since the al-Aqsa Intifada began twenty months ago.

May 17, 2002

Michelle organized a community gathering last night to support me in the Israel/ Palestine trip. I shared what I know and what I don't know about what I will be doing with ISM. I think I took on some of the fears of some of the folks who came, because I awoke in the middle of the night with a feeling of anxiety. I've been waking with that feeling often ever since I made the decision to go. I must be working with my anxiety in my dreams.

I'm feeling most unsettled and anxious right now with the uncertainty about whom I will be meeting and what I will be doing upon my arrival. I've learned that the two Georges with whom I have had e-mail contact are both here in the USA doing a speaking tour right now; that means they will not be there in Palestine when I arrive. Yikes! What am I doing?

At the same time, I am feeling like I'm getting stronger and stronger about this whole idea.

In my process of connecting with everyone in my life about my plans, three different people from three different parts of my life have urged me to contact David Hartsough, who is one of the founding members of the new organization called the Nonviolent Peaceforce (NP). The Nonviolent Peaceforce hopes to carry out Gandhi's vision of having a large trained "peace army" of civilians from around the world who are non-partisan and unarmed to be deployed in places of violent conflict such that their presence reduces the likelihood of violence and opens the political space for local peacemakers to do their work nonviolently.

I finally make the call and speak with David Hartsough today. He tells me that ISM members are very committed and that most of the people are younger. He also tells me a little about NP. According to David the focus of ISM is on supporting Palestinians, and NP will try to be non-partisan wherever they end up going. NP is considering doing a pilot project in Israel/Palestine as one of three possible locations (Sri Lanka and Columbia are the other two), but NP is currently still working on developing infrastructure and will not be getting people into the field until at least June of next year.

I am sending a bio and purpose statement to Michelle in case she has an opportunity to submit something to the media. Here are my thoughts about my purpose: 1) as a US citizen, I want to get in the way of abuse that is funded by our tax dollars; 2) I want to do what I can to bring peace with justice to the area; and 3) I want to listen, observe, feel, and let my intuition work on what my right action is while I'm there and for determining next steps after I return. My commitment to addressing this particular conflict is not any greater than to any other conflict in the world, but I see Israel/Palestine as a possible leverage point (like an acupuncture point) in a dysfunctional global system.

Intentions I identify are: to raise local media visibility by making a local connection to an international event, to help boost the growing non-violent resistance movements in Israel/Palestine, to build relationships with civilians and activists in Palestine and Israel, and to return home and inspire others to take action.

Michelle helps me list ways to take care of myself while I'm there: getting adequate rest, breathing deeply, eating regularly, finding time alone, and also spending time with other internationals to discuss and listen.

May 18, 2002

Today is Mom's birthday. My family (Dale, sister-in-law Judy, and niece Angie) and I visit her at her house. Michelle comes by for a bit to meet the family while I am here. My plan is to be in touch with Michelle fairly regularly while I am in Palestine and to call Mom twice a week, if I can. Michelle will be sending out emails to my list and will call Mom on a regular basis to tell her what she has heard from me and to reassure her that I'm okay. Dale and Michelle will be in touch in case of emergency.

After Dale, Judy, and Angie leave Mom's house, I ask her if she wants me to stay to talk anymore and she says, "No," that she doesn't want to think about it anymore. She is angry that I'm going.

May 19, 2002

I speak with a friend who is a Native American of the local Pomo tribe. She tells me that in her tradition, women are the keepers of peace and that we can make a difference. She says, "Listen," and warns me not to let the Western educated political person I am dominate the grandmothers' voices. She asserts when the grandmothers tell me to step back, that I need to step back. They will also tell me when to go forward. "That's part of the protection," she says. "We're not led by ourselves—we're led by the women that came before us. Those women over there know to listen to the voices of their grandmothers. Men don't. Women will help each other learn to listen for those voices."

She reassures me that the voices are loud and clear, so I won't have a doubt, and she emphatically warns, "Don't be alone over there. Not for a minute. There is no reason to be alone. Be in numbers. A rare person walks this earth alone. Only prophets and medicine people do that."

May 20, 2002

Though I felt strong and ready the other day, today I feel weak, doubtful, and hesitant. I'm really concerned about Mom. Also, some of the people with whom I spoke on the phone yesterday don't want me to go and I seem to be taking on some of their fears. I wonder, "Is it my own fear or other people's fear for me that I am feeling?" And if I can't tell when I am here by myself in my place of power at home, how will I be able to discern that when I'm over there?

I'm currently quite preoccupied with writing a message to the big e-mail list I've created to whom Michelle will be sending updates whenever she gets a call from me. I wish the Georges would respond to my last message to them, but maybe they aren't reading e-mail while they are traveling in the States. I am feeling frantic again.

Breathe deeply. Just keep breathing deeply.

May 22, 2002

I speak with a friend's brother who is from the United States and recently traveled in Israel. He tells me about his experience while he was there. He warns that as foreigners, we don't know the danger clues; and he says that the secret is to hook up and go out with people who understand. He also reports that time frames aren't exact because of all the complications of living and traveling there, so people don't show up when expected. He advises me not to get upset when this occurs; it's just a cultural difference.

May 23, 2002

I am feeling anxious. The preparation for this trip is taking a lot of psychic time, energy, and space so I am barely able to accomplish anything else. Mom still wants me to decide not to go. Yesterday, I spoke with my co-leader for the June women's vision quest to be sure she feels prepared to do the pre-trip meeting by herself, just in case I don't make it back in time for the meeting.

I speak with a colleague's student (Judith) who lives in Israel. I ask if I can use her name at the airport for my story of why I am coming to Israel. She is fearful of letting me do that. Also, she thinks I need to learn more about the situation into which I am going. She agrees to meet me at the airport when I arrive in the country to help me rent a mobile phone and find a taxi.

I wish I knew more about what to expect once I get to the hotel in Jerusalem. I'd like to know whether any other ISM folks will be there, who I'll initially be meeting and when, and what I'll be doing. Recently, I read advice about traveling in Jerusalem that I need to pay people who give me help with directions and that I need to bargain to buy anything. Learning that just adds to my anxiety because I'm thinking, "How much should I pay for directions?" and the whole idea of bargaining is disturbing to me. I guess I could still decide not to go.

Then there is what I learned in the phone conversation yesterday—that I may have to wait for a long time when meeting up with people—coupled with my Pomo friend's advice to not be anywhere alone. I hope I can hook up with some ISM women soon after I arrive in Jerusalem.

I send an e-mail to the hotel asking for directions from the airport and they respond quickly. I speak with my friend Penny who has spent some time in Palestine and ask about appropriate gifts, bargaining, tipping, and eye contact. She gives me contact information for people she knows there. She says that if I get there and can't reach anyone to call her. That's reassuring.

Penny gives me a much-needed pep talk. She says that I have the resources to get through this. She suggests making it an adventure and trusting myself. Trust that when I run into a problem, I can figure it out or find someone to help. Trust that I'm being guided and that I have the information I need inside me. She advises me to feel the fears, but not to let them be in control—to dispel panic and discipline myself to think clearly. She reassures me that people are hospitable and will take care of me. I can say I need help, ask them what to do or which way to go, and take their lead. They want to protect me. She says that it's less volatile there now than it was a month ago, and she advises me to let my reason for being there guide me.

Tonight, I wait up late to contact Yvonne in Israel at a time that works for her; it is late for me due to the time difference. Penny gave me her name and phone number. Yvonne is a member of Women in Black and is willing to let me give her name and address at the airport. I can say that I'm visiting her as my reason to come into the country.

May 23, 2002

I ask to trust what Penny says that I do have all the resources that I need in order to take care of whatever situations arise; and also what my mentor in Iona said about the protection and guidance that I have. I ask for a sense of adventure. That's something new for me, to be feeling excited about travel as opposed to dread. I'm dedicating this trip and everything I say and do to the good of all beings.

I am a tough woman who will survive every challenge, and learn from it. Just like what I would tell participants on a vision quest—everyone who comes my way is my teacher. Unlike in the wilderness, my teachers during this trip will most likely be in human form. For me that takes more trust and courage.

May 27, 2002

The members of my community and a few other friends say goodbye to me at a gathering at my house that Michelle initiated. During the gathering, they put together a necklace of beautiful beads; each bead is given a blessing. One of the teenagers gives me the blessing of optimism. She says, "I respect you so much for what you are doing. Stay optimistic for my sake."

I am also gifted with the following poems from two community members.

To Linda By Ken

tonight I heard someone say that you were in one another's
spiritual-support-group

tonight as I seek to find
words or thoughts
that can fuel your vision
and nourish you
in some phantom-felt
dark hour—I simply smile
and nod my head
in YES
and ADMIRATION
and APPRECIATION
and probably other 'tions"
but most of all
for being in
my spiritual-support group
(even when I didn't realize
I had one)!

tonight I am sending
you something from my heart....
yes, you are definitely
"walking the talk" Yes!
and being courageous
and a lot of other "things"....

but you have inspired
many by your actions
and convictions and
your friendship and
leadership inspire me
and help me grow

help me examine my own beliefs and will travel
with me always
you know this
but I do so
love you and
walking along side
of you in this lifetime!

For Linda From Pen
_____

The grass in the meadows
The cool leafy shadows
The speckled fawns
will be here

The hills turning golden
The raspberries ripening
The throaty frogs calling
The waters deep, cool, and green will be here

The velvet cattails swelling
The night sky spinning
The cool morning air breathing
 The golden light at dawn
The rosy tint at eve
Will be here awaiting your return.

Go with our love—Be there in strength—Come home to us soon!

2

Israel/Palestine

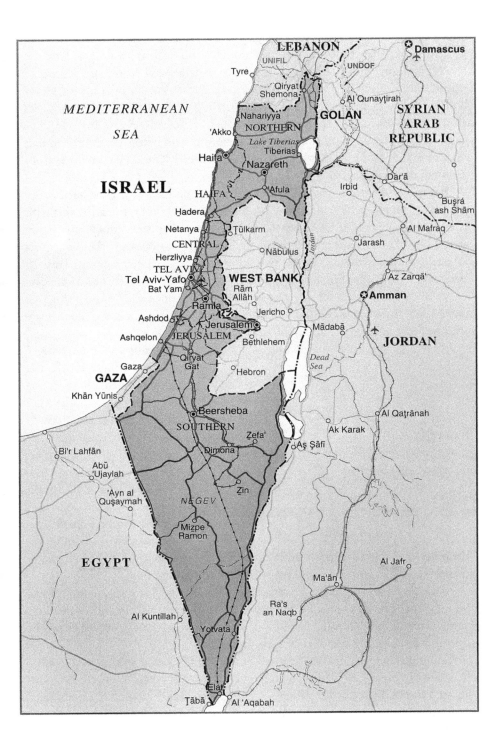

May 28 and 29, 2002

A T JFK IN NEW YORK, even though my San Francisco flight is late arriving, they take their time and put me through a full security treatment. First the officer questions me about why I am going to Israel and who I am visiting. I stumble in my answers because I can't remember what Yvonne does for work, nor do I know whether or not she has any children. I think to myself that it is probably difficult for him to believe that she is such a good friend that I would want to go visit her at this time, and I am relieved when he moves on to the familiar questions about who packed my bags and whether I have taken anything from anyone I don't know.

The officer escorts me to the carry-on baggage check where after putting my daypack through the machine, they open and search it. They are doing this with two other men from the USA as well. One of the men has been through this many times. He jokes about it and I relax a bit. Two Israeli guys escort the three of us into a back room where there are two other Israeli men and a woman. They do body checks on each of us with the wand. Then the first two escort us to the gate where our checked-through luggage awaits us. They open each piece of luggage and go over it with a wand. The last call for boarding is announced while they are still checking our luggage and holding us there at the gate.

I arrive in Israel May 29, 2002

© Mats Svensson

Getting on the plane, I see that the flight is full. The flight attendant shows me to one empty seat in the very center of the center row with two seats on each side. I'm thankful that the people on either side of me are kind. An Israeli man who speaks English is on one side and an older Israeli woman who does not speak English on the other. The flight is already an experience of Israeli culture. All the announcements are first in Hebrew and then in English and kosher food is served.

As we de-board the plane, I overhear a man talking with someone on his cell phone. Once off the phone, he tells his wife that there have been major warnings about terrorist attacks in the last couple of days. I wonder to myself what people are supposed to do in response to such warnings.

Going through customs on this end of the flight is a breeze compared to what happened in New York. The woman questions me, but seems to believe my story about Yvonne. In retrospect, I realize that this is probably when I should have asked that they not put the Israeli stamp directly into my passport. Having an Israeli stamp in my passport makes it impossible subsequently to use that passport to get into any Arab country. I had been warned about this, but I hadn't been clear about exactly when and where I needed to actually make the request.

As planned, Judith meets me at Ben Gurion Airport in Tel Aviv. She calls herself a Jewish mother because of her concern for me. I'm sorry that she won't be there for my return trip through Tel Aviv; she's going to the States for a weekend class. Judith helps me rent my cell phone and find a taxi (service). She gives me her cell number to stay in touch, explains that the best way to respond to the warning of a terrorist attack is to avoid crowded places, and asks me to call her when I get to the hotel.

Along the ride from Ben Gurion Airport to Jerusalem, we stop at a checkpoint where there is a man behind a machine gun pointed in our direction—quite a powerful image, which I probably won't forget for a long time.

Two women ride in the service (that's what they call a taxi here) with me—both Jewish New Yorkers visiting family. They had met on the plane. They can talk with the Israeli service driver who speaks only Hebrew. The one woman who is most friendly to me is appalled when I tell her where I am going to be staying the night. "That's Arab! What do you want to go there for?" She is really frightened for me even though I'm not Jewish and warns, "It's like going into Harlem." She wants me to change my mind. "The friend who told you to stay at that hotel is not a friend," she says.

The service driver is afraid to go inside the wall in this Arab section of Old Jerusalem and drops me off at the New Gate, a block away from my hotel. I am relieved to find that it doesn't feel scary at all. I stop to ask a woman shop owner if she speaks English and I confirm the directions I have. After checking in at the hotel I call George N. at the ISM office (still another George); he says there is an English woman named Josie who is currently on her way back to the hotel.

Once settled in my room, I call Judith and then Mom. It isn't long before Josie arrives. I note that she is young, probably in her 30s (I'm forty-nine). She tells me of her adventure getting back here from Bethlehem today. Her service dropped her off in the wrong place and she had to walk alone for a while. She encountered two men with whom she didn't feel comfortable and then she found another service to take her where she needed to go. Her story unnerves me. I share with her that people I trust have told me not to be alone while I'm here. We acknowledge that we are glad to be together now.

We meet Michael, who is another ISM team member. I note that he also appears to be in his 30s. The three of us call George to learn what to expect tomorrow. Plans are not complete yet, but we may be going to Ramallah.

Josie and I walk about ten blocks down narrow shop-filled streets to Jaffa Gate. Some of the men at the shops make comments as we pass. I think they are interested in us both because we are Western women and because they wish to sell us something. Josie seems comfortable enough and that helps me feel more comfortable. We are charmed into a shoe shop and I buy a pair of sandals. I figure that I am probably paying more than I need to pay since I don't bargain, but at least my money is going to a Palestinian (who I assume may be more in need than an Israeli, given the current situation). He offers us tea and at first, I refuse. But Josie accepts and I remember learning somewhere that it is offensive to refuse such offers, so I also accept.

The shopkeeper goes off with Josie to show her a cash machine, and I am left back at the shop with the shopkeeper's brother, who flirts with me. I make it clear that I'm not interested. He says not to trust anyone but his brother and himself. I think to myself, "Why would I trust you and not anyone else?" It's dusk. Josie returns and as we walk out of the shop, there are other male shopkeepers wanting our business and/or our attention. The shopkeeper's brother catches up to us and offers to show us a place for dinner. Josie agrees, but when he starts to take us outside the wall of Old Jerusalem, I say that I don't want to get so far from the hotel. Josie decides to stay with me and we say goodbye to the shopkeeper's brother.

We find a great place to eat. Josie has a couple of beers. I don't feel comfortable drinking alcohol, because of the cultural norm that women don't drink in public. Besides, I don't want anything to hinder my sleep tonight.

The walk back to the hotel is a little scary for me just for being in this unfamiliar place of which others have shown fear, and feeling the vulnerability of being two Western women out after dark, but in actuality I find there is nothing to fear.

May 30, 2002

George will contact us this morning. There are eight internationals already in Ramallah and they are planning an action in four days; they will be breaking open a road block. Josie, Michael, and I will have to get to Ramallah from here; from what we have heard, the checkpoints between here and there are numerous and daunting.

I'm already thinking about the logistics of my return to the airport. The three of us have different return times, so I'm already fretting that I will have to do some careful planning in order not to be alone for my trip back out of the Palestinian Territories. At the same time, I muse over the fear of the Jewish woman from New York whom I met in the service and how limiting fear can be.

I reflect on my feelings about traveling. I recognize that I might be more likely to enjoy traveling if I were to do it in such a way as to get to know the people to some extent, rather than just seeing the sites as a tourist. I also think about my misgivings about flaunting privilege. Perhaps as an international peace activist I can use white skin privilege to do something that really serves the local people.

At breakfast, a Palestinian man who works here at the hotel asks me where we are going today. I tell him we might go to Ramallah. He says that he tried to get there yesterday, but was detained seven hours at the checkpoint and then he came back here. His home is in Ramallah, he grew up there, and all of his family is there. He's grieving what is happening there and he seems pretty hopeless. Later he asks me to deliver something in writing that he says is medical; I think it may be a prescription. He needs help delivering it because now he needs to be working here the next couple of days.

After breakfast at the hotel Michael, Josie, and I go out into a part of Old Jerusalem where there are many shops. There are so few tourists that all the shopkeepers are desperate to sell their goods. When we go to lunch, we see two cafes right next to each other both vying for our business. We have to choose one and when we do, the other café owner looks angry. He seems desperate. Then a boy comes by selling postcards. I don't want a postcard. I think about just giving him some money; then I realize if I did that, I'd be swamped by other children also wanting money.

An incident that occurred in Bethlehem is on the news. I can't understand the language, but the voices of the people on the street are angry. Our waiter translates: There have been curfews in Bethlehem and a mentally retarded girl was arrested for being out on the street. When the Israeli authorities arrested her, other Palestinians came out to protest. The authorities wouldn't even let her talk to her parents and then they took her away.

I manage to nap one to two hours in the afternoon. I think I need time alone as much as time to sleep right now. I feel pretty full of grief from these glimpses inside people's lives here. Another international named Annie arrives.

One of the guys who works here seems to think I'm interested in him. At first, I don't realize what is happening. Once I do, I feel uncomfortable. He catches up to me when I'm walking back to my room after dinner, and asks to get together later.

I say, "No."

He says, "Why?"

I say, "Because that's not what I came here for." He apologizes and turns away.

After dinner, the four of us internationals go to a hostel just outside Old Jerusalem at Damascus Gate, where we meet with Starhawk and Neta (who are to be our ISM trainers). I am happy that Starhawk (Star for short) is here. I've read several of her books and I trust her. Being in her presence gives me confidence.

Star and Neta had been chatting late the night before. Neta is very tired and asks for help "organizing" the training. I don't know exactly what she has in mind, but I think to myself that I'm good at organizing things, so I volunteer. After the meeting, Neta takes a cigarette break, and then we talk. She needs someone to help her focus on all that needs to be done—which is mostly contacting various people. She takes time to chat with others while I'm making the calls.

I stop making calls for Neta at 11:00 pm. Josie and I walk back to our hotel. The streets of Old Jerusalem are still quite full of activity—not as much as during the day, but much more than I expected this late. The people who are out are all male. I wonder whether I'm being naïve or if it is just because Josie seems confident that I don't feel afraid.

For the second night in a row, I don't sleep much; I am wide awake well before sunrise.

May 31, 2002

When we begin the training, there are sixteen of us (men and women). Star barely begins introducing consensus decision-making when we decide to attend a Women in Black rally in central Jerusalem. During the rally, Neta hears that Israeli tanks are moving into Nablus. After multiple phone conversations, Neta and Star in consultation with the ISM office decide that we will go to Nablus rather than Ramallah; and that we will go even before we do more training.

We pack day packs with things we think we will need for a few days and leave much of our luggage at the hostel where Star and Neta have been staying. While we are traveling, all sixteen of us seated in a fifteen-seat van, Star demonstrates how to use a bandanna to protect against tear gas. Neta asks if we are willing to risk our lives. I take a moment to check in with myself, and then I say, "Yes. I made the decision to come here because I wanted to demonstrate that my life as a US citizen is no more precious than anyone else's life."

© MATS SVENSSON

Palestinians at windows inviting us in.

The van takes us as far as it can go before we come to a roadblock (a pile of rubble that we can only cross on foot). From there, it is a bit more than an hour walk through the countryside into Nablus. When we are at the top of a hill, I manage to get a call through to Michelle.

As we enter the town of Nablus, the people come out on their balconies to welcome us. Because they are under curfew, they are not out on the streets. I perceive their expressions of joy in seeing us; my eyes fill with tears. I imagine how it might be for them to view this group of sixteen internationals walking into town showing that we care, after the threat of the Israeli tanks that entered earlier. In our group are ten from the USA; a woman from England (that's Josie); men from Japan, Iceland, Denmark, and Australia; and Neta, who is an Israeli citizen of Canada married to a Palestinian man who lives in Nablus. The curfew only applies to Palestinians.

Once we get into Nablus, we split into two groups. Six go to the hospital where they will accompany doctors and drivers in ambulances. The other ten of us walk at least an hour further into Balata Camp, which is now more like a village of permanent homes for Palestinian refugees who moved there generations ago. Along the way through Nablus, we view much destruction that took place in April. A journalist from Jordan joins us. Three Palestinian men walk in the middle of the group for a short while until they get to their homes.

It is late in the day as we get close to Balata. A Palestinian ambulance passes us. Ambulances are the only Palestinian vehicles that are out on the street during curfew. A tank further ahead fires a line of machine gun fire at the ground in front of the ambulance and us—a very scary warning not to proceed further. At first, we are jolted and swerve to the side in unison. Someone reminds us of Starhawk's teaching to "ground," and then we turn to walk the other direction.

The ambulance stops and we all climb aboard. The two Palestinians in the vehicle are grim as they drive us around to another entrance into Balata Camp. It is growing dark and we know that it is dangerous to be out after dark because soldiers can't see who we are. We see that we have to walk past another tank. The eleven of us clump closely together and put our hands up as we pass. I keep reassuring myself with the idea that it would be bad public relations for an Israeli soldier to hurt a US citizen since their operations would not be possible without our funding.

It is dark by the time we get into the outer edge of Balata. Immediately, Palestinians are at their windows inviting us into their homes. Two of the men, one other woman, and I go into one of the houses. The others go into a neighboring house.

There has been a power cut; family members lead us up the stairs in the dark. I really have to use the toilet and ask for that immediately. It is a Western toilet, but there is no toilet paper. Instead there is a squirty thing that I don't know how to use. I fumble in the darkness, managing not to squirt too much water all over myself and the bathroom, and then re-join the others.

I'm relieved for a moment just to be inside a comfortable home. Then one of the men of the house uses a flashlight to point out the bullet holes in the ceiling from shots during the April Israeli invasion. Star and Neta come to the door. They have decided to stay in this house as well. I'm glad, because I feel more secure being in the same house with our two trainers assuming they have more knowledge and experience about this situation than any of the rest of us.

The women of the house serve us a tasty meal of cold cuts and pita bread by candlelight on the floor in the upstairs room. We learn that during the day the soldiers had gone through the whole village of Balata Camp arresting every man between age fifteen and fifty. Members of this family want us in their home because two men within the age range are still in the house. One of them is mentally disabled and was traumatized by the April invasion, so he refused to go when all the men were called out today. His brother, who happens to be a school psychologist, had decided to stay back with him. Eighteen extended family members live in this house.

While we make phone calls to press contacts, the women and older children of the family spread narrow mattresses with pillows and blankets on the floor. We four women offer to sleep downstairs in the front room so that we are the first encountered if anyone comes to or through the front door. The two international men sleep in one of the upstairs rooms.

We go to bed about midnight. I lay next to Starhawk. At 1:30, she is on the phone in a live radio interview. I don't sleep much and it seems that I spend a lot of the night listening to the other three women snore. The next day, I hear from them that they didn't think they had slept much either.

June 1, 2002

We gather around a tablecloth laid out on the shiny tile floor of the sunlit upper room that had been our candlelit office last night. The family serves a delightful breakfast of eggs, potatoes, and a dish of something green and spicy. Caoimhe is an international from Ireland who has spent a lot of time here in Balata Camp and is providing guidance to Neta. She arrives after breakfast and suggests that we go out for a little tour of Balata Camp. We leave our day packs behind because we expect to be back within about twenty minutes.

As we walk, many families invite us into their homes to show us damage caused by the soldiers. In one house, a gunshot had exploded a gas tank used to fuel their

© Justin Mcintosh

Checkpoint

stove and the whole corner of the kitchen had been blown out. The soldiers had pulled everything out and turned things over inside the room as well. Neta listens to a woman who has six children and translates that they have run out of food.

Suddenly we hear a scream; soldiers are entering homes. We realize we need to get into action and try to split into three groups in order to cover more area; but it is difficult to divide into groups for several reasons: few of us have experience, we didn't really have any training, and not many of us know the language. I start out with Caoimhe, Starhawk, and the journalist from Jordan; but before we actually split away from the others, Caoimhe and Star disappear into one home that soldiers have entered. The Jordanian journalist seems fearful and I don't feel confident being with him, so I decide to stay with Neta and the rest of that group.

We enter a house where the soldiers are in the process of bashing through the shared wall from the neighboring house. Neta starts talking in English through the wall, pleading with the soldiers to come through the door instead of doing such damage. Neta speaks all three languages (English, Hebrew, and Arabic), but she later explains to me that she usually doesn't let the soldiers know that she can speak Hebrew.

We learn that the reason the soldiers are breaking through the wall is that they are making a passageway so that Israeli soldiers can pass through the Palestinian houses rather than walking on the streets where they feel vulnerable to snipers. After bashing a door-sized hole into the common wall between two homes, they spray paint graffiti-like arrows on the walls to mark the route through the rooms.

Neta asks that they at least let us move the family's belongings away from the wall so that the things don't get trashed more than necessary. We start moving the piles of mattresses, pillows, and blankets. Then we hear screams from a neighboring house, so Neta suggests that some of the group go over there. The others do and I stay back with her. After moving all the family's possessions away from the wall, we stay with the mother and her adult daughter while the soldiers continue to break open the hole.

At one point while the soldiers are in their house, the daughter offers them some tea and they don't even respond to her. Later she comes out with a tray of lemonade—with enough glasses for them and us. Again they ignore her.

The soldiers finish opening the hole in the one wall, then move the four of us into a back room and shut the door. They go on to the wall on the other side of the house. There is a cabinet of dishes and they do move it fairly carefully, but the mom is worried and upset.

I go out of the room to use the toilet. The soldier who is guarding the door speaks English and asks me why I am here. I say, "Because I disagree with my government supporting you in doing this." Later, Neta hears him tell his colleagues in Hebrew that I am crazy because I am disobeying my government. Upon hearing Neta's translation, I realize that questioning and disagreeing with decisions made by the government—something that I take for granted in the USA—is not necessarily a norm here.

The soldier does not allow the mother and daughter to go to the bathroom or get a drink of water. Some of the family's things do get broken. After the soldiers finish bashing through the wall on the other side of the house and pass through it, the four of us sit down for lunch and tea. The mother tells us that she is thankful for our being there because she is afraid.

While we are still at the table, a man of the house comes back. He tells us that he has been beaten. He describes how he and others were told to put their hands against the wall and then were beaten. He was hit with two weapons in his stomach and mouth and was bleeding from the mouth. The soldiers checked his ID and then let him go. He had been held from 1:00-10:00 p.m. yesterday during which time he was given no food or water. He and others were made to walk in front of a tank that was shooting into the air. When they were released, they were told not to come back home for three days. They are staying in a nearby mosque. I don't know how he managed to come back at this time. I miss some of the explanations about what's going on because of not knowing the language; Neta doesn't translate everything.

I feel stress and I feel Neta's intensity. I don't fault her for not translating everything, but I feel baffled and it adds to my stress not to fully comprehend all that is going on around me.

After lunch, Neta and I go down the street where the soldiers are continuing to carry out their orders. They have closed another family into a room in their house. Through the barred window, the family members beckon us and then beg us to come in and be with them, but the soldiers won't let us through the front door. After spending a little time at the window with that family, we go on to the next house in order to be there when the soldiers arrive. We meet a grandfather peacefully rocking a baby in a cradle and the mother with two other children. The house is gorgeous—sparkly clean, walls painted in rich colors, shiny floors, and house plants.

We visit with the family a while. Neta makes calls to see what others in our group are doing. We learn that the six who had stopped at the hospital when we arrived in Nablus yesterday have come into Balata Camp today. A Palestinian mom with a two-week old baby had been injured and taken to the hospital, separating her from her baby who needs to be nursed. Some of our group members are working on reuniting them.

Things quiet down while the soldiers take a break. The family next door is still closed in their room. Again we ask to sit with that family and the soldiers tell us that we can after their break, but that turns out not to be true. Every time the soldier who speaks English completes an exchange with us, he slams the door.

We return to the house with the grandfather and cradle. He says, "Let them destroy the wall. We will just rebuild it," and laughs. I'm impressed by how the Palestinian people we have met seem to be able to adjust to the situation whatever it is and still maintain kindness, hospitality, and a sense of humor.

While the soldiers are breaking through this wall, the English-speaking soldier says to me, "You just don't give up, do you?" Then we engage in a brief discussion.

"But isn't that being disloyal to your government?"

I say, "Yes, I guess so." Then I reconsider, "No, my government is being disloyal to me."

Kahlil, a boy on the street to whom I had introduced myself earlier, comes to the door asking for me by name. He leads us to his house where there is a man who has been injured. A soldier hit him in the face with the butt end of a weapon. His nose won't stop bleeding and he seems weak from loss of blood. The family wants us to accompany him to a hospital.

We walk with him and his sister out along the street. A soldier stops us and Neta tells him the story. He seems angry about what happened. He goes to another soldier and they write a note giving permission for us to pass out of Balata Camp. We are on the road where the tanks go, and a tank is coming in our direction. Once we are in view, the tank turns directly toward us and increases speed. It appears that the driver intends to run over us. This is one of my scariest moments (as was the machine gun fire yesterday). I'm supporting the man on one side and the woman is supporting him on the other as we rush to the side of the road. Neta waves the little note in the air and walks toward the tank. As soon as the soldiers inside the tank get close enough to see the color of Neta's skin and features that identify her as an international, they slow down and then stop the tank. She talks to them and learns that there isn't a hospital in the direction we are going, so we turn and head toward Huwada.

Huwada is another refugee camp and it is at the Huwada Mosque where many of the men from Balata are staying while they have to stay out of their homes. I go to fill my water bottle at the mosque and a few of the men there who speak English ask me about what is going on in Balata Camp.

We flag down an ambulance and get in. The ambulance takes us to a hospital. After the man checks into the hospital, we go to the store. With donated money, Neta buys food for the woman with six children who told us she needed food, and treats for the families with whom we stay. We buy two cases of milk and a big bag of rice, which she figured was as much food as we could carry in anticipation of walking back into Balata Camp.

The man's sister, Neta, and I wait for the ambulance to take us back to the edge of Balata. It is getting towards dusk when it is finally ready to go. We learn that the ambulance is not allowed to carry the milk and rice, so we have to leave it behind. I hope they will be able to use it at the hospital.

It's getting dark again as we enter the camp on foot. There are tanks in both directions coming toward us. I feel the woman between us get tense and I myself feel frightened. Again, Neta flags the note in the air. We get through and into the camp, again at dark and escort the woman to her home. She doesn't invite us to stay there, so we go to the home of the family whom we were unable to join while the soldiers were in their house.

This is a difficult night for me. I don't have my daypack with my toothbrush, phone recharger, and other things. Neta is exhausted and she stops translating for me. She spends a lot of time on the phone. While I sit silently, the children demand my attention. The family is loud and the energy feels chaotic to me. They (including the two little children) are wide awake well into the night, Neta with them. While I try to sleep in another room, I hear explosions all around and shooting down the alleys. (Later, I learn that many of the explosions are just sound bombs and that one can learn to distinguish that sound from real explosions.) I'm feeling alone and like I'm probably more of a burden than a help to Neta and to the whole operation here. I don't sleep much for the fourth night in a row. Having heard that some of our group will be leaving Balata Camp tomorrow, I entertain the idea of going with them.

Back home, Michelle gets an interview with a public radio station and reports on what she has been hearing from me.

June 2, 2002

We gather with teammates in a Palestinian home and we learn that seven members of our team were arrested yesterday. They had made the mistake of giving their passports to soldiers who had cornered them. We learn that we don't have to give our passports to military, even if they ask. We only have to give our passports to police. Once the military have our passports, they have more control over us.

Three members of our group do leave Balata today and before they go, I say that I am considering going with them. Neta reassures me that she wants me to stay. She says that she enjoyed being with me yesterday and that it does make a difference that I'm here, so I decide to stay. However, I don't want to be her partner today. In my current state, I feel too needy and I want to let her focus on the good work that she is doing. I really just want a nap and a shower. Neta offers me two options. I could go stay with a quiet family to rest in their home or I could rest in the clinic. Since I really don't want to interact with people especially because I don't know the language, I decide to rest in the clinic.

We pick up our packs on the way to the clinic. Jessica, Melissa, and Star have been spending time at the clinic in order to be available to accompany the women and children from their houses to the clinic and back. This is important because during curfew soldiers might harass them for being out on the streets. I plug my cell phone in to charge while I rest a bit and probably even sleep a little. The other internationals are not around when I emerge from my nap. Since there are no English speakers around, I find a seat outside and lose myself in my own little bubble, silently writing while Palestinian life goes on around me. It feels good to have some time alone. It has been intense for everyone ever since we got here, but spending the day yesterday partnered with Neta was especially intense for me. Furthermore, it dawns on me that as an introvert needing time alone, it is a particular challenge to follow the advice to avoid being alone.

Johan from a radio station in Wisconsin calls me on my cell phone. Star had given him my number. He says he wants an interview with Starhawk or me. I give him some of the story of what I've experienced so far.

It's getting later in the day and I'm thinking I probably need to get settled somewhere for a meal and a place to sleep. I call Star on her cell phone and the three of them—Star, Melissa, and Jessica—come get me. As we walk past a tank and soldiers, I notice that the soldiers seem to be ignoring us now. I guess they have grown accustomed to our presence.

We go to this lovely house where Star, Melissa, and Jessica had spent the previous night. There is a grandma, her two daughters-in-law (one six months pregnant), and five children. Neta joins us later. We sit with the family for a bit and then we hear a shot very close. Star and I go down to the street to see what we can see. Nothing is apparent to us. Soldiers follow us back up the stairs and invade the house to do a search. While they are searching, they tell us that their "intelligence" told them that they would find something here. I wonder if that comes from the fact that internationals are staying in this house and our presence is actually doing more harm than good to the family.

The four-year old child is screaming and crying as the soldiers enter the house. I notice that he remains standing in front of the family in a position where he is the family member closest in proximity to the soldiers while he screams and cries. Jessica encourages the soldiers to notice that they are scaring the boy. One soldier takes off his helmet, squats down, and extends his hand to shake the little boy's hand. Under his helmet, he has on a yarmulke (the Jewish skullcap).

The soldiers pull everything out of drawers and closets, and leave the family's things dumped on the floor. I note that although some soldiers seem to be careful about not breaking things, others seem to destroy deliberately. For example, one uses his knife to cut into a suitcase full of clothing rather than opening the suitcase in the usual way. Some soldiers rip off some of the wall paneling in the room where we wait, and they cut a wall in another room. They find two pistols. One of the women explains that one of the men in the house is a policeman.

A soldier asks me to come with the elderly woman downstairs. They have her unlock a door and then she seems to want to stay, so I stay with her. At one point, two soldiers are ripping up a pair of trousers and they come to show me the label. Apparently the label has some meaning (proof of terrorist activity?). At another point, one soldier is having difficulty opening the cover to the septic system, so the woman shows him how to do it and we both laugh. When he finishes, he deliberately leaves his tool behind (as if it is contaminated now). One soldier tells me to search the old woman. He has me put one hand on her chest and the other on her stomach.

He says to another soldier, "She knows what she's looking for."

I say, "No, I don't."

He says, "Bombs."

I say, "Well, there are no bombs here." And he leaves.

The soldiers have gone back upstairs. The woman and I check things out down below and then turn off the lights, closing and locking the door behind us. As we start to come upstairs, soldiers stop us. I ask, "For how long?" and one of them says, "A half hour." I call Neta on my phone to let her know and then I suggest to the old woman that we go in and start to clean up the mess they left behind, which we do until one of the family members comes to tell us that the soldiers are gone.

Later, I hear more of what happened with the others while we were downstairs. While other soldiers were searching the house, Jessica communicated with the soldier who had extended his hand to the boy. He was the one posted to guard the door of the room where the family and internationals were being held. Eventually, the little boy was comfortable enough with this soldier to give him a kiss; and then the soldier actually kissed him back and gave him a little Israeli flag, which the boy took with great pride.

We all walk through the house to look at the damage. Money that was stashed in one room is missing. One of the women shows me money she has stashed (wrapped in plastic) in the freezer.

We straighten the rooms on the main floor as much as possible, and then the women begin preparing a meal. They do not accept any help from us in the kitchen, so we sit in the front room while they work. It is about 11:00 pm. During the meal, we sit around the tablecloth on the floor eating, chatting, and laughing as if nothing had happened.

One of the two younger women gives me her pink frilly nylon pajamas to wear for the night—not my style at all, but what a treat not to have to sleep in the clothes I've been wearing for several days.

Sometime in the night, there is a racket outside. Neta thinks that soldiers are raiding the house next door. I pull my clothes on over the pajamas. During this night, twice I put on my clothes and twice I take them off. I offer to sleep closer to the front door, but the grandmother insists on staying there herself.

June 3, 2002

Even with the interruptions last night, I awake in the morning feeling I had the best night's sleep since I arrived.

Of the original sixteen in our group, seven were arrested the other day and three left the camp yesterday. Annie has been staying day and night where she stayed the first night. And there are the five of us here in this house. Caoimhe who was already here when we arrived has been moving throughout the camp on her own to see where her help is most needed.

We have a quiet morning in the house. I notice the children carrying up containers full of water and it doesn't occur to me what that means. Later I go into the kitchen to refill my water bottle. When I reach for the tap, the little girl says, "No, no, no." She takes my bottle to fill from one of the containers they had carried up the stairs. At that point, I realize that when four of us took showers, we had emptied the water tank and now they have to carry all the water they use in

© MATS SVENSSON

Palestinians ask for escort past the soldiers

the house until the next time the water truck can come to refill their tank.

The family has been busy making pita bread all morning and when we internationals finally get ready to leave the house, they want to know when we'll be back for lunch (the biggest meal of the day). Neta responds, "Probably not," and they look disappointed. Melissa and Jessica are going to spend time with a family whose members are terrified because the soldiers have already raided and searched their house three times for something in particular. The soldiers told the family that they will be there to search every day until the family produces it. Neta is planning to spend the day resting in the house where she and I stayed the night before last. That leaves Star and me to escort families to and from the clinic.

When we walk past the soldiers, one who was on duty with us last night asks us about two children who he heard had been injured. We don't know anything about that incident, and I am impressed that this soldier seems really concerned.

Star and I accompany one woman and her baby from the clinic to her house. On our way back to the clinic, Star is taking a picture of a grapevine outside a house when the women of that house notice and invite us in. One woman is an English teacher so we are able to communicate well. An older woman who lives alone down the street is staying here for now because she was afraid to stay in her own house. She is very sad and worried about what has happened to her house while she hasn't been there. This house we are in has passage holes in the walls. The women tell us that now the soldiers come through day or night. Furthermore, during the last four months, they have felt imprisoned in their homes, because soldiers have been stationed on a nearby rooftop so close that they could fire down on them at any time.

Back at the clinic, a woman asks us to accompany her home because she wants to bring her sick baby. This woman lives in a different part of the camp further away from the clinic. The woman's house is much poorer than any we have seen thus far. She serves us a sweet artificial fruit drink and offers a meal, but I don't want to accept a meal here because it looks to me like she may not have much for her own family. As we head back to the clinic with her, five or six other women with babies join us. Every time we go by the soldiers, they ask, "Where are you going?" even though we have had contact with them many times and they know where we are going. After the visit to the clinic, we walk with all these women part of the way back, but once we get past the soldiers, the women insist that they don't need us to go any further with them.

While in the neighborhoods, we are asked to accompany young men who have been staying at the mosque but are walking in the camp for one reason or another. A family asks us to go with three men who are heading back to the mosque, so we start walking with them. This time, a couple of different sets of soldiers stop us. They question the men briefly and then let us pass. As we walk away from one of these encounters, the tall man next to me holds up his hands and mutters mournfully, "Why, why, why?"

We come to three soldiers who are posted down the street from the clinic. They stop us, take the men's IDs, call in the numbers, and direct the men to stand facing the wall with their hands up against it. Star asks one soldier what is going on and he says that he is waiting for orders. Meanwhile, two more Palestinian men are walking into Balata Camp from the mosque. The soldiers stop them and direct them to face the wall in the same way. I talk to one of the Palestinian men. The soldier orders me not to talk to them and he also makes it clear that the men at the wall are not to talk to each other. Several more men arrive and the soldiers have them line up next to the others against the wall. Twice we see a tank escort a small group of Palestinian men to the base of the road. The men come up the road with their IDs in their hands and the soldiers stop them all and add them to the lineup against the wall.

This whole time, I've positioned myself between the soldiers and the Palestinian men and Star is standing off to the side. Whenever a soldier approaches one of the men, I move close to them and carefully watch the body movements in the interaction even though I can't understand the words that are spoken. The soldiers seem to be trying to ignore me. Later, Star (who understands some Hebrew) tells me that the Israeli soldiers were saying things that would humiliate the Palestinians.

My cell phone rings while I am on the street between the soldiers and the Palestinian men. It is Johan, the radio reporter from Wisconsin, and I describe exactly what I'm doing in the moment. While I'm on the phone, about thirty-five soldiers come swarming up the street and are suddenly all around me, but still ignoring me. So here I am, standing among about thirty-five Israeli soldiers who have about twenty Palestinian men lined up at the wall, and I'm describing the situation on my cell phone to a radio station in the USA.

After I hang up my phone, one soldier catches my eye and tells me to go home. I say, "No."

He says, "What's the matter? Don't you speak English?"

I boldly say, "Yes, I speak English, but I'm not going to go."

He appears not to know what to do about me at that point, so he walks away. I feel strong and good about our presence here.

Star calls me away and I argue with her saying, "If I get out of the middle of them, I will have difficulty getting back into that position." She is concerned that the energy has shifted and that I might be antagonizing them. Just then, almost all of the Palestinian men are sent back toward the mosque. Three are held behind (one is a man we had been accompanying—the one who had said, "Why, why, why?"). Groups of approximately seven soldiers go with each one of the three, directing them down the street toward the clinic.

We keep our eyes on the one whom we had been accompanying, watching from a safe distance. He is taken to the front porch of a house where three soldiers position themselves around the door with guns pointed at the door. Four other clusters of soldiers position themselves away from the house in several locations also with guns pointed at the door of the house. The Palestinian is directed to knock at the door and stand in front of it. When the man and woman of the house open the door, the soldiers all converge forcing the couple and the man we had been accompanying inside. A bunch of soldiers go in. Star just wants to get back to the clinic. Later when we tell Neta about the incident, I realize that Neta probably would have followed the soldiers in, asking what they were doing. In retrospect, I think I would have been up for doing that if Star were, but with the fear of getting arrested now in the group, perhaps it is best that we didn't.

We go back to the clinic, where we sit on the side of the building in the shade and do further interviews with Johan. Melissa and Jessica come and we discuss where we want to spend the night. Melissa and Jessica want to stay at the same house as last night, but they are aware that the family they accompanied today would also like company overnight, so Star and I go there. I am happy about that, knowing that some members of this family are English speakers.

There are many family members in this household, including four or five sisters, several wives of brothers, all of their children, and the elder mom and dad. One woman who is a sister/aunt is in her 50s and was never married. That is unusual in this culture. One woman (the most fluent and outgoing English-speaker) is married to one of the brothers. We hear a bit of the story about the second time the house was raided: the eighteen family members were shut in a room for five hours.

The elder man sits off to the side and doesn't interact with us at all. He is smoking a lot and one of the women tells us that he started smoking so much because of this situation. I think how hopeless, helpless, and humiliated he must feel being the only man left in his house and having to worry for his whole family, his house, and all of their possessions without being able to do anything about the situation.

Star gives Tarot readings to the young women one at a time while I sit with the other family members. The English speaker who is married to one brother is very worried about her husband, because the family has heard the whereabouts of all the other husbands and brothers, but nobody knows where this one is. She has been trying to get pregnant and has gone through an expensive treatment (costing $750) in order to be fertile. Her fertile time is now; being separated from her husband and not knowing where he is makes it look like all that was for naught.

Meanwhile in the house where Jessica and Melissa are staying, the soldiers are conducting another search. While the soldiers trash the house this time, the woman who is pregnant goes into shock. Jessica is a street medic and recognizes the symptoms. She immediately begins talking to the soldiers about getting the woman to the clinic. One of the soldiers also recognizes the symptoms and the seriousness of the situation. Finally, they allow Melissa and Jessica out of the house to go to the clinic. Some nurses come back to help the woman, and they decide to take the whole family to the hospital.

Caoimhe arrives at our house before dinner. After dinner, Star gives her a Tarot reading. They disappear upstairs. I sit and chat with the family. One of the women receives a phone call and tells me that they have moved all the people out of the houses on the street where Jessica and Melissa are staying. They explain that moving neighbors away from a house is a sign that the soldiers are going to explode the house. I call Jessica and Melissa to give them this information. They are at the clinic at this point and the house is empty. They decide to go check on the house. I disturb Star and Caoimhe. Caoimhe recognizes this is probably just a rumor. She calls Jessica and learns that she and Melissa had found no activity in the neighborhood. When the whole family left the house to go to the hospital, the neighbors thought that they were going to explode the house—that's how the rumor began.

Caoimhe goes elsewhere in the camp. Star and I move into the room where we are going to sleep and about five of the women join us in our room. The women are really enjoying our company and they comment on how much safer they feel because of our presence. It is a slumber-party atmosphere. They show me some of the pictures the children have drawn and I ask if I can bring the pictures back to the USA. We exchange contact information. I yawn and they decide that it is time for them to leave the room.

Star and I lie on our mattresses on the floor talking about future possibilities of our work on the Palestinian-Israeli conflict. Star thinks we need to work with Israelis; I think we need to work with US citizens. In either case, we agree that being with Palestinians is much more fun.

At 3:00 am. the news spreads throughout the camp that the soldiers have left. We go out on the street in front of the clinic where a number of people have gathered, all expressing a huge sense of relief. I notice one woman busily sweeping up the mess the soldiers left behind. The Palestinians seem to have adjusted to this life with soldiers coming, committing various abuses, and then leaving, while other soldiers stay in posts as long-term guards. The Palestinians seem accustomed to cleaning up the messes of the soldiers repeatedly, erasing the evidence of their presence as soon as they leave and bouncing back to lives of normalcy as much as possible just like our dinner in the house the other night after cleaning up the mess the soldiers had left there. I feel sad and somewhat ashamed that these destructive disruptions are such a common occurrence.

June 4, 2002

We emerge this morning onto a street already transformed back into the bustling place I imagine it usually is with shops open and full of people. People are separating the ruined from the still useable, piling wreckage and trash, sweeping, and washing. It is very lively, actually too lively. I notice the contrast with how much calmer it felt during the curfew and with very few men around.

We ISM folks gather at the clinic to decide next steps. Jessica and Melissa are feeling very sad and spent; they want to leave as soon as possible. They tell us that the previous night, among the other atrocities, the soldiers had urinated on the family's things even though Jessica and Melissa were there. Decision-making is difficult, but two things become clear. Jessica and Melissa are going back to Jerusalem and we need to get all the gear of those who were arrested back to Jerusalem.

Star, Neta, and I carry the gear with Jessica and Melissa to the checkpoint, where they can take it in a service from there. On our way out of Balata, we experience the chaotic aliveness of the street. Even with no curfew, the women and girls tend to stay inside. And the boys swarm around us.

"What is your name?" "How are you?"

"Where you?" means "Where are you from?"

Some are attracted to and curious about what is in our packs. At one point, one boy gives Star something he has taken from her pack. She asks me to walk behind her after that in order to keep an eye on it.

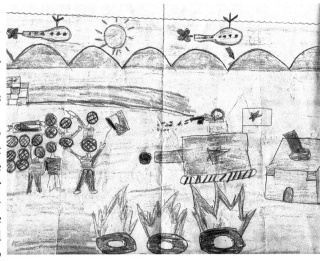

Drawing by 9-year-old Palestinian - Tires burning in the foreground

After we get Melissa, Jessica, and all the gear into a service, we continue to struggle with our decision about what to do next. We find shade and Star does a Tarot reading. I'm intrigued that she uses Tarot to help with making such important decisions, but why not? What would be a better way when there is no obvious rational decision?

We end up walking through Nablus toward the hospital. We walk through the old city past a whole block where several soap factories have been demolished. Nablus is famous for this soap, a product that brings income to Nablus. We stop at Neta's husband's family house for tea. I'm happy to have a toilet. We leave Neta behind to be with her husband and to get some much-needed rest.

Star and I arrive at the hospital to meet other ISM people—Brian, Enam, and Hyun-Mi who have come (or come back in the case of Brian—he was one of the three who left Balata earlier). Brian arranged for an ambulance to take everyone to the checkpoint in order to go back to Jerusalem. Before we can fill our water bottles, we get the message that someone shot at the ambulance and it is not going to be able to take us. The five of us begin walking up the hill, back the way that we had come when we first came into Nablus. It is hot. Thankfully, a service driver comes who is willing to take us to the roadblock. From there we walk to the place where Brian had arranged for another service to pick us up and carry us to the checkpoint.

At the checkpoint, the policeman asks me why I am here. I tell him that I am here to witness and pray. He searches my pack, jokes a little, and flags me through.

Star, Brian, and I come back to the hostel in Jerusalem. Star is flying out tomorrow. She wants to do some laundry because she fears they will never believe her story at the airport about visiting friends if they open her luggage and find her dirty clothes. She also wants to meet with Sam, an Israeli acquaintance of Neta's. Star invites me to join her in this meeting. After showers, some time to rest, and

© Mats Svensson

Walking through Nablus

dropping off our laundry in the Old City, we take a service to the West Side— the highest-class area in Jerusalem, where professors and government officials live.

Sam considers himself a "leftist" Israeli. My perception is that he carries much unconsciousness about Palestinians—much like the way progressive white people in the USA can be unconscious of what it is like to be a person of color in the USA. I silence myself a couple of times so that I don't put him on the defensive; thus I can gain more of what I have to learn from hearing his perspective. He talks about the views of some of the various primary parties in the Israeli government. The Greens and Conservatives are at one end of a continuum. He describes those in the middle as being "wishy-washy, not taking a stand one way or the other." The stance of the "leftists" is to go back to the pre-1967 borders.

Sam treats us to dinner at a café that is within walking distance of his house. A guard at the door checks through our purses. From dinner, we walk to a community center where there is free admission for a dance with live music. The place is fenced with a guard at the gate, again checking purses; and we go through a second security check before entering the building. Sam points out how inconvenient all these security checks are for the Israelis.

We view a series of photos on the walls inside. At one picture Sam boasts that Israel has a museum of Palestinian culture and points out that the Palestinians would not have a museum of Israeli culture. I ask what the Palestinians might think about Israel having a museum of their culture. He acknowledges that it might appear like co-option, but brushes that idea off saying, "There's always going to be something to complain about."

June 5, 2002

Star and I walk together to get our laundry before she says goodbye and leaves for the airport. The ISMers who are here now plan to go to Jenin City, but while we are waiting for our service, we hear that there was a suicide bombing of a bus near that city. The response of the Palestinians in this area seems mostly of discouragement and fear about what the retaliation will be. The service that was going to take us to a point where we could walk in to Jenin City gets caught in checkpoints and never gets to us. Michelle (a reporter here from the USA) interviews me about my experiences in Balata Camp.

By the time we finally get going at 1 pm, nine of us ISM teammates are boarding the service. I am riding in the front seat. I'm a little concerned about my being one of the more-experienced ones now, and still having had very little formal training. In general, this group seems more confident than the other group did when we were driving in to Nablus.

Michelle and Brian, both journalists from the USA, and I are the only ones still here from the group who went to Balata Camp. Enam (US American of Palestinian descent) and Hyun-Mi (South Korean currently going to UCLA), whom I had first met when we were leaving Nablus, are with us; as well as Micheline from France, Junaid (Indian heritage living in the UK), Jim from Ireland, and his partner Julianna from the US.

We drive past the site of this morning's bombing, a blackened piece of road the size of a bus. A suicide bomber from Jenin City had hit a bus, killing seventeen people and injuring forty others.

The authorities at a checkpoint ask where we are from and why we want to go into Jenin City. We hadn't discussed what we would say and there follows what feels to me like an awkward silence. Someone weakly says, "Visiting." The official asks, "Why?" and I decide to speak up with conviction using what I said yesterday at the checkpoint into Ramallah, "To see and to pray." He says that there is a "mine war" going on, so there are restrictions on tourism; and he refuses to allow us passage. Enam says that it was because of what I said that we were not allowed entry and that we should have said that we were visiting one of the settlements. I try not to feel defensive about what she said and think to myself, "Why didn't you speak up, then?" Someone says we should choose a spokesperson, and I suggest Enam. She says she will, and Julianna also says she will, but it turns out we don't need it again.

We go to Salem, which is a village on the Israeli side of the Green Line, the line that divides the Palestinian Territories from Israel. We walk a short distance across rough terrain to a place where a service picks us up and carries us over four-wheel-drive terrain through olive orchards. We pass through various villages and into Jenin City, arriving at the Red Crescent, just outside Jenin Camp. We made it!

The guys at the Red Crescent are welcoming because that is part of their culture, but they don't seem to be pleased to meet us. They give us tea and show us what is left of an ambulance that was hit by a missile. In the incident, the doctor had been hit in the abdomen, and when the missile also exploded an oxygen tank, three male nurses were badly burnt. The three burn victims had just been released from the hospital this very day. The Red Crescent men say that the missile had a liquid in it that is illegal. We guess that it was napalm. They point out the charred skin stuck to the seat of the burnt ambulance. They also describe how another ambulance had been hit by a tank.

Later we all board an ambulance and go to the house of one of the burn victims. Brian videotapes and Michelle audiotapes the man telling his story. He has one bandage that covers his left hand (each finger separately) and arm all the way up inside his shirt. Some of his right hand is exposed. His fingers on that hand are deformed and the whole hand looks like a burn. On that side, he has bandages wrapped around one finger and his forearm. He talks with that hand and uses it to point even though he can't move his fingers into pointing position. He says that he cannot go out in the sun at all for three months. Because of curfew, he cannot go out at night, so he is essentially imprisoned in his own house.

The burn victim's brother talks about how he would never have wanted to hurt anyone and about how the Palestinians are loving people. But after this happened to his brother, now he understands the feeling of wanting to kill someone. His story makes it clearer to us that what the Israelis do keeps feeding the occurrence of suicide bombing by some Palestinians.

June 6, 2002

After mid-morning coffee in the house where we spent the night, we are finally ready to visit Ground Zero in Jenin Camp. It is a hot day.

Ground Zero is atrocious—a huge pile of rubbish the size of 5x5 street blocks. Some members of our group are taking photos. We come upon a group of men and one woman. The woman comes out to greet us in English. "Hello, where are you?" Jim responds, "Ireland" and she says, "Welcome, Ireland," and then starts into a tirade. She thinks that we are taking pictures in order to make fun of Palestinians. She addresses several people in the group similarly, asking what we can do to help her. I want her to know that we are taking pictures in order to let people know about the atrocities that are going on here, but it seems she really isn't ready to hear anything from us. She just seems to need to release the anger. The Palestinian men and boys silently watch her. They seem amused. My interpretation is that perhaps it is dangerous for any of them to express anger, and that probably much of their anger is also being expressed through her. The last one to whom she speaks is Micheline who starts crying with compassion. The woman seems to soften a bit, tells her not to cry, and walks away.

We walk to the uphill corner of the massive pile of rubble. From that viewpoint, we can see much of the destruction. We meet a family whose house had been saved because it was the house that the soldiers had occupied while they were destroying the rest of the houses. The family invites us in for tea. They tell us how they had been closed into one room during that time. The soldiers had trashed their house while they were occupying it. For example they carelessly broke things and urinated on the floor.

We walk around the outskirts of the destroyed neighborhood and see uninhabitable houses that are still standing, and a few inhabited houses. We had seen a tent village when we first entered Jenin City and that is where many of the people who lost their homes are staying. Many are staying in homes of other families as well.

We take a service back to Salem following the same route we had taken when we arrived. Another service is supposed to meet us in Salem at 7:00; but by 8:00, it still has not arrived. Enam calls and we learn that the driver is still in Tel Aviv.

A local Palestinian invites us to sit with him in a covered part of his house that is outdoors. It is very neat and clean. He speaks English, but prefers speaking Arabic with the Arabic speakers, so again I miss out on a lot of the conversation. At one point, the locals are talking about their Jacuzzis, and I realize that they are accustomed to a much different lifestyle than the families we had gotten to know in Balata and Jenin Camps. Later, Enam explains to me that these are Israeli Arabs who have been benefiting from the privileges other Israelis have. She says that generally they aren't interested in giving up their privileges in order to stand up for the rights of Palestinians who live inside the Palestinian Territories. Some of what they say triggers anger in Enam. Among other things, she points out to me that although they had been hospitable, they hadn't invited us into their house.

There are mosquitoes, lots of smoke from smokers, only sweets to eat, too much noise, and not enough English being spoken. I'm tired and not enjoying myself. The driver finally arrives more than two hours late. When we get back to the hostel, I go straight to bed.

June 7, 2002

I wake up early. Activity and noise on the street begins very early here even though people seem to stay up late at night also. I don't know if it ever quiets down completely on the street, but inside the hostel right now, everyone else is still asleep.

I notice that there is a voice mail message on my cell phone. It is from Michelle back home. She says that she is going to be away from home (and thus unreachable) for a couple of days. Suddenly, I feel like I've lost an important lifeline to all the people back home and I immediately feel how this sense of disconnection weakens my spirit. I worry especially about being out of communication with my mother. I realize that when I'm distracted by thoughts about people back home, it is difficult for me to stay fully present here.

I call George to let him know that we intend to come to Bethlehem today; the ISM office is close to Bethlehem. Then Micheline and I go for coffee and she shows me around the hostel where she is staying. I enjoy these brief moments of connection with her. I feel less alone and a bit recharged. I remember that Michelle back home had encouraged me to take care of myself here by spending some time when I am just with other internationals.

Micheline stays at her hostel to rest and I head back to my hostel, where I find Enam and Junaid also ready to go to Bethlehem. Everyone else is still sleeping, so the three of us decide to go ahead.

Seeing the Church of the Nativity is both sad and wonderful. As soon as we arrive, a tour guide approaches and says, "You are the first tourists we've had in two months." We hire him to show us around. We have the whole Church to ourselves, which is a very special experience; in different circumstances we would be among crowds of tourists. Our guide says that this is the oldest church in the world, that when the Persians were destroying other churches, they saw the picture of the three wise men and saw that they were Persian, so they "decided to preserve this church only." Currently Roman Catholics, Greek Orthodox, and Armenians all worship here. The original tiled floor is about a foot beneath the newer floor that was built above it when the tile started to break. An old painting hangs on the wall—a portrait of Jesus in which his eyes are both open and closed.

The most special moment for me is stepping down into the cave around which the church was built. I feel enveloped in a powerful sense of sacredness. The guide then says this is the actual location where Jesus was born. An altar down low full of oil lamps honors the site of the birth and then there is another altar area where the manger sat. Though I don't identify as Christian, I'm overcome with awe being at the birth site of this sacred man and teacher who was open to letting the spiritual energy of love flow through him and out into the world. I learn that Muslims also worship Jesus as one of their prophets.

We enter the chapel where St. Jerome translated the Bible. This chapel reminds me of a kiva (Hopi place of worship in the southwest of the USA) because the original entrance was through the roof with steps down into the center of the room. A window now blocks the steps and there is a different entrance.

In the symbol known as the Jerusalem cross, two lines cross each other, equally dividing it into four quadrants. Each line is crossed at each end, and inside each quadrant there is another cross. I see similarity of this symbol with variations of the medicine circles of many indigenous cultures around the world.

Recently, Palestinians and protesters were locked up inside the Church of the Nativity with the Palestinian leader Arafat. Neta was among the protesters who were there. Outside, our guide points out the bomb and bullet damage to the building that occurred during that time.

This evening I call Michelle at home, thinking that I am just going to be leaving her a message about what we did today. I'm surprised when she answers the phone. When we sort out my confusion I realize the message I thought she left last night was an old message from a week earlier. What a relief to know that my connection to all my people at home was still intact.

June 8, 2002

Brian and I go to Ramallah today. When we pass through the checkpoint, an older Palestinian man points out to us that the soldiers are hassling a fifteen-year-old girl, who doesn't have a passport (because she is too young). The man says that she is on her way to school. Brian videotapes the encounter. A soldier tells him that we are in a restricted area and shows where he can go, which is further away. At first, I go with Brian but then while he is taping from there, I move back to where we had been in order to get a clearer view. They release the girl soon after I get back to that closer spot. I see that her eyes are tearing and red and perceive a look of humiliation, longing, and sorrow. She looks past me, and continues to do so even when I ask her if she speaks English. Brian thinks they released her because I went over there. I would like to think that is true—that our presence really does have a helpful impact on the lives of the people here.

We take a service to President Arafat's compound, another site where much demolition has occurred recently. More has been destroyed here just in the last couple of days in reaction to the suicide bombing that took place near Jenin the day we were there. Men are building up scaffolding under a second-story walkway between the two buildings. The walkway looks close to collapsing.

Four others of our ISM team arrive. Some of the Palestinian men are watching the World Cup and some members of our group go over to see the score. We walk around the destroyed compound. Cars that have been run over by tanks are scraped up into a pile against the walls that remain of the buildings that have been demolished. A few Palestinian men approach. At first, they are reserved and they ask about President Bush and politics. When they realize that we are anti-Bush, they begin to chat and show us around. One soft-spoken man carrying a

Jenin camp wreckage

© Gary Moore

pair of tennis shoes in a bag is laughing as he shows us his demolished office— the place he worked and slept. One wall and remnants of the ceiling are all that remain of the office. Rebar stretches out from the ceiling like octopus tentacles. I marvel once again at this man's ability to laugh at the situation.

Men are busily hosing down the compound with a fire truck hose, once again washing away the mess of the destruction in order to bring back some sense of normalcy. Some of us go over to sit in the shade of the building and one of the Palestinians warns us to move away because loose pieces of the building could fall on us. They refill our two water bottles and give us a fresh bottle of water.

We take a service into town for a great lunch. I'm annoyed when people leave behind the water they were served at lunch. Up until this point, I'd been generously sharing my water, but witnessing this, I feel stingier about it. I'm used to drinking about three quarts a day, so I always carry a lot with me. Although it looks like I have plenty to share, I don't really because it is difficult sometimes to get refills when needed.

We leave the restaurant in plenty of time to get across the checkpoint and into

Jerusalem for a demonstration. We are early and the first to arrive at the demonstration. The first organizer who comes is one of the Women in Black. She smiles and says, "Hi, I am Yvonne."

I ask "Yvonne who?" and am delighted to learn that she is the woman whose name I had used as my story for getting into the country. I tell her about the questions that they asked me when I was getting on the plane in New York. She tells me that she's a social worker and has two children, so now I have that information if I should face similar questions on my return trip.

As the demonstration begins, I'm feeling hot and tired and not much like being there. The speakers speak mostly in Hebrew, and it is quite boring for those of us who don't understand the language. Five of us decide to leave.

We stop for a meal and it becomes the most enjoyable evening that

We take a service

I've had since I arrived. I get into a meaningful conversation with Mark. He is interested in my work in education and curious when I say that I see teaching as a political activity. I tell him about the consensus classroom and about students I had in sixth grade who organized a non-violent protest at the school when they were in the eighth grade. I learn that he is a Palestinian living in New York with his wife and two children. He works in his family-run travel agency business here in Palestine connecting with groups like Global Exchange—a social justice oriented organization in the USA that provides international tours. I feel inspired when Mark says he sees that Palestine may be a key leverage point in efforts against globalization. This thought renews my hope and sense of why I'm here. After dinner, I enjoy smoking some special-flavored tobacco through a water pipe that we pass around the table, part of the culture here.

Mark's car is parked close to our hostel, so he walks with Hyun-mi and me. On the way through the Old City, he points out the video cameras that are always surveying the streets. I hadn't noticed them before.

June 9, 2002

Up early again this morning, Hyun-mi joins me in the common room and later, Brian. Brian interviews me on video. I have enough to say to fill the whole tape. What I hear myself saying confirms the importance of being here.

At noon, I go to court as a witness. Of the seven internationals who were arrested in Balata Camp, some were deported and those who chose to fight the deportation are still detained. The reason given for the arrest is that they had been in a restricted zone, but their argument is that they had never been told that. Brian has a video of the moment when five of them coming from the hospital the second day spoke to soldiers in a tank as they entered Balata Camp. The soldiers had allowed them to pass. Furthermore, the other two were with my group when we entered Balata Camp by walking past the tank with our hands up that first evening. No one had stopped us or told us that this was a restricted zone.

After hearing the story from the opposing lawyer in Hebrew, the judge says in English that she will let our teammates out on bail for now and they need to return to court on Tuesday. But since my flight out is Tuesday, she asks me to testify today. I describe how we entered Balata Camp and how for four days we freely moved among the soldiers, having many conversations with them. I make the mistake of saying that one soldier told me to "Go home" at one point. The judge and the two defending lawyers quickly guide me to explain that the soldier meant for me to get out of his way in the moment and not literally to leave Balata Camp. This distinction is important, I guess, because the argument of those arrested is that we had not been told by anyone that we weren't supposed to be there.

I enjoy the informality of the court scene and I especially appreciate the judge, who seems sensitive to our cause. The courtroom is small and crowded with a disorganized array of chairs and tables, which contributes to the sense of informality of it. A lot of side conversations take place throughout the session; some of these are translations, but sometimes two lawyers are talking to two people at once. One woman works for an organization that supports women who are in prison for political reasons. Another woman is researching translation during legal procedures. Representatives from the UK and Japanese consulates are in attendance, but no one from the US consulate even though one of the defendants is from the USA. Some press, a bunch of ISM team members, and the owner of the hostel where we have been staying are all here. At one point, the translation researcher passes a note to Josie.

People cheer when I get up to testify. They also say, "Good job," when I sit down. I don't know why, all I did was tell the truth. I appreciate when the judge warns those who have been arrested not to go back into any of those potentially restricted areas between now and Tuesday. It seems she is trying to make clear that she is not saying they can't ever go back into the Palestinian Territories, just until Tuesday.

After the court scene, ten of the ISM team members head for Gaza, but I decide not to join them. I still have in my mind that I want to avoid being out alone and I'm afraid that if I go to Gaza and the group decides to stay, like we did in Balata Camp, I could end up in a situation where I'd need to travel alone.

Back at the hostel in the evening, I meet Kiki, a young outgoing Japanese woman. For five years, she has been traveling the world and telling her experiences in two series she is writing for two different mainstream journals in Japan. She tells me that a Palestinian man was shot while she was at a checkpoint in Gaza today. She didn't see the man, but she heard the shot and saw the bloody hand of another Palestinian, who had raised it over the crowd and shouted, "Why?" Kiki seems quite shaken—even traumatized—and I recognize I am probably fortunate that I have not had to witness a killing while here. She reflects that she and her international companions could walk away, but not their Palestinian friend who had come with them to the checkpoint. The Palestinian woman had to turn back and go home; she didn't have a choice to leave. I appreciate hearing Kiki's thoughts and I point out to her how great it is that she is writing about this and reaching mainstream people in Japan.

June 10, 2002

I have a free day and spend it mostly alone walking around the Old City of East Jerusalem. I have spent enough time in the Old City in the company of others now that I'm comfortable being alone during the day here. This is a touristy area because of the history here and because all three religious groups (Muslim, Jewish,

Border guard at West Bank checkpoint

and Christian) have neighborhoods inside the walls of the Old City.

I think about how I want to organize presentations when I get home. I want it to do more than simply share my experience. I want to inspire people who are already supportive of the cause (my assumption about anyone who would come to such a presentation) to push their edges a little further into some sort of action.

June 11, 2002

During my service ride to the airport, I speak to an Israeli professor. Even though I don't admit it, he recognizes that I am a peace activist and seems amused. I don't have any problems or delays getting on or off the airplane during my return journey from Tel Aviv to New York and then San Francisco.

3

Feeling More Alive Than Ever

June and July, 2002

I AM GLAD MY TRIP TO ISRAEL/PALESTINE IS PAST NOW. My life is coming back to some sort of normalcy. I recall images of the houses left in shambles after searches in Balata Camp and the expanse of rubble in Jenin Camp alongside memories of the warmth and hospitality of the Palestinian people I met. I feel grief for the people and I realize I probably numbed myself to some extent while I was there; yet I'm not aware of any sense of traumatic stress.

I am having difficulty keeping up with reading all the e-mail messages I receive about what's going on in Palestine. I am now on a number of e-mail lists of organizations that are maintaining a presence there. Christian Peacemaker Teams (CPT) is among these organizations. Besides Palestine, CPT currently has teams in Columbia and other places in the world where people are being abused. I appreciate the work that they are doing in the world.

Maybe I'll know more from the Nonviolent Peaceforce soon. It feels totally right for me to apply for their pilot project, even if getting accepted would completely disrupt and change my life since it will require a longer commitment (like two years). I have felt drawn to the mission of the Nonviolent Peaceforce since I heard of the organization. My experience in Palestine gave me a taste of what I imagine the work of the Nonviolent Peaceforce will be and even though that Palestine experience was challenging in many ways, that kind of work still seems to be what my heart is telling me to do. The Nonviolent Peaceforce is definitely worth pursuing, but David Hartsough reports they are still not ready to get people into the field so I continue to ask myself the question: Is there something else calling to my heart? I'm wondering about Afghanistan and Iraq.

I hold a vision of a peaceful world, a healthy planet, and a sacred way of life for all. That could be a beautiful pledge of allegiance: "I pledge allegiance to a peaceful world, a healthy planet, and a sacred way of life for all."

I'm aware of my deep sadness about war. I am feeling sad about the similarities between what my European ancestors did to Native Americans while settling this country and what Israelis are doing currently to Palestinians. Now, there is a common sense of regret for the long-past abuses of large numbers of Native Americans, yet right now while the world sits back and watches, large numbers of Palestinians are being abused. And the USA is paying for it with our tax dollars.

I ask for openness to guidance and I reaffirm my willingness to carry out whatever instructions I'm given from that guidance. Without having any idea how I will get through this dark night of the soul through which it seems we in this society are passing, I commit to doing whatever I can to support the process such that this world has less violence and abuse.

Violence and abuse may be what is part of our reality for now and must be accepted as that, but I don't have to accept it as what always shall be. Sometimes I get caught in a paralyzing sense of discouragement, but I have to accept that what "should be" simply isn't. I need to just hold that—fully experience what is occurring, and fully bring myself to that—while at the same time not giving up the vision of what could be. Eagle (that inner guide who coaches me in reaching my full potential) says:

It isn't that you have to push yourself, it's that you have to relax into your own way to leadership. You have to let go of the defenses that keep you apart from recognizing yourself as a leader—melt, relax, expand.

There's something far greater in terms of spirit that will occur as you white European Americans recognize the violence that you've brought into the world. Recognize that violence so that you can actually work with it, move with it, and go beyond it to synthesize what is to be, that which is longing to manifest and crystallize through Western humans becoming more a part of the natural systems of the earth.

August 3, 2002

I am out in a base camp guiding a vision quest. My co-leader and I are talking about fears. He notes that we Western humans often respond to what we fear by killing it, and I see the truth in what he says. The conversation stimulates further

thoughts about the relationship between fear and killing. I reflect on some observations I've made about human fears of nature. For example, the initial response of many of my neighbors is to kill rattlesnakes found near our houses. And I remember when I was camping in Alaska, many people believed it was necessary to carry a gun in order to be safe from grizzly bears. Yet I have noticed how I feel safer around rattlesnakes

Linda with co-leader

and grizzly bears when I learn more about them and the reasons for their behavior, and then I don't feel a need to kill. For example, rattlesnakes really don't want to use their venom on anything other than their prey. I can be safer around them when I am mindful of their possible presence and look before I put my hands or feet anywhere. I can diminish fear when I gain some understanding and as a result, not need to kill in order to protect myself.

In the case of war, there are whole systems (nations or factions of peoples within nations) that fear other systems and wage war. President Bush is capitalizing on that right now. He is using the fears that the media has reinforced since 9/11 along with the idea that Iraq has weapons of mass destruction that Sadam Hussein might use on us to justify the USA bombing Baghdad. This conversation with my co-guide about how fear has led to killing confirms my belief in the great power of being with and understanding or embracing fear. Gaining understanding of the threat and then thinking about how I will respond can be helpful in dealing with fear so that I don't have to kill in response to it. Furthermore, many fears are unfounded and the perceived threats are not necessarily real dangers. Becoming aware of my fears and getting into a learning relationship with them can help me see whether or not the thing I fear is really a threat and if it is, how I can most effectively take care of myself in the face of it. This can eliminate the feeling of needing to kill, while denying fear just allows it to continue to have an unconscious power over me that limits my potential responses.

My spirit is thriving these days. Before going to Israel/Palestine, I feared that I would return traumatized. I realize instead I'm feeling more alive than ever in my life. For all of my life I've been bombarded with the violence that is in the news on a daily basis, and while witnessing that violence I know something has to be done to change it, but it has always been too big or too distant and I haven't been able to see how I might affect it. Having "gotten in the way" of violence to the small extent that I was able is energizing, like when the Palestinian men were all lined up against the wall and I was standing between them and the Israeli soldiers who were exerting their power.

August 6, 2002

I recognize the joy that I've been feeling since my trip to Israel/Palestine. I am excited about that further insight about fear that came while guiding the vision quest. I see how our Western cultural belief in survival of the fittest can lead to seeing the stranger as a danger and that can feed the fear that leads to violence and abuse.

August 9, 2002

The sense of joy I felt a few days ago has diminished. I receive many discouraging e-mail messages about Palestine every day. The atrocities continue and get worse. I feel like going back to sleep; the situation in Palestine is weighing heavily on me.

August 20, 2002

President Bush is still talking about bombing Iraq. Many people here in the United States seem to think daily life can go on as usual despite the havoc our country is creating in the world in our names with our money. I have been considering joining Voices in the Wilderness (Voices). Voices is an organization that for many years has been providing a presence in Iraq to witness the devastation to the people caused by the sanctions that are now in their twelfth year. Now Voices and Christian Peacemaker Teams (CPT) are working together to organize the Iraq Peace Team to witness or prevent the further devastation of war.

When I shared with a group of friends last night some of my ideas about helping to heal the world situation by working with people to overcome fears, I got a sense that one of my friends was trying to give me a less grandiose sense of reality. I want to figure out some way to get people like that to see that my vision isn't as far-fetched as they seem to think, that my vision is possible, and that all of us humans are simply unconditional love inside. Love is what is truly wanting to flow among us—whether friends, acquaintances, or strangers—and if we could remember that truth whenever we are interacting with anyone, we would not have to feel afraid and put up the defenses that eventually drive us to war and other forms of abuse.

August 26, 2002

I've decided to apply to join the Iraq Peace Team even though that may be dismaying to Mom. That decision feels right, but applying doesn't mean I've decided to go for sure. I'm not as clear about this as I was when I decided to go to Israel/Palestine.

With encouragement from my brother, sister-in-law, and me, Mom has decided to move from her current house, which is about 100 miles away from my house, into an independent living facility for elders that is about twenty-five miles away from me. I'm happy that she will be living closer but at the same time, my plans to join the Iraq Peace Team and hopes to get hired by Nonviolent Peaceforce to be part of their pilot project seem to be at cross purposes with Mom's move to be closer to me, and this contributes to further doubt about joining the Iraq Peace Team.

I am aware of the weight on my shoulders of what the USA is doing in the world. I want to do something to shift that, but it seems too big. I want to let myself expand to however big I need to be and then I want clear guidance about what it is that I'm supposed to do.

I'm thankful for Eagle who's always there on my shoulder and reminding me about thinking big and coming into my full power, holding my vision for the planet/world and continuing to strive to realize it, dreaming the impossible dream and then working toward making it come true; step by step, letting myself expand fully into all that I am. I ask for guidance as I communicate with the people in my life and go about my daily work. I offer all my daily words and deeds for the good of all beings.

Eagle says, You are all that is. All the conflicts and abuses that are part of the life of humans on the planet are within you and you are within them, so that you can make a difference. You do have some effect on what happens. Find the Iraq situation within. Find the Palestine situation within. Notice that it is in you to be abusive.

I remember when at age fifteen, it was time for my pet rat to go back into his cage, because I was going to leave the room. I grew more and more frustrated with him as he evaded being caught by getting out of my reach under the bed. When I finally did catch him, I was so frustrated that I squeezed too hard and he squealed. I so regret having hurt him. I don't think I can forgive myself.

That's part of the process to forgive the you who did that, who hurt an animal that's smaller than you because you were frustrated. You hurt an animal that you had power over. Repressed anger can drive one to do what she wouldn't otherwise do.

I also recall the time as a teenager when I was trying to frost a cake and crumbs kept coming to the surface and messing up the frosting. I got so frustrated that I hit the cake with my fist. A couple of other incidents come to mind: when as a young adult I threw a wine glass across the room, and the time more recently when I hit my computer. These are times when I let my anger burst forth in harmful ways that feel out of control. In each of these incidents, my anger was in control of me so that I did things that I wouldn't otherwise do.

Then there's also fear that can cause me to do things I would rather do differently, like when I was on a walk outside and a skunk was coming my direction.

© Dale Sartor

Linda's mother

I reacted without thinking by making a loud noise to scare it away, and only after doing so did I recognize that I would rather have stayed quiet and let it get closer. The most significant fear that controls me is when I hide out instead of speaking up, especially at those times when my contribution is most important because my perspective isn't matching someone else's.

I see the fear and the anger that can cause me to do or not do what creates or allows abuse. So what can I do about it? I can pray strongly for Palestine and all the other parts of the world where the USA has had a hand in causing problems. I can expect that there has to be a shift and then I can work in ways that I don't yet know exist toward making that shift occur. I'll just keep staying open to possibilities—possibilities that make sense rationally and possibilities that my heart just knows I have to consider—like joining the Iraq Peace Team, going back to Israel/Palestine, or joining the Nonviolent Peaceforce. Maybe it means I'll have to give up my current jobs, teaching graduate school and guiding wilderness trips.

August 30, 2002

I was so clear when I was preparing to go to Israel/Palestine—my inner voice was relentlessly telling me I had to go no matter how many good reasons there were to decide not to go; this decision about whether and when to go to Iraq is not as obvious.

September 8, 2002

Former chief UN weapons inspector in Iraq, Scott Ritter, says that the USA is using the "rhetoric of fear" to justify an attack on Iraq. That reinforces my belief that fear is a cause for violence and it also supports my decision to go to Iraq. If my heart is telling me to go to Iraq even though I feel fear, then my going there will model what I think would be good for all of us—the more that we follow our hearts even when we feel fear, the better off our world will be.

September 15, 2002

My niece is visiting and we do Medicine Card (Sams & Carson, 1988) readings for each other. Some of the cards that come up for me seem quite relevant.

Buffalo is in the position that is supposed to represent the dream within, which leads to my real purpose in life or the goals that my higher self suggests. Buffalo signals a time of abundance and plenty, praying for the good of all things in harmony, and accepting the great Mystery as part of that harmony. The description says that this may be a time of reconnection to the meaning of life and the value of peace. This confirms much of my inner journey of late.

Turtle is situated in the North of my spread of cards on the table. The North position represents inner wisdom that I may not recognize in myself. Turtle teaches how to use protection. This portends the work I hope to do both in Iraq and with the Nonviolent Peaceforce.

In the center of my spread is Fox reversed. That position represents integration, the taproot of my personal consciousness. This one says that I may have to dig deeply to find what excites me enough to scurry across the wasteland of my dulled senses and live. Wow! That resonates with my recent inner process as well.

September 16, 2002

I imagine a world in which everybody realizes how absolutely ridiculous and atrocious it is for anyone to abuse anyone else. In this imagined world, economics is in balance with ecology. There really is peace on earth: peace that is full of diversity; full of conversations; full of disagreements and even conflict, which we honor, respect, and celebrate. We know how to utilize conflict as a way to nurture love and good relationships. Everyone is given the respect that honors his/her uniqueness and gift(s).

A wall-hanging over my hearth says, "To you the earth yields her fruit and you shall not want if you but know how to fill your hands" (Gibran, 1968, p. 37). My boyfriend during my young adulthood gave this hanging to me because he thought I always got what I wanted. The hanging has always had a prominent place in my home, and I know there is more to it than what he thought it meant at the time. If all of us really knew that truth, we would be less likely to hoard. There would actually be enough resources for everyone to have what we need and there would be less reason for wars.

My resolve is to learn always to love unconditionally. I need to love even George W. Bush, in spite of the fact that I don't accept what he's doing and I am compelled to do something to change it.

I am also committed to doing all that I can do to have this next phase in my mother's life be the best ever for her.

September 23, 2002

Eagle reminds me that it isn't an impossible dream to stop the war.

Your intention is more powerful than you can imagine. It can be the beat of the butterfly wing that changes the course of events and all you have to do is keep loving in all of your relationships. Keep your heart open, keep your intention right where it is, and have faith that you really can make a difference just in fully being in integrity with yourself. Intend the strength and conviction you need in order to do that.

You're not going to get reassurance from the world outside when you are contributing that unique gift which is only yours to bring forth into the world. And it's a gradual process of bringing that forth. Every time you take a new baby step, you will feel vulnerable.

September 24, 2002

We are in the midst of global warming. If the United States were addressing that, it would be much more helpful to the rest of the world than creating this farce of a war on terror, which adds more to the problem of global warming as well as providing a huge distraction from it.

Over and over and in many ways, I've been told by inner voices that I can make a difference and that I need to let myself expand fully in order to do so. But today, CJ (my Critical Judge voice within) fears that my thoughts are grandiose and he is concerned about what someone might think reading this. When CJ's fears are strong in me I tend to hide out. But now is a time when my unique contribution is much needed. No, it is not grandiose. We all carry a unique contribution that needs to flow forth into the world in order to change the destructive course that is in progress. It is time for all of us citizens who see ourselves as insignificant to let ourselves be grandiose, because "it takes the best in each of us to bring out the best in all of us" (words on a button I was given as a graduation gift). CJ, I want you to really "get" this, so that we can start living into it more and more with each passing moment in every relationship.

October 10, 2002

I am one of six members in a research and writing group called the European-American Collaborative Challenging Whiteness (eccw.org). Yesterday we were talking about whom each of us has learned to see as "other." In the discussion, I came to recognize that for me, the "other" has been every human in my life. And I've learned to be afraid of all humans! So when I talk about the importance of being with fear in such a way that it doesn't stop me from doing what my heart is yearning to do, it opens the possibility to improve my relationships with all the people in my life.

I'm showing up very differently than before I went to Israel/ Palestine. I have more confidence in myself and am less dependent on other people's responses to define who I am, feeling more comfortable being just who I am without needing to pretend to be something I'm not. Maybe other opportunities like I had in Israel/Palestine will further liberate my soul.

October 20, 2002

I am feeling low today because I'm worried about Mom and the world. Mom has completed her move. Now that I am spending more time with her, I see that her physical health is failing more than I realized and probably because of the medications she is taking now, she doesn't seem to be thinking as clearly as she once did.

October 28, 2002

It is the time of the Celtic New Year, a time for reflection on the year past and the year to come. As I reflect, I note two insights that seem significant right now: 1) my best defense is an open heart; and 2) the more I avoid coming fully into myself, avoid being fully in relationship with others, and avoid showing up, the more I am complicit with the state of the world as it is.

© Frankie Sottile

Members of Linda's community

I think the coming year will have to include doing all I can to shift the energies that are charging toward a war on terror. I suppose that intention will carry me forward with the appropriate actions, which still aren't clear. I see that I can continue vision quest guiding and on-line teaching for sources of income, and I will also have the time to focus on Iraq, Israel/Palestine, the Nonviolent Peaceforce, and/or other ways to shift the nation's direction.

November 8, 2002

The UN Security Council has passed a resolution that says outstanding questions about Iraq's armaments should be answered through assertive inspections, not war.

November 29, 2002

The United States seems to have extreme power in the world and our government is supposedly by and for the people. Yet as a US citizen, I don't have any idea where to tap into that power and how best to affect change in support of the good of all beings, other than to hold my intention there and move in alignment with that intention as much as possible in everything I do and say.

December 2, 2002

As far as going to Iraq, I still just don't know. Christian Peacemaker Teams (CPT) has sent a couple of delegations that have joined the Iraq Peace Team during timeframes that I have not been able to fit into my schedule. A third CPT delegation is going to Iraq over Christmas.

December 10, 2002

I am present to support a civil disobedience action at the Recruitment Center in town. I find the event fun and rewarding. The action causes the center to close at 5:30 pm. when they normally stay open until 8:00. Starhawk participates and it is fun to reconnect with her. Michelle is there also. Neither Star nor Michelle is enthusiastic about my idea to go to Iraq.

December 20, 2002

The danger at this time is hopelessness, helplessness, and denial. So you must do all that you can to not fall victim to those. In order to do that, you must embrace any of those feelings when they come up; and they will. Don't deny denial, you'll get into trouble if you do. That's why it's good that there's this time to slow down enough to notice.

You've committed to opening up more time in your life to follow your spiritual path and follow your heart. That will continue to lead you to peace and justice activism, and it's for the earth. It's all connected. It's also connected to changing the economic system. You must continue one step at a time. The steps will lead you into the unknown. You have a contribution and you're making it. When you feel doubt, let that be an indication that something's off track. You're probably stuck in a 'should,' which is somebody else's expectation, somebody else's projection, somebody else's medicine.

I create myself and re-create myself and co-create myself with each word that flows forth. I'm new in every moment; and in any moment, there is the opportunity to co-create a relationship that gives birth to something new that didn't exist in the world before these two or more hearts/souls/spirits came together. This is what I am in the world to do—to be fully present with whomever I'm with in every moment.

I need to challenge myself to live my life more like a vision quest, moment to moment living in uncertainty about what is next. Just the thought of that is scary.

January 8, 2003

I've been waiting for clarity about going to Iraq, similar to the clarity I had about going to Israel/Palestine. I have watched e-mail announcements as three Christian Peacemaker Teams (CPT) went to join the Iraq Peace Team in the past few months. I considered each, but none of the timeframes worked for me due to other commitments. Now, there is a CPT delegation scheduled to go during the first two weeks in February. I look on my calendar and see that it is possible for me to get away during that time, so I decide to apply.

The notice specifies that since we don't know when President Bush is going to begin bombing and it is looking more and more imminent, CPT organizers only want people who have had experience in a war zone to join this delegation. I wonder if my time in Israel/Palestine is enough to qualify.

CPT in Iraq serves as an affinity group within the Iraq Peace Team. The Call for the Iraq Peace Team describes the following intentions while war is at hand:

- We will live among the Iraqi people.
- We will be with the Iraqi people during any aggression directed at them, including continued economic sanctions.
- We will use our presence and non-violent actions to protect, if we can, both the civilian population of Iraq and the facilities like water purification plants and electric power plants, which make daily life possible for the Iraqi people.
- We will use our experiences to speak truthfully, from Iraq and through supporters in the US, to all who will listen about the effects of sanctions and war on the people of Iraq.
- We deplore all human rights violations.
- We pledge our continued efforts to rebuild open and mutually beneficial relations between the Iraqi people and the rest of the world.

In the application for CPT, I sign the following agreement to accept personal responsibility in the face of the possible dangers:

> I am aware that I am entering a situation that may be tense at the present time and that there may be danger of war or other violent conflict occurring while I am there. I understand that I could be imprisoned, taken hostage, injured or even killed. I also understand that access to health care facilities; adequate shelter and food may be difficult on occasion. I assume and accept full responsibility for any risks of personal injury, illness, damage, imprisonment or other deprivation that may occur as a result of my participation in this program including, but not limited to, the risks described above. I understand that Christian Peacemaker Teams cannot ensure my safety or well-being while on this trip.

Further in the application, I write why I want to travel to Iraq and become part of the Peace Team: "I am appalled at the idea of the US going to war against Iraq and I need to make a statement that is greater than what I can do by protesting here in the US. I want to take a strong stand against the violence my country is committing in my name with my money."

January 15, 2003

I have been accepted to join the CPT delegation. The Israeli stamp I now have in my passport makes it impossible to enter Arab countries, so I have to get a second passport as soon as possible. In order to get a second passport, I need an official letter explaining why I need it. Claire at the CPT office tells me that they have a letter, but someone recently tried to use it in Chicago, and it wasn't accepted there. Yet it seems that's my only option, so she faxes the letter to me. The letter says that I am going to be traveling with CPT on a tour that includes some Arab countries. It does not specify Iraq. My flight will actually be going into Jordan.

CPT needs me to have the new passport in order to buy my ticket for a flight that is only two weeks from now. In order to get an expedited passport, I have to go to the San Francisco office. I call to make an appointment and "speak" to an automated system. The only appointment time that is available is in two hours. Given that my home is a ninety minute drive to San Francisco, I have less than a half hour to spare. I have to stop for passport photos on the way and I don't know exactly where I'm going in San Francisco, nor do I know the parking situation once I find the office. As I'm driving down the freeway with the CPT letter, I think to myself that if I am able to get the passport, that's my long-awaited sign that I am supposed to be going to Iraq at this time.

I manage to get the passport photos, find the office, find parking, and arrive in time for my appointment. The clerk who processes my application accepts the CPT letter. I have to come back tomorrow to pick up the passport, and I'm going to Iraq!

I'm feeling tired tonight. I don't think it's completely hit me what I've just committed to doing. I hope that it goes as well as Israel/Palestine did. I'm sure it will be different. One of my inner teachers gives me some advice (or reminders) about fear.

Think about fear and all the ways that it limits you. Fears stop you. It's good not to be so driven by fear. You're challenging that in a big way. It's no wonder you're tired. Give yourself a break, nurture yourself, let there be time to feel, clear out that schedule as much as possible. Give yourself time just to be with the fear. It's an important part of the experience. Feel the fear and know that you're not going to let it stop you.

I have to tell Mom.

January 16, 2003

I have to make another trip to San Francisco today. I awaken this morning, feeling burdened. I try to list the things on my mind: the syllabus for a course I'm teaching next semester; telling Mom and Dale, and my thesis students I'm going to Iraq; figuring out how to set up my e-mail address list as a list serve; taking time to myself to feel my feelings fully; taking care of loose ends; and discerning what's mine and what's not when confronted with other people's fears for me.

The needy child within me is feeling fearful and also trying to accept the idea of going to Iraq. She says, "You did a good job of taking care of me in Palestine, so I guess I can trust you to do so in Iraq; but I must say that I am not excited at all about doing this." Overall I'm feeling excited and looking forward to being part of a more solid "affinity" group than I was in Israel/Palestine. I'm happy; I have my feeling of aliveness back now that I've finally made the decision.

January 20, 2003

Claire from CPT calls today to find out my preference of airport. She says that she mailed materials to help me prepare. I look forward to seeing those. This prep feels much saner than my prep for my trip to Israel/Palestine because it's a formal delegation that is more supported by the organization.

There's nothing like putting myself in the face of death in order to appreciate all that I really love about life and to put priorities in perspective. I did so much coming to completion with people in my life when I went to Israel/Palestine, I don't feel a need to do it all again. I just need to stay current with everyone and everything, which is a good idea anyway. It feels quite right to be doing this. Even Mom seems to have taken it okay. Dale and my sister-in-law Judy went to the anti-war demonstration Saturday. I don't think they have ever done that before.

I have my range of feelings back, maybe more than I have had since they were conditioned out of me as an infant. One community member expresses his fears about what I'm doing. I appreciate his concerns and I'm glad he tells me about them so I can be more aware, but I recognize that they are his fears and I don't have to take them on as if they are my own.

Besides the threat that President Bush may start bombing while I am there, there are also the potential consequences of breaking US law. It is technically illegal to go to and spend money in Iraq because of the sanctions. I'm proud to do civil disobedience, and in this case the penalties for doing so seem small. In all the years that Voices in the Wilderness has been having a presence in Iraq, only a few smallish fines have ever been administered.

I prepare for a meeting with Michelle. She is not as available to help me as she was for my trip to Palestine because she has just adopted twin baby girls. The main requests I have for her are to call Mom on a regular basis and to send updates from CPT out to my listserve. I also pass on instructions for depositing checks and paying bills if I am not back by the end of the month. Finally, if my return is delayed further, I have a few calls I want her to make with regard to work responsibilities and appointments that I have scheduled in the next two months.

January 21, 2003

I question the relationship between being fully present and staying focused, because I see that being fully present means being aware of everything that's going on around me, and doing that might be a distraction to staying focused.

Clear intentions help with focus. Once your intentions are clear, then you can discern what of everything that's around you, you really want to let come into full awareness. You can discern and focus on that which supports your intention and ignore the rest. So staying focused is a way that you can hold your power and maximize it.

I see that when things appear chaotic, a focus on intention orders things in such a way that it doesn't seem so chaotic. The key is discernment. My heart communicates with me through feelings and I need to have access to all my feelings in order to discern where to focus and what to express—both what I let in and what I let out.

You are just a vessel through which many cycles flow like water. Energy finds the channels through which it is able to flow. It can't flow freely when the channel is blocked or dammed and in our society there's a lot of blocking and damming of energy flows. Much of that blockage is caused by fear. As a vessel, your job is to stay open so that what wants to flow through is able and if you hold that intention, then when you're in chaos that intention will keep the flow moving. Then only what shows up to block the flow needs your attention. The rest of the chaos that isn't blocking the flow is of no significance at that moment. When your intention is clear, the rest of the chaos is just distraction. There are a bunch of structures our society thinks are important for making order out of chaos. Many of these structures are insignificant if what's important is the flow of love.

© Ralph Portillo

Linda's brother, sister-in-law and niece

One practice that helps is meditation—not removing yourself from the world, but clearing the channels. The idea is to move in and through the world, being in relationship with whatever is present in the moment, and letting your spirit flow while staying grounded and centered.

I want to keep the channel open and expand the channel, so more and more of that love energy can flow through and out. I want more of my love energy to flow into the world wherever I am, whatever I am doing.

Just let it flow and trust. Surrender is not giving up. It is giving into that which is wanting to flow through; following your heart, whatever situation you find yourself in; not hiding or withdrawing, but staying fully present in the situation and in so doing, bringing your full contribution to it.

So what do I need to know to be preparing in the best way possible for this adventure? I ask.

You need to recognize that which you don't want to see in yourself and fully see it. Dance with your fear, don't let it stop you; accept it, learn from it, be with it, appreciate it.

January 22, 2003

I receive the materials from Claire. I read that I need to be prepared for an intense schedule, long days, and limited personal time and space. Also the basics of everyday life in Iraq can be very difficult and an attitude of flexibility is mandatory. In case of US military attack, travel could be difficult or seriously delayed. The past twelve years of sanctions have seriously undermined Iraqi infrastructure. Specifically the health care and sanitation system in Iraq has seriously deteriorated, so I should be prepared for some bouts of gastro-intestinal illness.

In reading the CPT materials, I am confident that this is exactly what I want. We will be living in Iraq among the ordinary people; and just by being there, we will be making a statement to our government that the lives of Iraqi people are as valuable as our own.

January 23, 2003

I'm excited about the trip. I talk with Claire, and feel a little self-conscious about some of my questions—that they may reveal the vulnerability that I always feel when traveling. CPT is so well organized that it gives me a great sense of security. I hope it isn't a false sense; I think I understand the reality of the situation.

I speak with a woman who is going to try to set up a talk for me upon my return at the graduate institute where I earned my PhD (the California Institute of Integral Studies). I am feeling much more ready to reach out and make presentations now than I did earlier. I can use these opportunities to get the message across that Iraqi lives are just as precious as our lives as US citizens. I need to experience fully the horrible ways people are being treated around the world because of the capitalistic values and the influence of my country. As a US citizen, I feel a sense of responsibility to present these realities to others.

January 26, 2003

I'm excited about the others from the United States who are also going to be in Baghdad while I'm there. David Hartsough says that Rabia and Elias (a couple whom I met at a Deep Ecology conference several years ago) are already there, and I see that Medea Benjamin is leading a group there as well. I have heard Medea speak and I respect her highly.

Tomorrow I intend to call the media contacts and to write to President Bush and my congressional representative.

Looking beyond this immediate trip to Iraq, I learn from David Hartsough that the Nonviolent Peaceforce is planning to send a delegation to Sri Lanka in July to explore the potential activities of having the pilot project there, with training scheduled for May.

January 27, 2003

I just realized that I could use help deciding to which office to send my letter. Is Congress in session currently or not? I don't know. Just that little need for help has me feeling down.

With what you're preparing to do, it's totally understandable that you get easily set off balance. So be kind to yourself and trust that whatever you're doing is right even if you can't know that rationally. Know that you've got a lot of good support within and without.

January 28, 2003

I didn't sleep much last night. I suppose that whatever I was doing besides sleeping was important. I have this media contact business and final prep for Iraq on my mind. I ran into some resistance from media contacts I made yesterday. I really had no idea what to expect, but I am disappointed with my results so far. I wish someone were helping me with this like Michelle did so generously when I was preparing to go to Israel/Palestine.

I recognize that in Western (European-influenced) society, we've been conditioned to separate and to defend. For me, these manifest as holding back or with-drawing. I've been conditioned to fear and to protect myself from much that is just illusion. I can understand these truths very well in my mind and yet, I have fifty years of patterning with which to contend. Actually, the patterns have been in place for more than the fifty years of my life; belief in the illusion of separate-ness has been passed from generation to generation. Yet the spirit within has not burned out and it won't. That spirit continues to yearn for connection.

Any bit of love that doesn't get to move might turn into the opposite—into a block such as a defense, into an action that hurts, or into what has been labelled 'evil.' Evil was created by Western ways of thinking. It was created by the mind that blocks the love from flowing and sees itself as separate. Love is life giving, life affirming, and life fulfilling. Thriving aliveness is cut off in separateness. Those Native American peoples who were known to have been so open and generous upon arrival of the Europeans learned to fear Europeans only after experiencing their abuse.

You're working at unlearning fear right now in a very big way. When you reach out to connect, some people see you and some people don't, but you can't control how your love is received. Others have their own blocks that blind or don't give the full picture. Sometimes it's about you not showing yourself, and of course if you don't show yourself then you don't have a chance of being seen ever by anyone; but all you can do is practice showing yourself because that's what you need to do and then let go of attachment to how you are received. Just keep refining the giving. You can get better and better at reading the 'other' to figure out how this relationship is going to work, how this channel of love is going to flow between these two people at this time. It's a craft. It's an art. It's a pursuit on which it is well worth focusing time and energy. It's about communication.

Some religious leaders (and witches) have carried that teaching. At some times in history, they let their love flow, and were killed for it. It's a different time now and the ability to connect or love is not in particular individuals as in religious leaders or trained healers, but it's in every one of us as we come together. Some of us may have easier access because there is less in the way or maybe just more of a yearning for it.

January 29, 2003
Today is a productive day. I now have four media e-mail addresses to give to Claire for distributing reports when we (the delegation) send them to the CPT office.

January 30, 2003
Claire sends an e-mail: "The possibility of war breaking out while you are there is real. Please talk with your loved ones about your motivations for going." She suggests that writing out a statement about intentions would allow me the oppor-tunity to collect my own thoughts, and that leaving a copy with my loved ones would help them understand what I am doing. So here goes!

My Statement of Intentions for Going to Iraq
Since my rational mind can't really understand nor explain why I

am moved to go to Iraq at this dangerous time when my country is threatening to bomb that country, I ask my intuitive mind to do its best to communicate from my heart. As I said before when I was preparing for my trip to Palestine, I cannot sit back and watch the atrocities that my government is committing in the world in my name with my money without doing all I can to shift that. I am going to Iraq in order to make a clear statement that the lives of the Iraqi people are just as sacred, precious, and important as my own. I am going to let the Iraqi people know that not all US Americans are represented by our president who wasn't even elected. I'm carrying with me to Iraq many prayers and blessings of many people who for many reasons are unable to get away to do this themselves. I go with an open heart that only wants to give love toward the healing of the earth and all of her beings, including humans. I go to witness and report real life stories of real life people to the media back here. I go while confronting and dancing with fears, and in so doing I want to challenge the power fear has over us especially here in the US (I'm thinking of Michael Moore's recent movie, "Bowling for Columbine"). I intend to do whatever I can to inspire others into actions that will contribute to these intentions in their own ways. I promise to strive to stay fully present, centered, and grounded so that I am as safe as possible; and also such that I am "standing in my own medicine"—thus bringing forth the best that my spirit has to bring to each and every situation and the people present. In all of this, I continue to hold the intention that all that I do and say be for the good of all beings.

I want to let you all know that although I feel that there is still a lot that I need to and want to do with this life, and it would be quite inconvenient, I'm not really afraid to die. I think the thought of that possibility (of my dying) is probably more diffi- cult to all of you and others whom I leave behind, but for me death is something that I think that I can accept fairly freely. I trust that my death will happen in its own timing. I trust the voice within that has made it clear to me that this is the right thing for me to be doing at this time and thus, though I do feel fearful at times, I rest assured that all is as it should be as long as I follow that voice (and please rest assured that I do take into consideration what the rational mind says as well).

I hope this piece of writing does what it is intended to do. One thing that it did was to force me to "confront and dance with" my fear of not being under- stood and to go forward anyway with this attempt to express some of what is in my heart.

4

Iraq

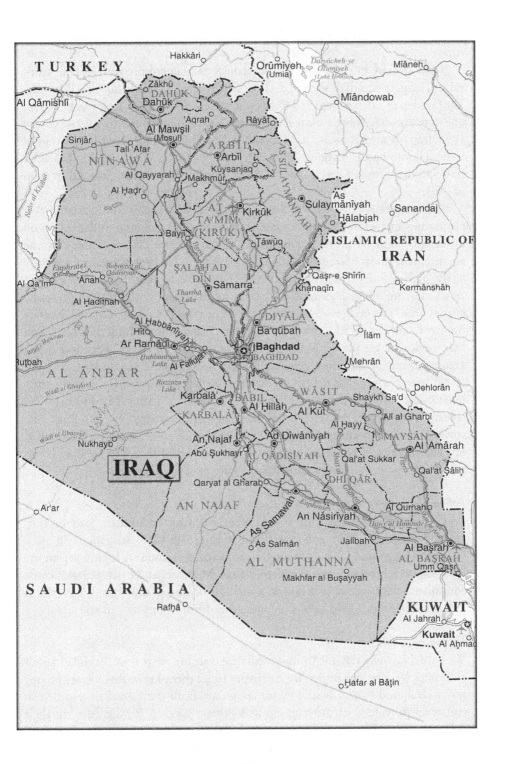

FROM THE MATERIALS SENT BY CPT, I glean the following brief background of Iraq's past as well as the situation between the USA and Iraq at the time of my trip.

It was around 4000 BC when the ancient Sumerian culture with its land cultivation, irrigation, urban society, and the first written alphabet flourished in Iraq. The Garden of Eden is depicted to have been here. Until 1990, Iraq was known as one of the most highly developed countries in the Middle East. Then in August of 1990, Iraq invaded Kuwait, and Operation Desert Storm followed—six weeks of intense bombing throughout the country led by the USA. After those six weeks, Iraq withdrew from Kuwait, but sanctions put in place at that time still remain in 2003.

Beginning early in George W. Bush's presidency in 2000, his administration was promoting a new foreign policy strategy of preemptive and even unilateral action utilizing US military power. Under International Law, the USA must demonstrate an imminent threat of Iraqi attack, so President Bush has been speaking frequently of the high risk that Iraq will unleash weapons of mass destruction in a surprise attack. Furthermore, President Bush's top administration officials continuously speak of the "mortal threat" posed by Iraq. When the UN asked National Security Adviser Condoleezza Rice to supply material evidence of the Iraqi threat, she said that we don't want the "smoking gun to be a mushroom cloud." Rice and Bush's arguments rely on emotions generated by the September eleven attacks.

My perception is that many US citizens as well as the international community remain unconvinced that Iraq really poses a threat to national or international security. Meanwhile, the US and UK insist on "regime change" in Iraq. Bush now vows to attack Iraq unilaterally if the UN Security Council refuses to authorize it. His administration is essentially demonstrating a belief that international law is an obstacle to be overcome, rather than a guidepost for US policy.

February 2, 2003

Peggy and Cliff meet us at the airport when we arrive in Amman, Jordan. They are both from the USA and have been leading the CPT delegations in Iraq. Counting Peggy and Cliff there are thirteen members in our delegation from the USA, Canada, Scotland, and the Netherlands. Members of the delegation include educators, scientists, social workers, a medical doctor, and a retired minister, as well as full-time peaceworkers. Our ages range from twenty-five to seventy-six.

February 3, 2003

We have a lay-over day in Amman while we wait for word from Baghdad about our visas. We visit our respective embassies to let them know that we are on our way to Iraq and to tell them why we are going. Both the Canadian and British embassies provide a warm reception and express concern for the safety of their delegates. The official at the US embassy warns us not to go "for our own safety" and gives a lengthy account of our government's position. As we talk longer with him, I get the impression that personally he has mixed feelings about the war in Iraq.

We ask why we continue to harm the people with sanctions and bombs when we know it is the regime and not the people who are the threat. He says that the concern is that there are products that were imported at an earlier time for which Iraq hasn't yet accounted that could contribute to biological and chemical weapons. According to him, Iraq, Iran, and North Korea are three countries who have chemical and biological weapons and who aren't cooperating with the international community. That sounds like Bush rhetoric to me.

Our embassy official acknowledges that the USA does not value morality higher than national interest. He divulges that he has a hard time trying to fit his own sense of morality into a position in which he is expected to simply follow US policy, and he admits, "It's not in my best interest as an American to cause suffering to other people." Further, the US American embassy official gives us his perception of the perspectives of Jordanians. Jordan's energy economy is dependent on Iraq and thus they would rather not have a war against Iraq. At the same time, there are a number of Jordanians who don't like the Iraqi regime. He says that most of the people here don't want war in Iraq and also that Jordanians have more anger and concern about US support of Israel. Furthermore, he identifies it as a problem that people reduce the complexity of the whole situation to East against West or Islam versus Christian/Jew.

This evening, several of us go to the Iraqi embassy to pick up our visas. We sit for over an hour in the waiting room, which Cliff says is typical. In the end, only part of our group receives visas and that worries us until we learn that this is only a technological glitch; one page of names had not been faxed from Baghdad.

Later this evening, we meet as a group. Following the CPT guidelines, different ones of us take responsibility for different roles and tasks to contribute while we are together in order for the team to function efficiently. I will be overseeing the writing of the final report.

February 4, 2003

The rest of the visas are issued this morning and soon we are gathering in our hotel lobby with our luggage. We are relieved that we all got our visas and our mood is jovial. We overhear a local person in the lobby: "I've never seen a group of people so happy to be going to Iraq."

By 10:30 am. we are settled in our bus and on our way. We stop along the highway for delicious kabobs and arrive at the Jordanian border around 6:30 pm. We show our passports and visas many times at this border crossing, both in order to leave Jordan and then again just across the border to enter Iraq.

I am particularly impressed by the welcome we receive at the Iraqi border. Iraqi men invite us into a warm and comfortable reception area adorned with a giant picture of Saddam Hussein filling the upper portion of the wall at one end of the room. Almost immediately two men present a tray with tea in glasses the size of shot glasses to a few of us. They don't have enough tea glasses to serve all of us at the same time, so as one person finishes hers/his tea, the men quickly whisk the glass away, wash it, refill it, and bring it back on the elegant tray to serve to the next person. Those who speak English chat with us while our electronic equipment is checked. They speak fondly of their country and of the city of Baghdad.

The whole process at the border takes about three hours, and then we are back on the road in the dark. Along the way, Cliff passes out thick wads of Iraqi dinar. These 250 dinar bills that were once each worth $750 before the sanctions are now worth twelve and half cents.

We finally arrive in Baghdad about 3 am.

February 5, 2003

Cliff and Peggy give an orientation that includes some tips about tourist life in Iraq. We should negotiate cab costs ahead of time and try not to overpay, because when drivers manage to get bigger prices from internationals, they will start to charge all of us more. Also, we should not talk with Iraqis about Iraqi government or leaders. That could put the people in jeopardy.

Iraq border reception room

We learn a little bit more about life for Iraqis here. The government effectively distributes food rations. The food that is distributed may not be completely nourishing, but everyone is eligible for the rations, so no one goes without food in Iraq and some people also sell some of their rations as a source of income. Before the Gulf War and the beginning of the sanctions, the government rations were a supplement; now, it is the full diet for some people. Since they have adequate food, the key reasons for child deaths are poor water and sanitation.

Two Iraq Peace Team (IPT) representatives join our meeting and share more about the situation here. Iraqis are tired and doing the minimum to get by. They say that the war against terror is really a war against civilians. Now, there are more internationals here than ever before: thirty-nine IPT participants including us (the CPT delegation) and fifteen CODEPINK women from the USA. Italians in a delegation calling themselves "human shields" are expected to arrive soon.

The IPT representatives give us some further practical advice. We should always carry our passport, visa, the "magic letter" that explains in Arabic who we are and why we are here, and the hotel business card just in case we need to find our way back to the hotel. Our bomb shelter is the basement of the hotel.

This afternoon, we visit the Amariya Shelter.[3] This bomb shelter is in a residential neighborhood where it was meant to provide safety to women, children, and elderly men in the event of war. During the Gulf War (on February 13, 1991 at 4 am.) the USA dropped two bombs directly on this shelter. The first bomb blew through the two-meter thick reinforced ceiling and went on down to blow through that floor which was the ceiling of the floor below. The second bomb was of a different type. It incinerated everything inside the shelter on both floors. 408 people died. Fourteen were saved because they were sleeping close enough to the door that the force of the blast blew their bodies out the door of the shelter. The oldest victim was an 80-year old grandfather, the youngest a baby who had been born four hours earlier. US military personnel said it was an accident and called it "collateral damage."

One team member describes what we see standing inside the shelter and looking up: "Twisted lengths of rebar that seem to be bent like pipe cleaners, the hole in the two-meter thick concrete ceiling looks like punctured tissue paper." We can see blackened imprints of people's bodies burned into the floor and walls.

I weep thinking about the horror of what my country has done in my name. The thought that we may be about to do it again is totally unfathomable to me. Our guide lives in the neighborhood. She says that now the Iraqi people will not go any of the thirty-three bomb shelters that are in the city because after that experience, they believe that they will be safer staying in their homes. The Amariya Shelter is now being maintained as a museum, a memorial to the horror of war.

Some of the other internationals here don't seem concerned about the bombing occurring before we leave the country on February 15. Cliff who has been here for two months is still hopeful that bombing won't happen at all. I am concerned and want us to talk about the possibility.

In the group meeting this evening, we name "what if" scenarios such as: What if bombs start to fall while we are together here? What if someone wants to leave before the rest of the group is set to leave a situation? What if someone is taken hostage? This is in preparation for a committee to consider the various situations and propose emergency plans back to the group. We also hear the distressing news that US Secretary of State, Colin Powell has made a very pro-war speech. I go to bed feeling agitated.

February 6, 2003

I am part of the committee who meets over breakfast to discuss our disaster plans for responding to the "what if" situations we raised last night. I may have

Ceiling of Amariya shelter

© Mike Hartnell

been the only one who felt a need for the plans, but at least several others come to this breakfast meeting. I feel safer once we have some plans in place.

I express a concern about having enough drinking water since I drink so much. Cliff takes us on a walking tour of the neighborhood and we buy many six packs of quart bottles of water. Cliff shows us to check to make sure the seals are still in place when we buy bottled water. Otherwise it might be a re-used bottle with tap water.

Many men whom we pass on the streets greet us by placing a hand over the heart. This is also a typical gesture that accompanies a handshake.

This afternoon, we have a first-aid briefing presented by Ted who is a seasoned IPT (Iraq Peace Team) delegate and war veteran. The disaster plan that we created this morning and this presentation help me feel more like I will know what to do if bombing begins while we're here, and this knowledge eases my fears. I think the discussions also give all of us an experiential glimpse at what it might be like to be an Iraqi living with the threat of bombing present all the time. Yet one big difference between us and them is that we are here by choice and will be leaving after a short stay. For the local people, that threat is their everyday reality and they cannot escape it.

At the first aid briefing, Ted distributes an IPT handout with safety recommendations. The handout warns that there might be a tendency to assume that since we cannot predict the future with extreme clarity we should do nothing. Ted says to hope for the best and prepare for the worst. In our rooms at night, we should have a "crash kit" ready that includes: flashlight and batteries, candles and matches, water, essential clothing, snacks, passport photos, passport, plane ticket, visa, emergency number, Iraqi money, toilet paper, and hand wipes. Before we go to sleep, we should put the clothes that we'll wear if we need to evacuate with the crash kit. Then if we do need to evacuate in the night, we can grab the pile and dress in the hallway as we make our way to the basement.

For safety on the street, we need to always be aware of where we might run for cover. For cover, we would want to get down and behind something—best would be to lie down in a ditch. While walking around the city, we should stay away from bridges because bridges are often targets. If we must cross one, we should take a cab so we don't stay on a potential target for long. Likewise, we should not walk on the side of the street where there is a building that might be a target.

IPT has prepared a news release and suggested talking points for us to use in response to Colin Powell's speech. We recognize that many listeners and viewers in the United States are likely to be scared following the speech. IPT is taking the stand that Powell's speech falls short of a legitimate justification for war. We say that war by the USA against Iraq is still not a war of self-defense. The UN Charter clearly states that all means of peaceful negotiation should be employed before any state declares war against another state and the USA has not employed all means for negotiated and diplomatic resolution of its disputes with Iraq. The Pentagon says it plans to drop more cruise missiles in the first two days of bombardment than were fired during the entire bombing campaign of the Gulf War in 1991. We maintain that this warfare would be immoral, illegal, unjustified, and counterproductive.

In fact, the US government seems determined to create the very conditions that will promote what they say they are trying to avoid. To show this, IPT points out Israel's collection of nuclear warheads and missiles, and that Israel is in defiance of numerous UN resolutions and is guilty of massive human rights violations. Yet the US is focused instead on the destruction of Iraq. IPT says that this blatant double-standard of US policy fuels national and religious animosities and undermines the prospect of peace in the region.

February 7, 2003

My sense of the likelihood of war starting while we're here goes up and down day to day, depending on the news from the United States. Colin Powell's speech was distressing and we hear today that President Bush said something like: "The game in Iraq is over." Yet, there are UN inspectors traveling here now and I think that while they are here, the world will be watching and President Bush isn't going to bomb Baghdad.

Today there is an Iraq Peace Team (IPT) meeting. We learn that thirteen people from France are expected to arrive today and thirty from Italy are coming soon. A group of Spanish dancers have also arrived. Many of the IPT people and some who are in my CPT delegation are planning to stay beyond February 15; some are committed to being here indefinitely at this point.

Elias of IPT shares plans for a series of actions that will take place next week in preparation for the mass demonstrations that are happening throughout the world on February 15. Every day next week the team will leave the hotel at 7:00 am. to gather across from the UN Headquarters in order to be there when the inspectors leave for their day's work. The message of our demonstrations will be: "Inspections Yes, Invasion No." One purpose is to gain media coverage and to appeal to people all over the world to come out on February 15. Then at 11:00 each morning, we will travel to a site such as a water treatment facility, electrical power station, university, or elementary school (places that were bombed in the Gulf War). At each site each day we will hang a banner that says, "Bombing this site is a war crime." We are hoping that people around the world will pick up on these demonstrations and place similar banners in similar places in their own home countries.

When we talk to the Iraqi people, we hear that the sanctions, which are "killing us slowly," are more dreadful than the threat of war. Some say that they can't think about war, when every day is a struggle for survival. They live one day to the next as our hotel receptionist said, "Waiting, just waiting. What else can you do?" The Iraqi dinar has decreased in value so much due to the sanctions that many teachers, doctors, nurses, and other professionals have had to quit their jobs. We meet a woman who used to be a teacher until her salary got as low as five dollars a month. She is now doing a day job that pays better than teaching and she is also painting pictures in the evenings and selling these for additional income.

While out in Baghdad today, some of us see inside a bus directly in front of our taxi a live brass band playing and children dancing. As we pass the bus, we realize that it is part of a wedding procession.

I join some of the women on the team to walk with Peggy from our hotel to visit a family she has gotten to know. Children play football (soccer) on the quiet residential streets while inside the homes, women clean and cook meals for families and guests.

The visit reminds me of visits with families in Palestine. We sit in the front room where several of the women serve us tea and sweets. The children love talking to us in their best English and they show us schoolbooks for learning English with English words and pictures. We are invited into the woman's bedroom and she shares some of her perfume with us. She gives us gifts—precious little trinkets.

UN inspectors starting their day

I hate taking these things because I know this family has so little, but I also know that it is important to accept what is offered. When we are ready to go, the woman insists that we come back for dinner in a few days to join the family for their Eid celebration, a three-day holiday. Peggy graciously declines.

This evening, some of us go to a music hall in which over two hundred Iraqi men (plus CODE PINK women and five of us) are gathered to listen to traditional Iraqi "macam" music. The hall is full of warm greetings as the men arrive and settle in the hard church-like seats. A fiddle player, flute player, percussionists, and several singers perform with high energy.

February 8, 2003

Today, I feel the best yet psychologically, even though I have diarrhea, so I guess I'm not so great physically. I talk with Michelle briefly to set up a time for her to call me back. I notice that being in touch with her makes a huge difference in my sense of well-being and realize once again just how important it is to have this key communication link with people back home.

Some of our team join an IPT action in which they meet the head UN inspector at the airport and then rally in front of his hotel with banners in order to attract media attention. They do get some media attention, so they feel successful. After

I hear what happened, I wish I had gone with them.

Instead, the group I join visits Cardinal Etchegary, the pope's "right hand man" who came from the Vatican to give a mass at the cathedral here in Baghdad. He tells us that Pope Paul would be here himself if he could because he is against the war, but he is getting too old and frail these days and unable to travel. I wish Pope Paul could be here; I cannot imagine that President Bush would bomb Baghdad if the pope were here.

After this visit with the cardinal, we take a trip on a small boat across the Tigris River to the Suk (outdoor market).

Later, I'm standing on the balcony outside my hotel room. I'm happy about this room location. It is a south facing window on the 6th floor overlooking the street and I can see the Tigris River to the west. I can see a good-sized section of Baghdad from here. Traffic seems calmer today, maybe because it's a national holiday (Independence Day). Tomorrow, we go to Mosul in the North of Iraq for two days and then there will be three days of a Muslim holiday (Eid). We will be returning to Jordan on the next day, so we don't have any more normal days in Baghdad.

I have 2½ hours before dinner at 7:00 pm. It feels good to have some time to myself, to reflect, write, shower, and rest.

We have a wonderful dinner here at our hotel. The hotel owners treat us to this feast to thank us for being here doing what we're doing. They serve platters of chicken, beef, vegetables, and salads. Some of my teammates don't eat any of the fresh salads because of concern about the quality of the water, but I take my chances and eat a little.

Matt tells the story of his conversation with a taxi driver. The driver said: "My wife's mother called from Detroit last night and she said we should get out of Baghdad." Matt marvels that even though he comes from the country that is about to bomb this driver's country, the Iraqi still seemed to want to establish a connection. The driver continued: "We love life. We love life and we are warm-hearted people. All we want is an easy life." Matt describes his struggle to know what to say in response when what he would say and what our government might do in our names are so different. When they arrived at Matt's destination, the driver turned to Matt and said, "My name is Riad. Welcome." They shook hands vigorously as Matt told his name. The driver repeated several more times, "Welcome here. Welcome here."

February 9, 2003

I'm frustrated that Michelle is unable to get through to me when she tries calling at the agreed-upon time and I think she may be pretty frustrated as well. I receive her response to my first e-mail and it is only one line, so again I feel out of contact with family and community. I console myself that since we don't have many more days before we leave Iraq, I can accept that it is what it is and endure it for now.

Today we are treated to another wonderful meal, a lunch with our "minder's" family. A minder is like a tour guide who is certified by the government to keep track of where we go and what we do as guests in their country. Our minder's family owns some beautiful farm-land with citrus trees. When we arrive, he and his brother lead us for a walk on the land and then the men of the delegation visit with the men of the family while the women visit with the women in a separate location. Soon, all members of the delegation sit down together for the meal prepared by the women and served to us by the men. The men stand behind us, and watch us eat. They place more food on our plates every time we finish something. I struggle with what to do because I don't eat beef. I nibble a little of the beef dish in order to be polite, but then I realize that the more I eat, the more they will give me, so I end up deciding that I just have to leave some of it on my plate.

After lunch, we travel with our minder the five and a half hour drive to Mosul. The land we cross is very open for the most part and then at widely spaced cross-roads, there are clusters of shops. Shepherds tend their flocks along the sides of the road. The homes range in quality from tents or old broken down buildings to new and beautiful adobe type structures.

Lulled by the movement of the bus, I marvel over how much history this particular land has witnessed. I decide to ask for guidance from this land. I want to hear what it has to tell me, but I think that we are moving too fast. To my surprise, as soon as I tune in, I get a clear and simple but profound message: "Slow down. Learn to breathe with the land, and then you will know how to be in relationship with the other."

When we arrive in Mosul, we visit Old Nineveh, an ancient historical site that was an active community 6,000 years ago. This is a place visited by Jonah, according to the Bible.

February 10, 2003

We visit the Children's Hospital of Mosul. Before the Gulf War and the sanctions, it was a modern, well-equipped hospital providing a wide range of services to children. After the effects of the sanctions set in, nurses could no longer afford to work and so they had to leave. Now there seems to be just one doctor and families rather than nurses take care of the needs of the children who are the patients.

Dr Shameh, a pediatrician in his mid-thirties, leads us from room to room explaining the difficulties of caring for sick, malnourished children when he knows what treatments they need but does not have the means to provide them.[4]

First, we enter a small room with five or six worried-looking adults standing around a cot with an emaciated eight-year-old boy. Five days ago, this boy was diagnosed as having viral encephalitis. Dr Shameh says that they cannot import enough of the antiviral antibiotic. The doctor explains that the boy is the long-awaited male child in this family, with five older sisters. The boy's anguished and angry mother hisses at us, gesturing wildly with her arms.

A three-month old infant lies gasping beside his mother; the oxygen mask is too large for his face. The doctor says that there is no treatment available; even oxygen tanks are hard to come by.

A girl tries to comfort her twelve-month old brother. He was admitted with fever and convulsions due to meningitis from an untreated ear infection. There was only enough of the needed antibiotic for four days, so the doctor switched to another antibiotic that was used twenty years ago. He hopes it does

Men of the minder's family

not cause severe bone marrow depression. "What else can we do?" he shrugs and shakes his head.

Another malnourished infant has acute kidney failure. Since 1991 there has been no dialysis in the North of Iraq. "We are treating her conservatively," the doctor says. The mom is breastfeeding and the infant is receiving an electrolyte solution intravenously.

Dr Shameh shows us the hospital transfusion center, and says that before 1991, 750 patients received transfusions every month. Now only a handful get transfusions and the limiting factor is not blood, but blood bags, intravenous lines, and cannulas, which are all products limited by the sanctions.

The doctor is distressed, but not in despair. He says he knows what's needed, but he can't do what's needed; he can't treat his patients in a way that they can leave the hospital healthy. Many of the children will die in the hospital and others will not fully recover.

On our way back to Baghdad, we visit an historic site that's being renovated called Hattra. It was active around 260 B.C.E. We see temples to the sun, moon, and Mars, plus some wells and places where animals were sacrificed. Both Greek and Roman architecture were used, and there are many beautiful sculptures in the walls—figures from myths of many cultures. Iraqis discovered and started digging this place out in 1951, but the renovations had to stop after the Gulf War because of lack of funds. I wonder what will become of it now in the approaching war.

No e-mail message from Michelle today; I will try calling her again tonight. I'm going to start working on the team report.

February 11, 2003

As planned, IPT has set up a tent across from the UN and we are getting out early in the morning each day this week to wave to the inspectors on their way to work. Today, one inspector crosses the boulevard to give us a big "Thank you." He tells us that our presence is really helping their morale. Many media people from all over the world (including England, China, Japan, South Korea, France, Germany) come to interview various ones of us. No reporters come from the USA.

We drive out to a power plant where we unfurl the banner that says, "To bomb this site is a war crime under the Geneva Convention."

We also learn that Iraqis have two six million-dollar generators that they bought but have not been able to use. The generators have been sitting here unused, because due to the sanctions they don't have the software and necessary supplies to run them.

Back at the hotel, I have a conversation with a man behind the desk. He confirms what I have heard from others. The threat of the war is not nearly as big a deal to the Iraqi people as the sanctions that they've been living under for the last twelve years. He says, "The war will come and go, but the sanctions are a threat to the economy here. It used to be a thriving place and people were healthy and well. Now there is a lot of poverty."

February 12, 2003

Having had so much difficulty ever getting to talk to Michelle, it's amazing that I manage to complete a live interview uninterrupted with Pat Thurston at a radio station back home. It is 4:00 am. here. Following are some excerpts.

Pat begins with a question about my reasons for coming to Iraq. I give the reasons I've named earlier and then I say, "I'm also confronting my own fear in a big way and I think that the atrocities of the system and the system itself are able to stay in place because of playing up on our fears. One thing I have to say to that effect is that being here is much less scary than thinking about being here."

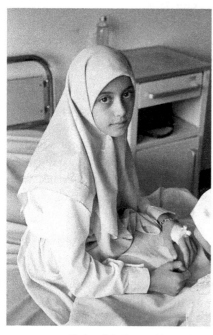
Girl with leukemia

© Alan Pogue

She speaks from her fear: "Linda, you're in Baghdad. You're in the heart of it and every indication is that within the next couple of weeks, we're going to start bombing and those bombs—there's not going to be a few of them. We're looking at 800 bombs falling in possibly a 24-hour period."

"Right, we've heard that. Actually before I came, I expected that bombing could easily have started while I was here. I'm already leaving now in less than a week. But we got a good sense of what it is like—I mean just a glimpse of what it is like—to be an Iraqi living here with that threat in the background of their lives every day and that's been going on for a long time."

I go on to say: "Also, the reports that you hear there are very much biased toward the sense that war is inevitable. And many of us here still hold out that it isn't inevitable, that there is still some sanity in the world that could keep the US in check. I'm sure you've heard that Germany, France, and Belgium have all taken stands against the war. They've come up with a good alternate proposal in the UN."

Pat asks about our restrictions and the need for a minder.

"I've been here for over a week. We had a minder two of the days. Otherwise, we've been free to move on our own. We have to get permission from the minder to go where we go, but I don't feel a strong sense of restriction, nor do I feel inhibited."

"But in talking to the people when you've had the opportunity to, were they receptive to you? Were they kind to you?"

"Oh yes! Totally. It's an incredibly different culture than in the US. These people are loving, generous, hospitable, and kind to us any time that we meet them. They know we're Americans and they're totally appreciative of us for being here for one thing, but it's just part of their culture to be hospitable and generous."

Power plant demonstration

I tell the story of the men serving us tea at the border crossing. "And this has been my experience every time we meet anyone and go into a home or place of work. We sit down and tea is provided. We have visited families and often a whole meal is provided. And these are people who have been living under sanctions that don't have access to a lot and they'll give whatever they have even to US citizens. The other thing is after spending time with anyone like the woman of the house, when she's saying good-bye it's like you've become family. You get a hug and a kiss on both cheeks. It's totally amazing—the loving generosity of these people."

Again, Pat speaks a fear: "Have you heard what we just heard this morning? Have the Iraqi people heard the words of Osama bin Ladin that were broadcast on Al Jazeera today? He says he's in solidarity with the Iraqi people, but he also calls for the Iraqi people to overthrow Sadam Hussein. He calls for them not to give any support to Christians or Jews, that if they do that they essentially become one of them, which would essentially be an enemy to Muslims. It was very scary to hear his words and were I you in that situation right now, it might make me a little more nervous."

I tell her that we don't talk to the people about Sadam Hussein. It would be dangerous to them to do so. I say that I'm not here to fight a political battle. "I'm here to stand in solidarity with people who are facing atrocious conditions."

I tell about the Children's Hospital, the Amariya Bomb Shelter, and the actions that are taking place this week.

In the end of the interview, Pat thanks me for my courage and for being here. "Linda Sartor, live from Baghdad."

February 12, 2003

This morning at the Peace Tent Vigil, we are singing and dancing in order to stay warm. Two of our Iraqi drivers join us and teach us the words to one of their songs. After we learn enough of it to start singing together, two Iraqi guards in front of the UN building across the boulevard start to join in, also singing and dancing in place. What a glorious moment!

After the morning vigil, we visit CARE International. This organization provides water and health care. We learn that there were no NGOs (Non-Governmental Organizations) here prior to 1991. Up until then Iraq was a prosperous developed country and didn't have a need for NGO support. In 1991 many people had savings and assets. By now, they have given all those up in order to support themselves. Now a new doctor is paid only $11 a month. Many women here are chronically anemic. This woman who works for CARE describes a teacher she knows who has no furniture because he had to sell it all. He has bought his own second-hand clothing on credit and hasn't been able to pay the bills, and he had to take his daughter out of high school because he didn't have school clothes for her.

About the possibility of war, this woman says, "You don't try to think. You just live day to day. You already have difficulty supporting your family now. You can't think about what will happen if there is war." Then she also identifies another concern, "It may start, but how will it end? When will it end?"

Later, we visit an art center in an elegant waterfront home where middle class people sell and shop. Amal al-Khedairy, the owner, welcomes us with the typical hospitality of tea and then we browse the handcrafted goods on display in multiple beautiful rooms and the courtyard of the art center part of her house.

February 13, 2003

Today we meet with a man at the United Nations Development Program. He tells us that in 1990-1991, power plants generated 9000 megawatts of electricity and now they are only able to produce 4000 megawatts. The water system depends on electricity. Without electricity, the sewage backs up into the water system. Though we foreigners have only been drinking bottled water, the Iraqi people drink the poor quality tap water and this leads to epidemics and disease, which often are untreatable because of lack of necessary drugs.

We learn that The Oil for Food Program is implemented by the government in most (fifteen) locations, and by the UN in the three Northern locations in order to protect the Kurds. He says that the food distribution administered by Iraqi officials is very good, but humiliating, that humiliation leads to revenge, and "people are exhausted. I'm surprised we don't see more fights."

He shakes his head, "We are one of the richest countries in the world," and goes on to say, "I'm amazed and humbled every day by the courage and values of the people." Yet three to four million Iraqis have left the country and are longing to come back. He also tells us that we all need to work together in terms of reconciliation—for the rehabilitation of the Iraqi mind/spirit and to give hope to the young people.

Later, we have a group meeting to discuss going home; addressing concerns about getting through the airport. At Immigration, we can tell them we've been to Iraq, and it's a good idea to hold onto our passports. It's our right to hold our passports when the officials take down the information. We are advised to write the CPT phone number on our arms just in case we should get arrested.

We conclude our time together as a delegation with a dinner together and a closing meeting. We sing songs and tell stories meant to inspire all of us to move into action. The ten of us who are returning home honored the five who are staying behind—Peggy, Cliff, and three from our delegation—for their commitment to staying here in solidarity with the Iraqi people. Then the five honored the ten of us who are returning to our hometowns with many important

Demonstration site across from UN

stories to tell. I am leaving with a renewed sense of possibility and the challenge, which I'd like to pass on: What does it take to stop a war?

February 14, 2003

One of the hotel clerks who served us behind the desk makes a special trip in to the hotel today on his day off in order to say good-bye. When someone asks about his family, he says, "I don't have a wife or child, but all of the earth community is my family. All of you are my brothers and sisters. If there's a war, if there is no war, it doesn't matter. I still have my smile."

We travel back to Amman today.

February 15, 2003

To be in solidarity with the massive anti-war demonstrations that are taking place in cities around the world today, the seven of us flying together from Amman through London hold a silent vigil in a busy corridor of Heathrow Airport in London. We display a large sign saying, "No War in Iraq." Several passers-by take photos, one woman joins the vigil, and several others express thanks or say, "Peace be with you."

After the vigil, three teammates have to get to their gates and four of us go to a restaurant for lunch. Police officers find us in the restaurant to investigate a complaint that "there had been a demonstration with a banner." Our conversation is amiable, although the officer in charge makes it clear that displaying such offensive banners can be grounds for arrest. One delegation member who is wearing a shirt that says "War is not the answer" inquires as to whether his shirt would cause a similar response, and the police officer explains that, indeed, the shirt might be considered offensive by many and that he could be arrested if there was a complaint.

Hotel clerk's goodbye

After the police officers leave the restaurant, a woman approaches from another table and says, "Actually, I was quite thankful for what you were doing there. I almost joined your group."

When I arrive in San Francisco, the immigration officer asks where I've been. I tell him that I've been in Iraq. After I tell him why I was there, he smiles and says, "Good for you."

I think the most dangerous part of this whole trip was actually my drive home in heavy rain after traveling for some twenty-seven hours.

March 3, 2003

I see in an email today that after being a diplomat for twenty years, John Brady Kiesling submitted a letter of resignation to Secretary of State Colin Powell. What he says in his letter reminds me of our conversation with the official in the US Embassy in Jordan. Kiesling says that his belief in the United States and its values was the "most powerful weapon" in his "diplomatic arsenal," and that with the Bush Administration, he can no longer believe that he is upholding the interests of the people of the USA and the world.

It looks like Russia is going to veto the US resolution to invade Iraq. Turkey is also still likely to oppose the invasion. I remain hopeful that we can stop President Bush from bombing Iraq.

March 6, 2003

The lobbying organization called MoveOn.org has sent a message reporting that in less than two days, 550,000 people from over 200 countries have signed their petition to the UN Security Council to not approve President Bush's war.

March 9, 2003

I learn today that under a procedure called "Uniting for Peace," the UN General Assembly can demand an immediate ceasefire and withdrawal even when the Security Council cannot come to a consensus. This gives me another reason for hope.

March 11, 2003

There are six countries in the UN Security Council who are undecided about a war in Iraq: Mexico, Cameroon, Guinea, Angola, Chile, and Pakistan. The US, the UK, Spain, and Bulgaria are for the war, while France, Germany, Russia, China, and Syria are calling for continued inspections and a peaceful resolution.

March 19, 2003

Congressman Kucinich proposes an Emergency Congressional Resolution, which would amend the October 10 resolution that handed over absolute military power to President Bush, and transfer war powers back to Congress.

March 20, 2003

Contrary to my hope that it could be stopped, President Bush starts bombing Baghdad early this morning. I spend the day in San Francisco participating in civil disobedience along with two members of my community. We stop traffic in the Financial District by taking over intersections. Our message is that we cannot continue with "business as usual" while the US is dropping bombs on Iraq in our names.

We step out into a crosswalk when the light turns green. The three of us spread out across the street, and then just stop walking, standing in place while the light turns red. Other protesters join us and soon there are protesters in the other crosswalks as well and we have managed to block traffic completely across the whole intersection. The police come and then we leave that intersection behind, moving on to do the same thing in the next intersection.

I have a blast. My "inner adolescent" loves the self-righteous defiance. This kind of action helps move my anger through my body. We manage to avoid getting a ticket and I don't see anyone get arrested.

I receive an e-mail report from my teammates in Baghdad. Lisa describes hearing the aircraft and the sirens at 5:30 am. She says, "There was an hour plus of sporadic explosions, some 'boom' and some 'rat-tat-tat.' They were not very close to us. One rattled the windows slightly. A couple of us stood outside in the hotel entrance for a few minutes. The Iraqi staff at the small hotel here are very helpful and comforting. One of the staff went home last night to stay with his wife who will have a baby any day now. He called this morning to tell us not to worry." Lisa says that there is much less activity on the streets, but men are still out visiting with each other and children are still playing soccer.

My teammates Cliff, Betty, and Peggy along with other Iraq Peace Team members set up a tent and are providing 24-hour presence at a Water Treatment Center that provides water to one sixth of the city and to a hospital.

At midnight Lisa, who is staying at the hotel in Baghdad, reports that the latest attack was really scary where she is. It was a lot closer, and she felt the building rattling. That attack lasted for 30-40 minutes. The team at the hotel took "shelter" on the ground floor, which has windows boarded over and stocks of food and water. Lisa says that the Iraqi people are amazingly strong. The people are calm and collected, encouraging each other and the team. A 15-year-old boy said to Lisa today, "I want you to go home. I'm used to this, but you are not."

The team is encouraged by all the anti-war actions around the world. They say to tell everyone we meet at vigils and demonstrations that we attend, "Iraqis thank you from the bottom of their hearts."

March 21, 2003

I hear again from the team in Baghdad. Bombs have been falling for the past hour and the bombing is more intense than it was the previous night. Inside the hotel, severe pressure can be felt when bombs explode. The bombing at the water treatment plant tent site is somewhat less intense. The telephone connection between the "tenters" and the hotel (a distance of four miles) continues to work, although connections to other parts of the city are breaking down.

March 25, 2003

My five CPT teammates are still in Baghdad. Peggy reports:

> Right now as I write this there have been two bombs exploding in the background. On the horizon in most directions we see plumes of black smoke coming up from buildings burning.
>
> Some cars are still on the streets and we have been able to get around in taxis. Yesterday, many of us went to a hospital where wounded people are being taken. We saw a twelve-year-old boy with a large cut in his abdomen from shrapnel. He and eleven other members of his family were injured by shrapnel while in their home two days ago. Many others are awaiting or just coming out of surgery for shrapnel removal.
>
> For the last three nights, I have slept out in one of two tents at the water treatment plant. So far I have appreciated being at the camp. The out-of-doors setting with grass, trees, and songbirds flying around has fed my spirit.
>
> I have been experiencing a mixture of fear and anger, but mostly grief about what is happening. There is no good reason for this assault on this society and these innocent people. I am impressed by their strength and courage and their continued openness and graciousness to us who are from countries who are bombing them. We don't know from day to day what we will be able

to do. Our 'minders' have just started wanting to know where everyone is during the day, and not allowing us to go out on the streets around the hotels unaccompanied; but up until now, we have been able to go to most of the places we have wanted to go.

March 30, 2003

Three of the five people from my team who are still in Iraq are asked to leave by their minder, probably for their own safety. They leave Baghdad with other internationals in a group of three cars. On their way out of the country, one of the cars has a blow-out and three US citizens are injured in the accident. My teammate Cliff is one of the injured. They are treated at the only remaining medical facility in a town that had been bombed just three days earlier. Their story captures well my experience of the generosity and loving compassion of the Iraqi people. I find myself sobbing as I read it.

As the internationals drive out of Baghdad, US and British planes can be seen in the skies and are actively engaged in bombing near the road; the drivers decide to spread their vehicles apart and travel at maximum speed so as to minimize the likelihood of their becoming "collateral damage." When the car in the rear has the blowout, those in the car don't know whether the wheel has been shot by a nearby Allied plane or the tire has been destroyed by shrapnel or debris on the road from earlier Allied strikes.

The car is totaled, and the other two cars in the convoy are well out of sight down the road toward the Jordanian border. Because of the intensive US/British bombing, there are very few vehicles on the road between Baghdad and the Jordanian border. The group is just beginning to panic, when an Iraqi civilian approaches in a car. He pulls over and asks if he can help. He drives them to the closest Iraqi town, Rutba. This civilian town with no apparent military structures had been devastated by US/British bombing three days earlier. Much of the town is destroyed, including the children's hospital. Two children in the hospital were killed in the bombing. The group is taken to the only remaining functioning medical facility in town, a 20-foot by 20-foot four-bed clinic.

The people of Rutba welcome the wounded, stranded US citizens, just three days after US/British aircraft had destroyed their town. One of the internationals asks, "How do you think Americans would respond to Iraqi civilians accidentally stranded in their community three days after Iraqi aircraft had destroyed their town?" The doctor is embarrassed because many medications are unavailable. Cliff has to get the ten stitches to close the gash in his head without anesthesia. The doctor says that he would have offered to take the wounded by ambulance to Jordan. But he cannot make that offer in the current situation. Once all members of the group are treated, they try unsuccessfully to pay the clinic and doctor for their services. "We treat everyone in our clinic: Muslim, Christian, Iraqi, or American. We all are part of the same family you know," the doctor says.

April 2, 2003

I receive an e-mail with inspiring words from Clarisa Pinkola Estes. She says, "Do not lose heart. We were made for these times." She acknowledges concern about the state of affairs in our world right now with "abject disregard of what the soul finds most precious and irreplaceable," and she implores readers not to lose hope. She states that we have been raised since childhood for this time precisely.

Estes tells us not to get overwhelmed by how much is wrong or un-mended in the world, and not to focus on what is outside of our reach or cannot yet be within reach. She notes we will meet resistance, but we have the resources that we need, and she encourages us to listen to the inner voice. She goes on to say:

> Ours is not the task of fixing the entire world all at once, but of stretching out to mend the part of the world that is within our reach. Any small, calm thing that one soul can do to help another soul, to assist some portion of this poor suffering world, will help immensely. It is not given to us to know which acts or by whom will cause the critical mass to tip toward an enduring good. What is needed for dramatic change is an accumulation of acts. We know that it does not take 'everyone on Earth' to bring justice and peace, but only a small, determined group who will not give up.
>
> One of the most calming and powerful actions you can do to intervene in a stormy world is to stand up and show your soul. To display the lantern of soul in shadowy times like these—to be fierce and to show mercy toward others, both—are acts of immense bravery and greatest necessity. Struggling souls catch light from other souls who are fully lit and willing to show it. If you would help to calm the tumult, this is one of the strongest things you can do.

April 8, 2003

I'm on a radio program with Pat Thurston again. She asks if I have great hope for what's going to happen when the bombing finally stops and I respond: "I grieve what's going on over there, thinking about the people whom I met there and how they were suffering before the bombing began and imagining how they are suffering more so now, although it is hard to imagine how it could be much worse because they were just living one day at a time as it was. I know that many of the people who were left behind at the time that the bombing started were the poorer people who don't have the money to get out of the country. I heard that there were richer people who had gotten out of the country and are just waiting to come back, so one of my hopes is that when things calm down there, the people who love their country will return and start building a new country.

"It's hard to feel hopeful about the conditions and the situation for Iraqi people in Iraq, but the hope that I carry is watching how the world community is rising against President Bush's bombing. There are many conversations happening worldwide about the morality of war, which to me is unprecedented. For thousands of years, war has just been something that we've taken for granted. It is now being questioned in a big way and that brings me hope for the longer term. But in terms of the Iraqi people, I hope that there can be some reconciliation made and care taken for these people who have been so devastated for so long."

Pat expresses the concern that some people have that not supporting the war may be demoralizing to our troops.

I respond, "There are those of us who don't support the war who are concerned about our troops and do want them to come home safely, and do want them not to suffer from chemical weapons or suffer from trauma because of being involved in a war over there that shouldn't be happening. I would say that those of us standing up and speaking against the war are not speaking against our troops."

April 10, 2003

Kathy Kelly of Voices in the Wilderness describes what it is like in Baghdad now after three weeks of bombing. "Early this morning, an Iraqi friend sat quietly in the hotel lobby staring at the parade of tanks, Armored Personnel Carriers, and Humvees that slowly rolled into position along Abu Nuwas Street. Tears streamed down her face. "I am very sad," she told me. "Never I thought this would happen to my country. Now, I think, my sadness will never go away."

Kathy goes on to talk about conversations she has had with US soldiers on the street: "Each of them has assured us that they didn't want to kill anyone."

Yet killing and destruction have not ceased. "Since I began this letter," Kathy says, "there have been four huge explosions nearby. Looting and burning continue."

I receive a clip of a newspaper article from one of my CPT teammates. The article titled "An Art Center Left in Ashes" is about the art center that we visited on February 12. Amal al-Khedairy has had a change of heart about the USA now that she has experienced the bombing and looting. The article depicts her as having been an admirer of Western culture while trying to sustain her native culture under the harsh rule of Saddam Hussein. Her house was bombed, and her cultural center was then ransacked by looters. Now she is angry and says that the USA has pushed her country deeper into degradation. She believes now that the destruction of her home as well as the looting of the national museum are evidence of an American plan to deface Iraq's culture and carry its treasures out of the country.

April 11, 2003

All the members of my CPT team are now out of Baghdad. The last of them decided to leave when food started getting scarce. They weighed the amount of good they were doing with the extra burden they were placing on the Iraqi people by being there eating the scarce food.

5

First Stays in Sri Lanka

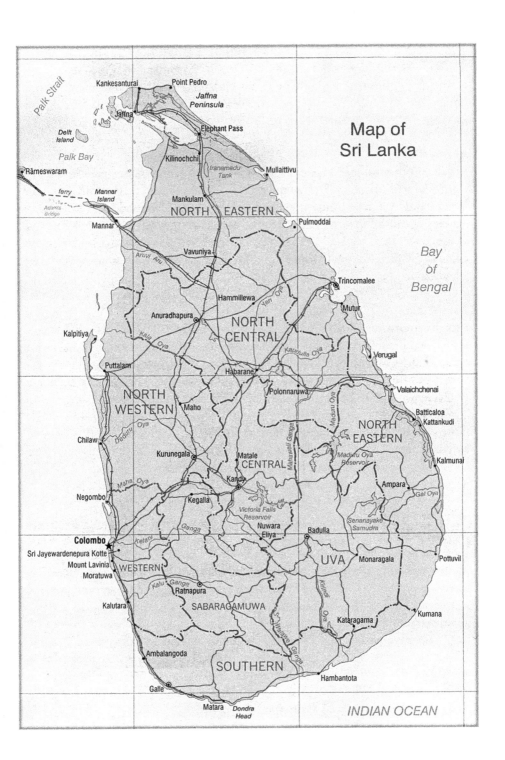

Map of
Sri Lanka

April 12, 2003

I JUST RECEIVED A MESSAGE from the Nonviolent Peaceforce (NP) that the directors are recruiting now for the pilot project in Sri Lanka. They are asking for a two-year commitment. Although two years is a long time for me to be away from home, compared to these other two trips that were only two weeks each, I intend to apply.

April 15, 2003

I have an opportunity to speak at the California Institute of Integral Studies on April 30. I will talk about both of my experiences in the Middle East this past year. What stands out most from my experience in both Palestine and Iraq is the loving generosity and compassion of the people, even when they have so little to give and so much reason to be angry at the USA. My intention is to inspire the people who come to my presentation to listen to and follow the call of their own hearts to take whatever actions (big or small) they can.

June 4, 2003

I receive an invitation from NP to come to the assessment weekend in Thailand. If I am accepted, I will stay for three more weeks of training, then I'll be home for a month before going to Sri Lanka for two years.

NP describes our role in Sri Lanka to be a "trained, international, civilian, nonviolent peaceforce sent to this conflict area to prevent death and destruction and to protect human rights; thus creating the space for local groups to struggle nonviolently, enter into dialogue, and seek peaceful resolution." We will live in and accompany communities threatened by violence as well as support local efforts in their ongoing peace process. The Sri Lankan government and the Tamil Tigers (also known as the LTTE) have recently agreed to a cease fire agreement in an effort to end the civil war, which has been going on for nineteen years.

July 20, 2003

I am attending the NP training in Thailand. We are staying in small individual rooms, each with a cot, a simple table, and a curtain hanging over the doorway. There are no showers; we bathe by scooping cold water from a trough and pouring it over our bodies. The grounds are lovely with blooming flowers; the air is warm and a bit humid; insects are numerous and huge.

NP is very proud of this training, which took one and a half years to develop. David Hartsough told me that the training brings together the best of what is already in the field. Four techniques of Third Party Nonviolent Intervention (TPNI) are central to the curriculum: 1) accompaniment, 2) monitoring and observing, 3) presence, and 4) interpositioning.

Accompaniment is being with an unarmed local peace worker or group who feels threatened and asks to be accompanied for a particular activity. During accompaniment the NP team member does not speak for the people being accompanied, but is passively present as an outsider, thus providing a sense of protection and boosting confidence for local peacekeepers to do their work in their own way with less fear and less chance of violence.

Monitoring/observing is witnessing an event for a particular purpose, such as observing elections for fairness. Often monitoring/observing includes taking notes and/or pictures to be shared internationally for public awareness.

First NP team in Sri Lanka

Presence is being physically and obviously in the location where violence might occur and thereby shifting the likelihood of violence actually occurring.

Inter-positioning is putting oneself physically between opposing forces. The first three techniques are actions we are likely to use in our work, while we have a choice whether or not to engage in inter-positioning.

July 22, 2003

I'm home from the training. Eleven of us committed to join the Nonviolent Peaceforce in Sri Lanka (NPSL) for two years. We are four men and seven women with one each from Kenya, Ghana, India, the Philippines, Japan, Germany, Brazil, and Canada; plus three from the United States. This represents five continents. There is still some uncertainty about funding and also we are awaiting registration with the Sri Lankan government so that we can get visas. Thus, we will not be leaving home before mid-September.

August 6, 2003

I speak at a gathering organized in my hometown by a local NP supporter. Twenty-four people attend. Most (if not all) of them are elder to me. In answer to the question why I decided to become a field team member with NP, I share my belief that we may be at a turning point in global history in that, after thousands of years of acceptance of war, people are now questioning war worldwide. NP has a vision of what might be possible. I feel fortunate to be a part of the beginning stages.

I also share a little of what I know about the complex situation in Sri Lanka. The major conflict in the country is between the Sinhalese government and the Tamil Tigers. The government was elected by the majority population, but the Tamil people are a large minority and both Sinhalese and Tamil people have a long history on the island. Tamils were privileged when the British were in control and the Sinhalese government has marginalized the Tamil people since they have been in control. The Tamil Tigers emerged to bring attention to the plight of the Tamil people. There is a smaller minority of Muslims also living in Sri Lanka. They generally live in the Tamil areas. The Tamil and Muslim people are also often in conflict. People have experienced much violence in the past thirty years, but a ceasefire in the last one and a half years has opened up some space. I explain that there are human rights violations on the part of all the parties in conflict.

The meeting ends with all of the participants enclosing me in a circle with their hands upon me as a blessing.

September 17, 2003

I receive some more concrete information from NP about my future in Sri Lanka and I find it comforting and exciting. The team will begin training in the Colombo (the capitol of Sri Lanka) area on September 29. Field sites will be in the Batticaloa, Trincomalee, and Jaffna Districts as well as a District in Southern Sri Lanka, probably Galle, Matara, or Hambantota. The in-country training will end on November 7.

The conflicts where NP hopes to make a positive non-violent impact are different in each field site. Mutur is in Trincomalee District. The team is likely to be placed in Mutur town to work with local peace committees and others involved in trying to bring peace and protection. The Mutur area has seen the most outbreaks of communal violence in the last eighteen months with over one hundred deaths. The town itself has a majority Muslim population, with less than ten per cent of the community being Tamils. Surrounding the town is a patchwork of Muslim, Tamil, and Sinhalese villages and it is within a short distance of LTTE (Tamil Tigers) controlled areas. All these ingredients have led to sporadic violence inside and outside the town. The NP team will be the only expatriates living in the town.

Batticaloa district has the largest concentration of Tamils in Eastern Sri Lanka. Muslims are confined to three towns, two in the middle of the District and one in the south. There have been clashes between Muslims and Tamils with loss of life here as well. Very often these clashes take place in reaction to events in Mutur. Unlike the Mutur area, Batticaloa has a very strong NGO community grouped together under a consortium in Batticaloa town. The consortium is concerned about threats to life and property from ethnic violence and is interested in obtaining support from NP. Additionally, Batticaloa district has seen continual reports of forced recruitment of children and also conflicts between different Tamil militant groups. This adds to the volatility in the area. Together with the consortium and individual NGOs, NP expects that it will be able to increase the sense of protection for vulnerable groups as well as help increase the capacity for peacebuilding amongst civil society groups and individuals in the area.

Galle, Matara and Hambatota are in the South. During the period of the ceasefire, political violence has increased resulting from disputes between local groups of the three main political parties that draw their support from the Sinhala community. In these areas NP's principal partner in Sri Lanka (PAFFREL) has strong networks, working for voter education and support of the peace process. Many political analysts predict that when the election comes, violence will be greater as has traditionally been the case at elections. NP's positioning of one of its first teams in the South of the country is not only intended to demonstrate its holistic and non-partisan attitude to violence, but also to help to forestall some of the potential for violence, in cooperation with PAFFREL colleagues.

The Jaffna team will initially consist of two members, while all the other teams will have three until the arrival of the next group of NP field team members, expected in April 2004. The task of the Jaffna team will be to lay the groundwork for a full site office. Jaffna has a weak NGO community, but many problems surrounding human security because of continuing tensions between the Sri Lankan government forces and the LTTE, whose main headquarters are to the south of Jaffna.

September 26, 2003

I am with another field teammate, Rita, in the Hong Kong airport during our twelve hour layover on our way to Sri Lanka. I'm reading an e-mail from Jan, our team coordinator. He sent some information about the demographics of the team in Sri Lanka. There are fourteen members all together. This includes the eleven of us who were trained in Thailand, plus a country director (William), the team coordinator (Jan), and a local woman who will help to manage the office in Colombo (Dharshini). We range in age from twenty-four to sixty. I am the fourth oldest member.

September 30, 2003

We have now completed two days of the in-country training. We have received our assignments and learned a bit about culture and customs; tomorrow we will begin our forty-five hours of language instruction. I have been assigned to the Batticaloa district team with a young woman from Canada named Angela and a young man from India named Sreeram.

October 1, 2003

We are staying at a center that is located about forty-five minutes outside of the city. Tomorrow we will take a bus into Colombo. We hope to acquire all of our work visas and then we will visit our various embassies. It will be an experiential lesson in getting around in Sri Lanka on the buses. I plan to shop for clothes appropriate for the weather and culture here. What I wear needs to be modest (covering my shoulders and knees) and light-weight because the climate is so hot and humid. I find that long skirts are cooler and thus more comfortable than trousers.

Due to the heat and humidity that never goes away, I realize that I just have to get used to being wet with sweat all the time. I find that I always want to be where I can feel the air of a fan blowing on me, even at night. Thunder, lightning, and downpours sometimes provide a bit of relief from the heat.

The food is spicy and tasty. The people are friendly and hospitable. It is part of the culture of the local people to do all they can to please guests and to strive to make us comfortable.

October 7, 2003

Today we learn more about Batticaloa district, where my field site will be located. The Tamil and Muslim schools have been separated for a long time and the two ethnic groups don't have much contact with each other. There is much farming in the area. There is also illiteracy. The children often drop out of school in order to work in the fields. Then as young men and women, they have nothing else to do but to join the military branch of the Tamil Tigers. Some children are abducted by the Tamil Tigers. Besides the Sinhalese/Tamil tension throughout the country, and the Muslim/Tamil tension in many Tamil-speaking areas, there is also tension between the Tamils in this area (the East) and those in the North. Soldiers are essentially the only Sinhalese speakers in the Batticaloa district.

Land mines are not a problem in Batticaloa district although they are in other parts of the country. And there are not bandits like there are in the South. The main thing we will be doing—especially in the beginning—is forming relationships with members of all the different divisions of people in order to develop rapport and trust. We will provide a "protective presence" just by being there as foreigners. The idea is that even tourists provide protective presence, but tourists rarely go to these areas now because of the violence. Next week we will be taking a field trip to the area.

We have had four days of language instruction. I am studying Sinhala. It is a phonetic language and each letter always sounds the same. We haven't started learning to read the script yet. It's going to be difficult for me to continue practicing the language once we are settled in our community since the only Sinhala speakers will be soldiers and I won't have much contact with them. The good thing about this language is that in the country as a whole more people speak Sinhala than Tamil.

Briefing for Sri Lanka

October 19, 2003

We are back in Columbo for a week. My field team along with our team manager Jan spent last week meeting with people in the Batticaloa district. Everyone we asked seemed to agree that the best place to locate our office/residence is on the street that is the border between a Tamil neighborhood and a Muslim neighborhood in Valaichchenai, a village that is about an hour drive north of Batticaloa town. People in the two neighborhoods are afraid of each other and there is very little interaction between them. Main Street has both Muslim and Tamil shops on it, so it is the one place where the two groups cross paths. People with whom we spoke generally believe that the presence of three foreigners there could make a difference in the fears and tensions that are present.

A favorite beach near our house

Although we were quite busy morning, afternoon, and evening with meetings among ourselves and with others, we did manage to get out to a couple of beaches. The cooling breezes and swimming in the warm tropical water provided an enjoyable break.

I was pretty tired of being in constant relationship with and listening to people after our first day of meetings. By the end of that day, it occurred to me that my introvert nature is one more element in just how far outside of my comfort zone this whole experience is for me. Then getting cut off three times during attempted phone calls with my mom seemed like a big deal and stimulated doubts that maybe are usually further under the surface. This was the first time since I started thinking about working here that I let myself consider that maybe it isn't the right thing. Fortunately, there is an opportunity to re-evaluate our commitment after the first three months. I comfort myself by thinking that I can focus on staying three months and by then, I will be more settled into my assignment and community and better able to make an informed decision about the suitability of this two-year commitment.

October 25, 2003

After another week at our field site, we are staying in a different place in Colombo to continue our language instruction and other in-country training.

Getting enough exercise is a challenge for me because it is so hot and because I dislike the intrusiveness of men when I'm walking alone on the streets. Rita and I discover a track next to the hostel where we are staying this week and we walk the track together early in the morning just after dawn—the coolest time of the day.

We have only one more morning in this location and then we will go on a third trip to our field sites.

November 2, 2003

Angie, Sreeram, and I had another productive trip last week to the Batticaloa district. First, some helpful folks from a local NGO in Batticaloa town took us to see three available houses in Valaichchenai that they had found. The one we decided upon is located on Main Street; much of it was burnt down a year and a half ago in a violent encounter between Muslims and Tamils.

The owner agreed to fix up the house for us. I was excited about seeing it, even though it didn't look like much in its current condition. When we walked inside the ground floor, a bat flew out and when I climbed the stairs to what is now the roof, there were six goats.

We met the government agent for the district, army and police commanders, a few members of NGOs, and a religious leader. Relationship building is our key task.

Activities on the streets here are very different than in the United States. There are numerous pedestrians, people peddling bicycles with amazingly large (both tall and wide) loads, cows, goats, dogs, cats, buses, vans, trucks, three-wheelers (taxis that look sort of like golf carts), ox-drawn carts, and a few cars. The human-driven vehicles are all bustling as fast as possible, swerving in and out of traffic, around meandering cows and sleeping dogs, cutting within inches of each other, and no one winces or swears. A driver will honk the horn as information to let others know when he/she is passing, which occurs often so there is a lot of honking.

We've seen monkeys playing in trees and elephants together with cows grazing peacefully in a garbage dump. As we ride out into the countryside on our way to Batticaloa from Colombo we pass through villages that have their own specialty products, including cashews, coconuts, pineapples, and wicker furniture. Mosquitoes have not been as big of an annoyance as I expected and I love that houses can be open to the outdoor air since it is always plenty warm. I really like the thatched roof open air shelters that are homes and shops. We plan to add an open air thatched roof second floor to our Valaichchenai house to provide shade for the house and a space where I imagine/hope I will enjoy spending much of my time.

We're now here in Columbo for our final week of training before we return to the field to stay. I am concerned about my mother back home. This week she is in a "Stop Smoking" program, attempting to quit once more after having smoked for more than fifty years with multiple failed attempts. She thinks it is crucial to stop right now, because her lung disease has developed to the point that she needs to use an oxygen tank. My brother and sister-in-law have been keeping me updated about her challenges.

November 4, 2003

The president of Sri Lanka has suspended parliament and released three ministers. This could set off violence. To date, I haven't heard of any problems, but the political situation here is very tenuous. For the first time the country has a president and prime minister from different political parties.

I don't fear for my personal safety. Currently we are all still together at a hostel in Columbo, but even once we get into the field, it seems internationals have a sort of bubble of protection from the political violence. I hope our work will make a difference that allows some Sri Lankans to feel safer as they work toward peace.

Ox-drawn cart

November 8, 2003

Friday was our last day of language training. Since I'm shy even when speaking my native language, I'm not one to initiate many conversations. To date, I haven't felt comfortable taking my Sinhalese public. The primary language spoken in our field location will be Tamil. Fortunately for our team, Sreeram is from southern India and was already familiar with Indian Tamil. With the language lessons we have had, he is able to get by in Tamil.

The eleven of us field team members plus the team leader will be going to a tourist site called Sigriya for an outing together. From there we will head out to our field sites. Dharshini in the NP office is still negotiating on the Valaichchenai house and then the rebuilding will take place.

November 13, 2003

We meet with one of our NGO contacts this morning in Batticaloa town and he asks where we are staying. We say, "A guest house." He says, "That's too expensive," and then shows us a perfect house for the time while we wait until the work is completed on our permanent residence/office in Valachchenai. He helps us move in to this temporary home immediately. I love this space. It is on the second floor and has a balcony overlooking the lagoon—a private place to be outside. We can walk to most places in Batticaloa Town, so I will get good exercise.

November 23, 2003

We continue to meet with various NGO and government officials in the Batticaloa and Valaichchenai area.

Power outages are normal and we have reduced power every evening. It gets dark at about 6:30. It is now 7:15 and I am sitting on the balcony with lights and fan. They are both operating at about half power and will be for another hour and a half. Lately, I have been plugging in to the telephone line downstairs, which belongs to the owners of the house, in order to send and receive e-mail messages.

We have cold running water and a western toilet. Showers are always cold. We boil and filter our drinking water. We purchased a gas stove with a propane tank. Angie loves to cook. It is her way of relaxing and she also describes it as her spiritual practice; I feel blessed that she is my teammate/housemate since I'm not much of a cook. We also purchased a refrigerator this week; now we can store leftovers from one meal to the next. Many households here do not have that extravagance. We will take our stove, refrigerator, and water filter with us when we move to the Valaichchenai house. The landlord hopes to have it ready by December 31.

I was sad to notice this morning that the landlady takes the garbage across the street and dumps it on the edge of the lagoon. I had a hunch that was what happened to it because I'd noticed garbage lining the lagoon when walking alongside it. When we were in Columbo, I noticed that people would burn their garbage, so the air was often full of the toxic smell of burning plastic.

December 1, 2003

I'm coming home for an indefinite amount of time. My mother was unable to quit smoking and has refused to bring an oxygen tank into her home. She was doing so poorly at Thanksgiving dinner that other family members (my cousins as well as

Sigriya

my brother and his family) are saying that I should come home. Even though Mom has been saying that I need to follow my heart and stay here, I am clear that I want to be with her at this point, so I am taking an unpaid leave. I intend to rejoin the team in Sri Lanka at a later date. Now that I've made the decision, I am looking forward to being home.

January and February, 2004

It was good that I came home when I did. On December 18th Mom fell and broke her hip. Since then, I've been busy with her in the hospital, a skilled nursing facility, a board and care residence, and finally back in her home. Her broken hip is healing without the need for surgery. While Mom was in the hospital, they put her on oxygen so she got familiar with the machine. She has continued to be on oxygen in the other facilities, so the transition to having an oxygen machine in her home is no longer a hurdle.

I become clear that I won't return to Sri Lanka for a long-term commitment as long as Mom is alive. Her energy increased quite amazingly after I came home, so it seems clear to me that it is important that I not be so far away for so long at this time in her life.

On the other hand, the work of being in NP's pilot project in Sri Lanka seemed quite meaningful and now I feel lost. I gave up my teaching and vision quest guiding jobs to join NP; then I came home to be with Mom, who is doing fine now and doesn't need much from me; so now what? My unpaid leave status officially ends February 29. I discuss with Jan over e-mail the possibility of my returning to Sri Lanka as a trained team member for a short term need. I also commit to teaching one course in the spring for the university where I was employed before joining NP.

Mid-February Jan invites me to return to Sri Lanka for a brief stay. I agree to be there for the last three and a half weeks of March. I will be able to pay for my flight out of the money I am paid by NP, so it is like volunteer work for me at no extra cost to them. Jan wants me to re-join my Valaichchenai team for this brief period. They expect to be gaining a new teammate soon and feel a need for a third member in the interim. Since national elections are now scheduled for April 2, it is probably a good time for me to be there. Election time, including the period just prior to the election, is often a time of increased violence. I am happy that I will be able to reconnect with my field team as well as the whole NP Sri Lanka team, since my leaving last December was abrupt.

March 2, 2004

I'm gearing up for my brief return to Sri Lanka. I'm excited about our plan to accompany local election monitors in order to deter the possibility of violence occurring as they do their work. That's exactly the kind of task we were trained to do. I am flying out of SFO on March 7 and returning March 31.

March 14, 2004

I am totally enjoying being back in Sri Lanka. It is great to see and spend time with many of my colleagues here. I also enjoy meeting visiting members of NP's International Governing Council (IGC) and reconnecting with David Hartsough, one of those IGC members. We have a productive meeting in Columbo with three of the Sri Lanka administrators (William, Jan, and Dharshini), five field team members, three IGC members, and a videographer who is doing a documentary for NP. I love being part of this kind of "thinking out loud" meeting. It is the intersection of the visionary founders with the on-the-ground pilot team and we have a lively discussion about what our mandate really means when put into action. I also get a chance to visit the field team in the South for an overnight visit.

Jan and William decide not to send me to join Sreeram and Angie in Valaic-hchenai because currently they are in the hot spot on the island where there has been some violence since the election process began. Two other field team members join them because it's better to send those who can stay for an indefinite period of time.

I am deployed to do pre-election monitoring in Puttalam, which is on the west coast north of Colombo. Karen from Germany is my NP field teammate, and PAFFREL (the election monitoring NGO) has provided a translator named Indonil and a driver named Chauminda to go with us. We spend today meeting with candidates. We will be meeting police and government officials here in Puttalam tomorrow, and probably moving on to do the same in Anuradhapura the next day. Folks are saying there is much less violence here in Puttalam than in the past. We're hoping that continues. Indonil has talked about going to see some of the ancient historical sites while we are in Anuradhapura.

March 19, 2004

I'm back in Colombo now. During our time in Puttalam and Anuradhapura, we met with local organizers who are members of PAFFREL and monitoring the elections. With the guidance of these local organizers and sometimes with their escort, we visited with candidates at their houses (which are also their campaign quarters), government officials, and heads of police. According to everyone with whom we spoke, the incidents have been minor and there is much less violence than during pre-election periods in the past.

I was able to take time at the Internet café to keep up with the students in the course I am teaching, which combines face-to-face and on-line instruction. The ability to work with my students over the Internet gives me the opportunity to do this work in Sri Lanka for short term placements.

I enjoyed being with the members of my team. Indonil turned out to be a great guide to the local historical sites and both Indonil and Chauminda were wonderful traveling companions. At the end of each of the three days when we were in Anuradhapura, the four of us spent the dusk hours visiting the historical sites.

At a meeting with PAFFREL tomorrow, we will be learning more about what we need to do during the next stage of the election process called postal elections, which will take place next week. Postal elections are when government people vote in their work places. Many people fear that things might still heat up as we get closer to the actual election date—April 2. I'll be going home before that date.

March 25, 2004

We have now finished our second week of pre-election monitoring. I went back to Puttalam with the same team (Karen, Indonil, and Chauminda). PAFFREL asked us to visit as many of the police departments, military places, and bus depots as possible in the Puttalam District during the postal elections. All was peaceful and we witnessed no indications of fraud or manipulation of voters.

On the day prior to postal elections, we visited several IDP (Internally Displaced Person) camps in the Puttalam district to see how these people were feeling about the elections. The people in the camps are Muslims who have been displaced from their homelands since 1990. We did not detect any problems particular to the election.

Village shops

We went back out to the one town where we learned last week that people had some concern about potential violence. When we asked at the police station they said that no incidences were reported since our visit last week. We stopped at the two main candidates' offices in that town after the postal elections and they confirmed no violence.

Each evening when we finished our pre-election monitoring work this week, we went out elephant watching at dusk. I thoroughly enjoyed getting outside the hustle bustle of the towns and into a beautiful and peaceful place in the countryside. We were blessed with good views of a herd of wild elephants coming to bathe in a huge reservoir called a tank. Some of the tanks in Sri Lanka are thousands of years old.

While I was doing this pre-election monitoring, I grimaced every time I was asked my country of origin because of what happened in the 2000 election of President Bush. During that election, there were questions about the count in Florida and the Supreme Court determined that George W. Bush was elected. That led to further investigations into other instances of miscounts, fraud, and voters being mistreated or misled at the polls in the USA. Because it was a Supreme Court decision that placed him in office, many progressives say that President Bush was selected, not elected.

This weekend many more internationals will arrive for training about Election Day monitoring. I am invited to attend the training even though I will not be here on Election Day. Since all the NPSL team will be present, I look forward to spending time with the other team members whom I haven't had the opportunity to see since I arrived in early March.

April 28, 2004

After being home for a month, I accept another invitation to return to Sri Lanka. This time, I will actually be joining my original teammates—Sreeram and Angie. Tensions continue to be high in Batticaloa district and that team has grown to five members due to the needs in that community for our work. I'm happy to be joining a larger team and pleased to be needed for the work I was trained to do. I'll be flying out on the night of May 17 and returning June 25. Right now I feel I can leave my mom for periods as long as two months at a time.

May 12, 2004

I still receive reports from CPT describing the situation inside Baghdad. This report depicts detainees at a press conference telling of torture and mistreatment by US soldiers. I include this description because it is the kind of atrocious information (not available through our usual media) which fuels my motivation to keep doing this international work.

One man lifted his shirt to show the long scars across his back from a whipping he said he received from US forces. He said, "They beat me, urinated on me, broke my arm, and raped me." A fifty-year-old man in traditional dress who was in Abu Ghraib prison camp last winter testified that US soldiers herded detainees into a room in groups of ten to twenty men and stripped them naked. The soldiers ordered one detainee to rape the others. The soldiers then ordered half of the detainees to sit on the ground and engage in oral sex with the standing detainees. The man also described how soldiers would form balls of fabric and shove them into the detainees' anuses. After this, soldiers would remove the balls and put them into the detainees' mouths. He explained that soldiers also gagged them with rags soaked in hot peppers, and held their nostrils under a running water faucet.

May 23, 2004

I arrived in Sri Lanka in the evening last Wednesday and spent the next day in Colombo. On that day, I got to visit Dharshini and her new baby in the hospital. I took the night bus to Valaichchenai, traveling with a local NGO employee. Rita—who is now brave enough to drive in Sri Lanka—met me at 4:30 am with the truck which now belongs to the team.

First thing in the morning, we went to a meeting at the UNICEF office in Batticaloa town. Local organizations and UNICEF are focusing on supporting child soldiers who were released after the battle in April when a faction of LTTE in the East split off from the main organization in the North and released many of the young cadres. There is a need to find school programs that will help these ex-cadres find a place in society and there is also a fear of these young people being re-recruited by LTTE military.

The field team has asked me to facilitate meetings, something I enjoy doing. I've also been helping to catch up on weekly reports. I'll be here in this field team location for a total of five weeks.

May 28, 2004

Since the office residence isn't big enough for the whole team, Rita and I were staying at a guesthouse which was a short drive from the office; but early this week we found a little two-bedroom house just three blocks from the office in the Muslim neighborhood. People in the neighborhood are so friendly that at first we thought we'd never be left alone. It may have been the novelty of two white women moving in; already it seems that we are attracting less attention.

Houses here are simple structures with windows open to the outside air, which I love. The better houses like this one are made of concrete, the poorer ones of thatch or mud. Ceiling fans are a blessing and essential both for staying cool and also for blowing away mosquitoes and flies. We don't need to furnish the house much since we spend most of our time at the office residence. A mattress on the floor on top of a couple of floor mats is my bed. We have a set of five plastic patio chairs that we use inside and out. The house is walled in with a very noisy gate, so the whole neighbourhood probably is aware when we come and go.

Our office/residence on Main Street is made of brick covered with concrete. Fenced in by a wall, the sand-covered yard is spacious. A caretaker who maintains the yard, sleeps there and provides a sense of security at night. Beneath a mango tree in the back corner of the yard is a favorite outdoor sitting/meeting space. That outdoor space is especially nice during the frequent power outages when the fans and computers stop functioning. The daily hustle bustle of Main Street is just outside our gate, where there is a bus stop. Several three-wheelers (little taxis) are stopped there when they are not transporting people. The street that intersects right across the street from our front gate leads into the Muslim neighborhood and our back gate opens to the Tamil neighborhood. We have good relationships with both groups of people. Sreeram and Angie have done a great job of creating a space that is welcoming to all of our neighbors.

We are currently a four-person team while Angie is in Colombo with health problems. Usually two field team members will go out in the field with our interpreter while two of us stay in the office. The NP field teams have now hired local interpreters because our language training was not extensive enough for the kinds of communications our work requires. Even Sreeram's superior Tamil language skills aren't enough. We try to keep the office open all the time and we call on a couple of other people living close by who can speak both English and Tamil when we need help interpreting at the office.

Often people will come to the office looking for help that we don't provide. They don't understand exactly what our purpose is—many seem to think we are mediators and others come looking for funds. They come with whatever problems they have because we are there and available. Because Angie and Sreeram have learned much about the NGOs, INGOs, and other resources in the area, we can make appropriate referrals.

A mother comes seeking a vocational training program for her son. He was among the recently returned cadres and being in such a program will help protect him from re-recruitment. The child soldiers were initially recruited (abducted) by LTTE who requires every Tamil family to provide at least one family member for their military. There is a rift between LTTE members in the North and those in the East. Karuna, the LTTE military leader of the East, led a battle in April that resulted in a separation between the two factions. After the battle, Karuna released a large number of young soldiers who returned to their homes in the Batticaloa district. Yet many Tamil people in the district are still loyal to the LTTE of the North and so because of this split, neighbors cannot trust their neighbors and the fear of re-recruitment is ever-present in those families with returned cadres. Another mother comes to the office after her child had been taken by gunpoint, presumably to be re-recruited.

When people might be better able to get their needs met nonviolently through our protective presence, we pursue the situation further with them. We strive to guide people to solve their own problems. We ask questions such as: "What do you want to do?" "What do people in your community usually do about problems like this?" "Would it help if you have a meeting with this person?" Once we are in

Photo by NPSL teammate

Front of Valaichchenai office

the field with someone, he/she often looks to us with a question like, "What should we do now?" However at every decision point we strive to give the responsibility of making the decision back to the individual(s) by asking, "What do you want to do now?"

A Tamil community leader asks us to accompany him into a Muslim area so he can talk to a Muslim community leader about a fear that Muslim land owners will eventually shut the Tamil people from passage to an important temple on the beach. We do this accompaniment and witness the Muslim leader reassure the Tamil leader that his people won't do that.

We visit a village where we had heard a rumor (even broadcast on the radio) about some violence, but as far as we can tell from talking to the people once we get there, things are peaceful. Then we are able to do rumor control from an informed perspective.

A lecturer at the Eastern University, located between Valaichchenai and Batticaloa town, was assassinated last week. He was the first civilian who has been killed since the elections. We are asking some of our local contacts in the area if there is any way we can support people due to the increasing fears that are probably arising because of that incident.

June 4, 2004

My five weeks are passing quickly. Rita and I went on a holiday to a popular surfing beach about a four-hour drive south of here last weekend. It was great to get away from the field site to do something fun and I enjoy spending time with Rita. Angie returned from her medical leave in Colombo and she's doing well.

A journalist was assassinated in a village between Batticaloa town and Valaichchenai, killed probably by someone who feels threatened by the stories that he published. Assassination seems to be a normal way of solving problems. Such acts of violence, especially when the perpetrators remain unknown, contribute to a growing culture of fear and silence among the people. We have been working to expand our network of contacts; however it is a challenge to find ways to support when everyone is afraid to talk or organize.

A *hartal,* a mass protest when all businesses are expected to shut down, is called following the assassination. A hartal can be strictly enforced by the members of the community who called it, so the villages become like ghost towns and no one feels safe going outside their houses. This hurts the livelihood (what little there is) of the people who are already hurting so much.

I was inspired by a meeting we had yesterday with a dedicated and sharp young Tamil man who has a strong sense of faith and believes in following his intuitive wisdom. He has been threatened a number of times over the years, arrested and beaten a couple of times, and even now he says that his life might be in danger, but he stays here and continues working as a community leader keeping as low a profile as possible while doing what he can to support his people. He believes the best thing to do right now is to work with people to develop peaceful ways of communicating with each other, beginning at the individual level. Looking at him, I think to myself, "Despite the hardships people here face, there is a wonderful sparkle in many eyes."

Today we go to one of the small Hindu villages close to Valaichchenai to meet with the villagers who are called together by their priest. The priest had expressed concerns about the fears of his people to my teammates when they met him on an earlier occasion. We go today to see what support we might give to him and his village. Perhaps we can help them tap into community resources. They tell us that they feel unsafe when the Sinhalese police and military forces come into the village in the evenings with their weapons, and they also feel unsafe in their relationship with the Muslim community with whom they share a border. One of their fears is that their cows (sacred to the Hindu people) will be harmed by Muslim neighbors who eat beef. We ask the priest if he would be interested in talking to one of the mosque leaders of the Muslim community. He says, "Yes."

June 11, 2004

Last week, we visited a delightful place called the Butterfly Peace Garden in Batticaloa town. This lovely facility and educational program brings together mixed groups of children from Muslim and Tamil communities in a program that uses the arts to encourage them to connect with their inner spirits. A mountain of clay and a two-story tree house are two of the attractive and imagination-stimulating niches in the compound. Adult "animators" provide materials and instructions for

Local demonstration

activities that include artwork, creative writing, and storytelling. The children move in and out of these activities by free choice and in their own timing, and all were so involved in their activities that few even noticed our presence as we toured the compound. The Butterfly Peace Garden provides transportation from the villages and groups are balanced in numbers between the two ethnic groups as well as by gender. The same mixed group is together at the Garden after school two days a week for nine months and is invited back in four year cycles; the children continue deepening their relationships with themselves and each other as they grow up.

We also had a productive "thinking out loud" discussion with a grassroots community organizer who was considering an offer by another organization to bring more internationals in for a two-week to several-month period of time with the intention of contributing in some way to peace here. We discussed the advantages and disadvantages of such an opportunity and how it would take much preparation of both the internationals and the communities served in order to make it a successful experience. It gave me a deeper perspective on the challenges faced by such organizations as the International Solidarity Movement and Iraq Peace Teams—how to bring internationals into a country for a short period of time and really give them enough training about the culture and context of the situation so that what they actually do is helpful and not unconsciously hurtful to the local people.

William, our project director was with us for several days. We had a joint meeting with the Mutur field team to discuss what we are learning about accompaniment from our experiences; accompaniment is one of the Third Party Nonviolent Intervention activities that is part of our mandate here.

The community leader with the sparkle in his eyes of whom I spoke earlier invited us to a People's Peace Congress that he is planning for local grassroots community peace organizers. He asked us to submit a proposal for a project we might facilitate sometime after the event. His idea would be to "feel what the people need right now" and attempt to create a series of workshops that would provide a space for grassroots organizers to refine their capacity for problem solving and peace building in their respective communities. This is an instance where we have to figure out what really fits into our mandate. We are not supposed to be offering trainings, but we do want to engage in capacity building to support local organizations to do their own peace work since the Nonviolent Peaceforce will not be able to stay in the country indefinitely. This is one dilemma of being a pilot project—we are refining our understanding of our mandate as we go.

We're developing a work plan as a field team because we are being called in many directions and we don't want to get over extended.

June 20, 2004

This past week, we accompanied a leader in the Mosque Committee to speak with the members of that Hindu village I described on June 4th. After that meeting with the priest and the villagers, we approached the Muslim community leader because we knew he has a commitment to peace. He was willing to go into the village to meet with the people, but he was uncomfortable about going alone and asked for our accompaniment.

I feel blessed to have gotten to witness the interaction. There were a large group of villagers (men and women) and two priests present. I couldn't understand the Tamil language spoken, but I watched the facial expressions, body language, and energy. One villager ranted angrily for quite some time and the mosque leader listened respectfully. I also witnessed laughter and good caring dialogue between the Muslim leader and several of the other villagers. The Muslim leader took notes that he will take back to the Mosque Committee and he gave the priests his phone number for future contact if they experience any problems with the Muslim people who share their border. All seemed very pleased when we were shaking hands at the end of the meeting. Even the one who had been ranting was smiling.

We hope to also arrange a meeting between some of the villagers and another friend the team has made, a colonel in the Sri Lankan Army.

It's the end of our day on Sunday, and we're finishing up in the office. We are going out to the beach this evening. I'll take one last "sea bath" in the warm ocean, where I enjoy the exercise of swimming as well as the buoyancy of floating in the warm salt water over gentle rolling waves.

There's now a good possibility that I will return to Sri Lanka again for six to eight weeks in September and October.

August 22, 2004

I have been back at home for two months. Today I receive an email inviting volunteer election monitors for the presidential election in the USA this November. "We can be a nonpartisan force for democracy, educating voters about their rights, monitoring the polls on Election Day, and ensuring that every vote gets counted." I consider doing this even though it is very close to the date I return from my next trip to Sri Lanka. I don't have to think about it long before I sign up and send out a message seeking a partner to join me.

September 5, 2004

I am back in Sri Lanka at my original field team site and will be here for two months. There will be six permanent members and me on the field team. I intend to make the most of my time. Each time I've returned, I feel more love for the place and the people.

September 10, 2004

It's been a fairly quiet, though busy week. In the area of child protection, we are still collaborating with UNICEF and other agencies (both national and international) in their ongoing protection for children and youth from involuntary recruitment and re-recruitment. With that goal in mind, we have recently been providing international presence at Hindu Temple Festivals and coordinating other INGOs (International NGOs) to support this effort by being present as well. The festivals take place through the nights in the temple compounds over periods of several days and have been a venue for abductions. NPSL is providing presence overnight and other INGOs are setting up booths and attending the festivals during the days.

As well as our child protection efforts, we are continuing to build relationships with local NGOs and nonviolence activists in general. We're working in partnership to form a local peace congress and also to identify local mediators who might be trained to work through conflict among local groups. The team helped launch a new Tamil/ Muslim Peace Group and we are now providing a neutral meeting space for this group at our office on Main Street.

September 19, 2004

We have been working with a married couple who are local activists not identified with any particular organization. She is Sinhalese and he is Tamil. They are initiating the district-wide grassroots Family Support Network and many activities to support families in protecting their children from abductions. They elicit our support especially when they think that our accompaniment or presence will make it feel safer for community members to participate in these activities.

Two days ago five of us spent much of the day collectively writing a draft document of suggested guidelines for providing conscious presence at temple festivals.

Today we pay our second visit to a Sufi community south of Batticaloa town whose members are feeling discriminated against and threatened by the Muslim community in which they are geographically embedded. Conflict arises partially because the Sufis see themselves as Muslims, but the traditional Muslims are offended by some Sufi beliefs and thus are antagonistic toward them.

Given that anything I say about the tensions present in Sri Lanka is a simplification and does not represent the complexity of the situation; here is a brief review of the conflicts as I have come to understand them. The overall conflict in the country as a whole is between the government representing the majority Sinhalese population and the Tamil Tigers (LTTE) who see themselves as representing the minority Tamil. The Tamil people generally want justice and some autonomy in terms of having their own language, beliefs, values, and practices respected. Some are appreciative and supportive of the Tamil Tigers, others don't support the Tigers, and many Tamils are afraid of the Tigers.

Furthermore, there is tension among Tamil Tigers in the North and those in the East, and as I said before, last April that tension led to a battle during which the Karuna faction separated from the LTTE. Now many people believe that the Sri Lankan government is allying with the Karuna faction against the LTTE. There are some Tamils in Batticaloa district who still support the LTTE in the North, others who support the Karuna faction, and other Tamils who just want to live their lives without threat from either. As I said earlier, this conflict between the LTTE and the Karuna faction causes neighbors to not trust each other and contributes to a growing culture of fear and silence that is prevalent in this area.

The Muslim communities are usually geographically located in Tamil areas, and though the Muslim people are Tamil speaking, they are not Tamils. There are often tensions between the Muslims and the Tamils. Like the Tamils, Muslim people want justice and some autonomy with regard to their beliefs, values, and practices. Now we've met some of the people in this small Sufi community within one of the Muslim communities, who similarly want autonomy with regard to their beliefs, values, and practices.

We strive to be (and to be seen as) non-partisan in support of any people who are attempting to secure and maintain their human rights through non-violent means.

September 26, 2004

Various festivals are scheduled this week. We are attending a smallish Hindu temple festival tonight. Tomorrow night, we will begin spending the nights at Verugal, a big Hindu temple festival that lasts a week. We will go in shifts. Mutur field teammates will also be coming to Verugal. Furthermore, we will be holding presence at a Sufi festival in early October. The Sufis are particularly concerned about the last few nights of their festival and a food give-away that they sponsor the final morning.

We spent one lovely day with a group of sixty-two ex-combatant youth who are in a vocational training program in Batticaloa town. They participated in activities at the Butterfly Peace Garden (see 6/11). Because of concern about re-recruitment, we were asked to accompany the youth for their bus ride from their boarding school to the Peace Garden and then we got to stay with them for the day. The "animators" (facilitators of learning) work very well with young people of all ages, getting them involved in creative activities and play. It was fun to watch these young people who were in military training and carrying guns just six months ago breaking down their defenses and playing, singing, dancing, doing artwork or craft projects, and listening to stories. The bus ride back to their boarding school was lively and delightfully rambunctious.

Another day, we met with about twenty-five men of the Muslim community in which the Sufi community is embedded. We listened to their "side" of that story. They feel threatened by the Sufi community and fear violence from them. It was an opportunity for us to develop our relationship with them. We were able to describe our work and how we might be able to support them if they want our presence while they are involved in peaceful attempts at negotiations anywhere. I think that meeting will make our presence at the Sufi festival more effective in terms of the possibility that it could actually deter violence while maintaining our image as non-partisan.

October 3, 2004

I was awake overnight Monday, Wednesday, Friday, and Saturday last week at temple festivals. The festivals were peaceful and we noticed no evidence of recruitment, and got to enjoy the cultural experience as guests. Nighttime at the festivals is like a giant slumber party with family members sleeping together in clumps on mats on the grounds surrounding the temple while rituals take place through

© Dschen Reinecke

Verugal temple

the night. Some of the activities that take place in the rituals look horribly painful. I see devotees suspended from crane-like vehicles and carried across the compound. The devotees are essentially hanging by the skin with multiple hooks piercing the skin down their backsides. Fire walking is another festival ritual.

In order to get to the Verugal Temple from Batticaloa district, we had to cross the Verugal River on a hand pulled ferry that carries up to two vehicles at a time. I enjoyed grabbing the cable to help pull the ferry across the river. I saw crocodiles swimming in the river when we were heading home in the gray light of dawn.

At one point when we were "patrolling" during the night, we walked up to a lovely little temple on top of a rock. There we spent a few peaceful moments away from the busy activity of the festival crowd.

Other than the festivals, we have faced some horrible family tragedies. One woman was killed in her home near a checkpoint when shots were fired at the checkpoint. The surviving family members were thankful that the projectile went all the way through the woman's head and then exploded outside of the house, because that way the four children who were with the woman inside the house were not harmed. The father, brother, and two community members came to our office seeking help because they couldn't afford to get the body from the hospital in Batticaloa town—where it had been taken—back to the village in order to perform the proper rituals. At first we called some of the official organizations and couldn't find anyone who could help because it was a civilian casualty and because it was a weekend. Looking discouraged and distraught the family left our office to figure out how to get themselves to the hospital. After they left, we thought of a few more of our contacts we might call for help with the situation and managed to find a couple of peace activist friends in Batticaloa town who were willing and able. They met the family at the hospital and helped them get the body back to their village.

There are magical moments as well. Incredible thunder/lightning storms and swimming at night under the stars are a couple of examples of these.

October 11, 2004

Project director William and field team manager Jan came from the main office in Colombo to our field site for a three-day work visit. The Mutur team joined us. We had some open-ended philosophical discussion and some important decision-making discussions. We worked on capturing some of what we have learned about providing presence at temple festivals and we worked on some of the difficult interpersonal dynamics that have been going on among members within and between the teams. There is a great difference among those of us attending these meetings in terms of how much time we are willing to spend in discussion, so we dance with that tension on a regular basis. I did some of the facilitating and felt good about managing to support good communication.

The meetings took place out at a beach house a short drive from our Main Street office. This location provided convenient opportunities to swim. Several of us spent one night sleeping on the beach and I swam in the beauty of the dawning day—brilliant florescent-red ball emerging from the water, turning golden and casting its gold across the smooth warm water as I swam further out than I have ever gone before.

We also spent two evenings and the final morning at the Sufi festival, roaming the perimeter and watching for anything that looked like harassment or something that could lead to violence. Nothing did. On the final morning of the festival, we shared the area with police who were in full riot gear with guns, shields, and tear gas. As far as we know, no

© Rita Webb

Verugal river ferry

violence occurred at all through the ten days of the festival.

Several incidences of civilians being killed for unknown reasons were reported in the district. This causes increased fear and tension for the people. Due to these recent deaths, we face the challenges of being with the people in their grief and fear, while wondering what (if anything) we might have done to provide protective presence. Sometimes we have to wrestle the tendency to feel too much of a sense of responsibility for things we cannot control. We need to recognize that we don't really have the power to prevent some things from happening no matter what we do.

In one case, we were able to accompany a local Tamil peacemaker who works for an organization called the Fellowship of Co-existence. He came to our office the morning after two Muslim men were killed during the night in a Muslim village. He feared the possibility that a violent response to those murders would occur and wanted to go talk to the people there, but would have been afraid to do so without our accompaniment.

I have only two more weeks here for this time around, but I'm happy to say now it looks like I might get to come back again in the early spring.

October 20, 2004

My field team decided to try cooperative inquiry as a structure for identifying some of what we are learning through our practice here. I introduced the idea because the process of cooperative inquiry as an action research method that provides a structure for learning from experience. A part of my work outside of NP has been facilitating cooperative inquiry, so it feels great that there is the interest among my colleagues here. I intend to continue to support the group in the process at a distance via e-mail after I leave.

The situation in the community here continues to be tenuous. I trust that we are doing good work to try to decrease the stronghold of a culture of fear and silence, but it is difficult to assess to what extent our presence really makes a difference.

I'm pleased to say that the decision is final that I will return again in February/ March. That makes it much easier on my heart as I prepare to leave within the coming week. I do look forward to being home as well—my heart continues to be in both places. I'm happy not to have been in the USA for the bulk of the election campaign and I look forward to going to Florida to do election monitoring with my good friend Doug.

End of 2004 and most of 2005

I'm home from Sri Lanka and from Broward County, Florida where I was election monitoring. I'm feeling grief and bewilderment about the election results—electing President Bush for a second term—and concerned about what that says to the world about US citizens. I feel inspired by an e-mail with an article entitled

"The Optimism of Uncertainty" by Howard Zinn (http://www.thenation.com). He says that revolutionary change comes from small acts multiplied by millions of people. Optimism in bad times is based on noticing that human history is not only of cruelty, but also of compassion, sacrifice, courage, and kindness. Zinn says that what we emphasize now in this complex history that we are living today will determine our lives. To live as we think humans should live in defiance of all that is bad around us, is itself a marvelous victory.

A tsunami hits on December 26, 2004, especially devastating Sri Lanka and Indonesia. All NP members in Sri Lanka are okay with one injury. One of our offices is destroyed, but no one was present there at the time. Among the dead in the Valaichchenai area are a husband and wife with whom Sreeram in particular had become friends.

Over time, I receive messages with glimpses of how it is in Sri Lanka due to the tsunami. I actually think that the many people who died may be better off than those who they left behind when I hear a story from the perspective of our interpreter in Valaichchenai. She and her family who live in Batticaloa town had managed to get up on their rooftop, where they watched as neighborhood children were swept away.

NPSL has expanded our mandate to include new needs in the areas where we work due to the tsunami, supporting relief and reconstruction activities that promote inclusivity and community participation.

I receive an e-mail with a lovely story about the US Military helping with the tsunami disaster in Indonesia. Helicopter squads have been bringing food, water, and medical supplies to people who are remote and stranded. In an interview, the head of this operation, a three-star Marine Corps General said: "I've been in the service of my country for over thirty-four years, and this is a different kind of service and it's one, perhaps when it is all said and done, that I'll be most proud of."

My mom gets pneumonia and is hospitalized. Her already stressed lungs are now in much worse shape. The doctor talks to us about hospice care. I recognize that it's time that I need and want to stay close to her. I postpone my trip to Sri Lanka for an indefinite amount of time. My intention is to support Mom to have the best possible quality of life for however much longer she is alive.

While I'm home, I am able to support the Nonviolent Peaceforce in Sri Lanka from a distance. NP recruits for a second group of field team members. I help score the applications. Once applicants are selected and preparing to come to Sri Lanka for the assessment and core training, I'm the one who responds to their questions. In addition, I give my perspective to the thinking that is going into the core curriculum for the training.

I also get to attend a retreat for major donors to NP, where I do a presentation on non-violence and contribute to an update about the situation in Sri Lanka. I enjoy spending time with a few NP folks whom I haven't seen for a long time, including a man from India and a woman from the USA, two of the three who were in charge of our assessment prior to our training in Thailand.

I am troubled as a US citizen by the torture that we now know took place in Iraq and the lack of our ability to be sure that this doesn't continue to happen. Human Rights First has documented how the administration blames low-ranking soldiers and is avoiding a credible, independent investigation of the abuses.

A friend on my e-mail list questions me about a non-violent response to a terrorist attack that took place in London: "I'm interested in what your Nonviolent Peace activists have to say about the cycle of violence we're in with Islamic extremists groups. What stops escalating violence? What is the appropriate, nonviolent thoughtful response to yesterday's attack in London? Does your network have rays of hope, too?" Following is my reply.

> I haven't heard any official response to the situation from other Nonviolent Peaceforce folks, so I can only speak for myself in response to your questions. The Nonviolent Peaceforce is non-partisan. This can be a challenge when there are justice issues involved. Violence and non-violence can be defined differently by different people, but in the work we do in Sri Lanka for example, we attempt to provide a presence that allows local civilian peaceworkers to do their work in their own way. The hope is that we can help to "open up the political space" for them by providing a presence that serves to reduce fear.
>
> Personally, I believe that as long as the US is doing the sort of violence that we are doing in the world, we can't really be surprised when something like this happens. The deaths and injuries in London aren't anything compared to what we've been causing in Baghdad for the last two years. So from my perspective, an appropriate non-violent response would be to get out of Baghdad and to clean up our own violent acts as US Americans on whatever level(s) we can. I also believe that the anti-globalization movement is a good place to focus energy, because global capitalism is causing many of the inequities and injustices that exist throughout the world.
>
> Furthermore, I believe that one thing that keeps the powers in place that perpetrate US American violence is a strong culture of fear that is created and maintained through the media. I think that whatever we can do on an individual level to overcome our fears, the more powerful we might be to eventually make the changes that are necessary to get out of the cycles of violence in which we are caught at many levels. And overcoming fear doesn't mean getting rid of it—it means being with it, even embracing it

Tsunami damage

as the teacher that it can be to us, and not letting it stop us from following our hearts. What brings me hope is my belief that the more we all can learn to follow our hearts, the more we will tap into unknown resources and healing possibilities.

Thanks for asking. It's always fun to talk about the world according to Linda.

In October and early November of 2005, I provide four weeks of 24-hour care for my mother. It is a blessing as well as a challenge to have that time with her. Once we find a primary caregiver whom Mom trusts, she stays with her around the clock and I continue to visit her almost daily.

Mom dies on November 18. I feel that I've been in the process of letting go and grieving over this whole two-year period, witnessing her go through physical, social, and mental changes; and watching her over time give up the things she loved doing one by one. Now, in addition to the great sense of loss I feel, it is also a relief not to be daily and nightly watching her deteriorate gradually and worrying about her comfort and care.

6

Two Final Years in Sri Lanka

Durinc December 2005, NP advertises for the third set of field team members to go to Sri Lanka and also announces plans to hire a team of five to begin work in Mindanao in the Philippines.

Furthermore, NP organizes election monitors to go to Palestine at the end of January. I consider doing this myself and even organizing a group to go with me, but the possibility of going back to Sri Lanka is pending. Toward the end of December 2005, I receive a confirmation that I will return to my field team in Sri Lanka for two and a half months from mid-January through March.

January 18, 2006

I receive an e-mail with another inspiring article by Howard Zinn. He believes that we may be at a time to end all wars. Zinn states that governments now have to do a lot to convince their people to go to war and he reminds us that the power of governments is dependent on the obedience of their citizens.

January 27, 2006

I've been in Sri Lanka now for more than a week. A couple of days ago, the Sri Lankan government and the Tamil Tigers (LTTE) finally agreed on a location for talks. They will meet in Geneva in February. This announcement has brought another (though tentative) renewed sense of hope to civilians and a reduction in the violent acts that have been taking place both in our district and country-wide.

I have enjoyed meeting my new field team back in Valaichchenai; Rita is the only member remaining on this team from the last time that I was here more than a year ago. Currently, eight men and three women make up the team—three from the US; two each from the UK, Ghana, and Sri Lanka; and one each from Egypt and Burundi. We will be opening another field team office in Batticaloa town soon and some of these teammates will move there. Currently, we live in four different households all within walking distance of the office, which is also still one of the residences. Rita's husband Marty is now living here with Rita. I will first stay in the house behind the office while one team member is on leave and then move to another house, which is a walk of about six blocks from the office.

Yesterday, three of us went out to a small rural village where the team is developing a longer-term relationship with a local NGO stationed there. The NGO builds houses and provides health education programs for the people in this poor rural village in an LTTE controlled area. The NGO workers are all from other places in Sri Lanka (no internationals) and they once spent nights on location in the village during weekdays; but as abductions and seemingly arbitrary killings increased especially here in the East of Sri Lanka after the November presidential elections, the staff stopped staying over nights. Their presence in the village day or night provides a sense of security to those who live there. They want to start spending nights there again and have asked us to join them overnight. We intend to spend two nights a week with them at first, and we hope that eventually they will be willing to spend additional nights without our presence.

While three of us were in the village yesterday, we sat out on the veranda of the NGO's office enjoying a gentle breeze and the silence of the lush green setting, a contrast to the hustle and bustle of Main St, Valaichchenai. While the local NGO office workers were doing their work inside speaking Tamil, we did our office work outside in English. We discussed a strategy for our team to collectively write work plans for several of our projects. The intention of NPSL as a whole is for each field team to have a work plan that will help to discern and prioritize so we might most effectively utilize our time and resources as we become increasingly aware of relevant needs. I remember we were already beginning to create work plans when I was here over a year ago.

February 9, 2006

In terms of violence, things have continued to be fairly calm since the LTTE and Sri Lankan Government agreed to engage in peace talks at the end of February. One of our primary activities has been supporting parents in doing what they wish to do after they have lost a family member in a forced recruitment. Sometimes parents wish to go to the office of the likely abductors to inquire about their child.

Some of my teammates accompanied two young Tamil women who had previously been abducted by the LTTE and then released by the Karuna faction to the police station to file their reports. The young women were held for more than twenty-four hours at the police station and they feared they might have been poorly treated had our team members not been present.

One teammate and I went to meet the new commander of the Sri Lankan Army in our division. He has been hired since the new president took office. The commander values openness and wants to find an alternative to war. That is a welcoming message in terms of our work. This initial contact is the beginning of what we intend to be an ongoing relationship with him; then it will be easier to call on him if we need help that he in his key role might be able to provide.

© Rita Webb

Assisting mothers in Vigil

February 26, 2006

I have been away from my field site much of the time in the last two weeks. First, I had to go to Colombo to renew my visa, which took two days of driving and five hours in the immigration office.

I just returned from a four-day holiday. Rita, her husband Marty, one other teammate from the USA, and I went to a town called Ella in the hill country. It was delightfully cool enough to hike there. We went to Lipton's Seat, where it is said that on a clear day one can see 60% of the island. It was not that clear that day, but there was still a great view all the way around and the trip getting there was spectacular—a very steep narrow road through beautiful tea estates. We also went to an ancient Buddhist temple built into a rock cave.

Tea plantation

© Bernard Gagnon

Last week, I was part of a meeting with a man from the UK who is an "Expert Witness." He researches the challenges of safety to civilians here in order to assist the UK in considering asylum cases. I learned that the only country that now accepts asylum cases directly from Sri Lanka is Switzerland. In other countries—like the UK— people have to be able to pay the cost and face the risks of getting to the country on their own (illegally) before they can apply for asylum.

February 28, 2006

The peace talks seem to have gone well and I feel a tentative sense of hopefulness here once more. Both the Sri Lankan government and the LTTE have recommitted to the ceasefire agreement made four years ago and to controlling violence of those within their power. They also scheduled another round of peace talks to be held in April.

Our articulation of work plans is getting more and more refined. Since NP Sri Lanka (NPSL) is the pilot project for this new organization carrying out a vision that has not really been attempted prior to this, we first had to discover what the work is or might be before we could start organizing our thoughts around work plans. I expect that the process we develop and the plans themselves will help the greater NP organization as we continue to discover what it means to bring our vision into reality. These documents now include purposes, strategies, activities, potential outcomes, and indicators in areas such as: Emergency Warning System, Responses to Violence, Local Capacity Building for a Nonviolent Society, Human Rights (in general), and Child Rights (in particular).

Next week we will be away from our field sites for a full week on a staff retreat. We will be meeting with the whole NPSL team, which now includes about thirty internationals as well as all of the local staff from four field sites and Colombo.

March 12, 2006

During an outing from the staff retreat, we did a midnight climb to Adam's Peak, locally known as Sri Pada and sacred to Buddhists, Hindus, and Muslims. It was quite a strenuous climb with some 5,000 uneven concrete/stone stairs. It was humbling for me to realize that my aging body is no longer able to do what it once could. We began hiking at midnight in order to get to the top in time to see the sunrise—a tradition here. Pramila, my hiking buddy, and I made it up to the top in time for sunrise. When we started down, I immediately felt pain in my legs—

Sri Pada

stressed from the climb—and they were wobbly almost like jello.

Fortunately, Pramila had the same pace and we hobbled down together, being the last to arrive back for the afternoon meeting. I felt better when I saw all the younger folks also hobbling around with sore muscles for a few days following that trip.

Back in Valaichchenai, yesterday, we attended a showing of two short documentary films produced by young people here through the help of an NGO from Canada. The films did an excellent job of capturing the depth of sorrow carried by war-torn families who live here in the East of Sri Lanka.

March 24, 2006

We have recently been seeing an increase in abductions. This is sad news; abductions did seem to slow down during and following the February peace talks in Geneva.

I just returned from an overnight with the NGO in that community I described January 27. With our support, the staff did decide to start spending some nights beginning March 1 and team members joined them in pairs for two nights that first week. It was unfortunate timing that we went away for our staff retreat the following week. During the third week of March, the increase in abductions was such that the NGO workers were feeling insecure again and decided not to stay, but this week they stayed last night because Rita and I were there with them. Since the presence of the NGO overnight provides a sense of security to the whole village of a few thousand people, we see this as one way that even with a small team of two we are able to increase the sense of security of large numbers of people.

Rita and I brought our own mosquito nets, a coffee pot, and a deck of cards. The workers—all men—were socializing in Tamil nearby. We were sitting out in the darkness of evening playing cards by the light of a lantern, when one of the men found a snake in the outhouse. There are a number of poisonous snakes in Sri Lanka, so people are quite afraid of them and their general practice is to kill any snake they see. It's disturbing to me to kill even poisonous snakes, but in California we only have to watch out for one kind of poisonous snake that is easy to identify—rattlesnakes—and still people feel a need to kill them. A giant insect, the size of a small bird, was flying around in the dark. One of the men caught it and showed it to us. It was ugly and creepy, but he was holding it in his bare hands. After everyone got a good look, he killed that too.

March 29, 2006

NPSL now has two offices in the Trincomalee (locally known as Trinco) district, the original office in Mutur and a newer one in Trinco town. Several weeks ago, the NP field team in Trinco town received a request for protection from a family who was being threatened. The Trinco NPSL team visits the family and provides night patrol near the house on a regular basis while the Sri Lanka Monitoring Mission (an organization from Norway monitoring the cease fire agreement) patrols the neighborhood during the day. One of the sons of the family was one of five Tamil students who were killed in Trinco in January. The father of the family is seeking justice for his son's death by appealing to the Asian Human Rights Commission's Urgent Appeal Programme. The father believes this activity puts him and the rest of his family in significant danger, so it takes great courage to do this. His appeal to send letters to increase the pressure on the authorities who can ensure the safety of the family has been distributed worldwide through e-mail and in the newspapers.

Unlike many of our cases that we need to keep confidential because of the danger to people who stand up for their human rights here, I can print the father's letter of appeal to the Asian Human Rights commission since it was made public. I include it here because it provides a good sense of the kind of experience that is common in the East of Sri Lanka. Many Tamil people live in constant fear of both the Tamil Tigers and the Sinhalese government and they do not feel protected by the Sinhalese government, police, or judicial system. I have removed names from the letter.

26-02-2006

Dear Sir:
I am submitting the following facts for your kind information with a view to obtaining your advice and guidance.
My second son aged twenty, was one of the five students who was murdered on the 2nd January 2006 in Trincomalee.
On the 10th of January 2006 there was a ministerial inquiry at the Magistrate court Trincomalee and I gave evidence on behalf

of my son. After the inquiry was over, that night and for several nights after that, there were a number of telephone calls, threatening me and the lives of the other members of my family for having given such evidence. I have already informed you about this in writing.

Furthermore, following this incident, late at night some people started banging at the door of my house and throwing stones at the roof. I was scared to open the door to go out and see who was doing this. But everybody knows. After the continuing problems, the whole city has become silent and no civilians leave their homes. But the forces still walk around the city.

I and my wife are Medical practitioners by Profession. But after my son's death we temporarily closed our Medical clinic. During the day strangers, coming by motorbikes, requested for treatment from me. But when my wife offers her services the strangers say they want to meet me personally, refuse her offer of treatment and leave. They do not leave their names and always wearing helmets to hide their faces.

After these fearful incidents my family members go to stay in different places at night.

After the death of my son a person helped in the purchase of household goods on one or two occasions. The forces asked him as to whom he purchased the goods for when his home was elsewhere. He told them he was helping me and they told him not to go to my house. My friends, regularly coming to meet my family to give moral support were also told them not to go to my house.

I often go to Magistrate' courts, after the inquiry till the case is taken up and I sit along with the parents of the other four victims. In my absence, the Police has been commenting that, we are kottiyas (meaning Tigers) and speak in virulent language. All of these incidents create a mortal fear in our minds.

I will bring to your notice, an incident to illustrate my fears: The Trincomalee reporter to the SUDAR-OLI Tamil Newspaper had taken photos of the five students murdered and has given a vivid report of this incident. This appeared on the front page of the paper. This report highlighted the atrocities perpetrated on the Tamils by the forces, to the outside world. This reporter was shot dead on the 24th of this month at 6:30 am while going for work. The normal version of the authorities is that an unknown person has killed the victim. Normally the murders perpetrated by the armed forces go unnoticed, and are classified as being murders of unknown people and therefore investigations cannot be done. In this case of murder of these five students there is clear evidence to show that it was perpetrated by the armed forces.

Now I don't run the Medical Clinic fearing murder at any time for me or my wife or my other two sons. My two sons are unable to attend school, because the forces ask them whether they are the brothers of the late kottiya. As the newspaper had published the photos of my late son along with my own and my other sons, it is also risky for us to settle in any other part of the island.

Sir, I think you can understand the risk to life I and my family are facing. We cannot get over the deepest sorrow of missing my loving son and we really do not want another death in our family. Can you help me in any way to at least safeguard the other members of my family.

I therefore urge you to take the necessary steps to have this matter investigated and to provide immediate protection to this family.

Yours sincerely,

April 18, 2006

I've been home now since the end of March and I have decided to return to Sri Lanka for six more weeks, April 24 through June 4. My placement this time is in Jaffna, the district on the northern tip of the tear drop shaped island of Sri Lanka. There are three other field team members on this team right now including Pramila (my partner in our trip to Adam's Peak). A third set of field team members are now in their Core Training and I will fill in during the interim before these new team members begin.

April 25, 2006

I am in transit from San Francisco today. I stay overnight in Colombo one night before flying to Jaffna. Last week, the LTTE pulled out of the peace talks claiming that a level of normalcy in the East will need to emerge first. Furthermore, the government of Sri Lanka has lobbied for the European Union to ban the LTTE, so increasingly the cease fire agreement is losing power here.

Today, a young woman, who pretends to be pregnant, visits the army hospital and sets off a suicide bomb that kills the Chief Commander of the Sri Lankan Armed Forces at the army headquarters in Colombo. In retaliation, a coordinated action by the Sri Lankan Navy and Airforce targets LTTE controlled seaside areas close to our office in Mutur. The bombs and shelling by a naval craft and fighter jets can be felt and heard by the Mutur team members in their office/residence. The town of Mutur has lost electricity and reports of casualties from the area targeted are coming in slowly, but the exact numbers will not be known until the fourteen hours enforced curfew has passed. For the moment, Colombo is also under curfew until dawn while the army is conducting house searches in certain areas.

Our NPSL project director reports that the environment in which we work is extremely complex and the circumstances are increasingly more dangerous. In recent weeks, there have been almost daily attacks on the Sinhalese government security forces in the East and North. Civilians have been injured and killed, including two local NGO workers killed by a claymore mine attack while passing an army convoy. Shooting and retaliation incidences have been carried out on civilians in response to mine attacks that are blamed on the LTTE. These incidences include mob killings, burning of houses and shops, gun fights, and displacement of communities.

NPSL team with villagers

The worst violence has been in the Trinco district. A bomb was set off in a busy market on April 12, killing at least five people, including one child. Within minutes a Sinhalese mob came and targeted revenge on Tamil shops, homes, and individual civilians, leaving at least nineteen more civilians dead and over thirty shops burned. The ethnic violence continued in other border areas where Sinhalese and Tamil communities come together. Thousands of villagers from the areas have moved for safety to temporary IDP (internally displaced person) camps in public places of worship or schools.

Our Trinco team witnessed the aftermath of the bombing of the market and assisted several of the injured people to a hospital. Then they were attacked by an angry crowd of Sinhalese youth who surrounded the NP vehicle. The youth slapped and punched the driver (one of my teammates from Kenya), who was trying to turn the vehicle and move away from the hostile scene. Parts of the truck were ripped from the side. The team was also threatened with a hand grenade. Before they could leave the area, heavy stones were thrown at the vehicle, smashing the side and back windows. Luckily, no one on the team was seriously physically injured. The team recovered quickly from the attack and continued their work the next day, providing protective presence for the delivery of relief to the IDPs.

With the diplomatic skills of their local translator during the days that followed this incident, the team managed to reach out to the gang who had attacked them. Subsequently, the attackers apologized and agreed to take part in a local peace meeting between the communities.

April 26, 2006

I fly in a small plane from Colombo to Jaffna early this morning. The wait for the plane to depart takes twice as long as the flight. We also have to wait at the other end because everyone has to travel in government buses from the government airport to Jaffna town.

Once I get to Jaffna, my new teammates welcome me with a delicious lunch, which the team driver picked up from a local restaurant. We share the meal around the table in our office/home. Already, I see that this team operates with quite different norms than the Valaichchenai team did and I like it. There is more of a feeling of abundance and support for the team provided from the team budget. The house/office is much nicer than any of our houses in Valaichchenai and we also have a housekeeper!

Furthermore, this team has never established the practice of keeping the office open at all times, so we can all go out to do our fieldwork together. I like that too. After lunch, we all climb into the air conditioned van to "make rounds." We drive together around Jaffna town, so I get to see the town and we get a sense of how the people are doing. This is a big city compared to the tiny village of Valaichchenai.

April 28, 2006

The highway to Jaffna has been shut down because of increased security measures due to the increased violence in other parts of Sri Lanka. With the highway shut down, fuel trucks are unable to make deliveries and the district goes into a fuel shortage which leads to power cuts (or power rationing). Yesterday we had only seven hours of power: from 5:00 to 6:00 am, 10:00 am until noon, and 6:00-10:00 pm. We aren't sure for how many days we will be on this schedule, but we are busy adjusting. For me, the most difficult part is not having a fan. April is known to be the hottest time of the year in Sri Lanka. Fortunately, a wonderful breeze (even a wind) provides good air circulation in our house/office.

Jaffna house and office

Yesterday, two of us accompanied a journalist—who believes his life is threatened—to Columbo. There I was back on the time consuming plane trip I described earlier. This time, the windows of the government bus that took us from Jaffna town to the government airport and back were all covered with paper so that no one could see out. The window coverings also meant that there was no air circulation in this non air-conditioned bus, so it was stifling.

May 2, 2006

Last Saturday (our day off), Pramila and I walked from our house to do some shopping. While we were in the clothing store, a shooting occurred and the street was immediately shut down to the local Tamil people by government security forces. The two of us stood on the street for a while to provide international presence while the Sinhalese government forces interfaced with the Tamil people who live and shop here. The authorities sent away any civilians who were on the street and demanded that shop doors and windows remain closed, probably out of concern for their safety. When everything seemed pretty calm and fears on both sides had apparently subsided, Pramila and I walked down the street where the dead body lay. The body had to remain in place until the judge came to look at it. The killer and motive remain unknown. Killings allegedly by unknown people for unknown reasons often occur here.

May 6, 2006

The situation has gotten very tense. There have been bomb blasts, grenades, and shootings in various locations around Jaffna district and in Jaffna town several times a day the last few days. Sometimes I wonder how we can best focus our time and energy.

One road across a causeway provides the only access to and from a group of islands off the coast close to our house/office. Navy checkpoints are distributed along that road, and when something like a bomb, grenade, or shooting occurs out on the islands, the civilians living there are not allowed to pass over the causeway back to the mainland until a search is completed. A man was shot there in the village of Allaipiddy the other night and because they were unable to move him across the causeway to the hospital, he died in his home early the next morning.

We are focusing some of our attention in that village; the people are frightened and feel like there is no support for them. The Catholic priest there, Father A has asked us to consider opening an office there or at least plan to spend some nights. Some of the villagers definitely appear comforted by our presence.

We are also questioning various key people in Jaffna town why there was no ambulance to take the man to the hospital that night.

May 12, 2006

Life is definitely tense here, but there are still more calm moments than not in our daily lives. We have security plans in place addressing our own safety. Any time we decide to take a new action, we have another security discussion.

In general, the local people seem pretty discouraged about the situation and are preparing for war. We have determined that the downstairs bathroom would be the safest room to go into if bombs are falling and we have stocked up on some supplies like extra drinking water and propane. Yet, there is also a strong belief that neither the LTTE nor the government wants to be responsible for officially starting the war. It appears to me that both parties are attempting to provoke the other party into starting a war. Some people expect this sort of action will continue rather than a declared war.

We are making arrangements for a couple of team members to spend at least one night in Allaipiddy this coming week.

While we pursue the question of what resources are available to help civilians who need to get to a hospital (especially after dark), we have uncovered many weak points in the system. The Red Cross has one ambulance, but the local drivers need permission from the army to get through checkpoints, which is not always possible after dark. Today, we attend a meeting to discuss with other NGOs how we all might work together to address this issue and make ambulance service available to everyone twenty-four hours a day.

Pramila and I are walking almost every morning, early before the day gets too hot. During these walks, we find opportunities for friendly exchanges with both the local Tamil residents and the Sinhalese armed soldiers who are posted on almost every corner. We distribute a brochure that explains NPSL in three languages—English, Tamil, and Sinhala.

May 17, 2006

Current experiences in Sri Lanka are reminding me how precious life is. The people in Allaipiddy are particularly vulnerable to political acts of violence from outside the village with uncertainty about the perpetrators. Last Saturday night Father A called us, saying that there was shooting occurring right at that moment and to please come imme- diately. Unfortunately, we were unable to go because we couldn't find a driver. When such acts of violence are occurring, especially at night, local people are afraid to go out. We had no means to get to the island until the next morning when our driver (who keeps the van at his house) would feel safe to come from his neighbor- hood to pick us up.

NPSL vehicle in village

That night, Father A managed to drive his own car past the checkpoint to take three of the villagers who had been shot to the hospital. He then came to our house/office. As he entered, he said, "Now I have to figure out what to do with the bodies," referring to dead bodies he left behind in the village. We made some phone calls to crucial people we know in NGOs and local organizations who might have been able to help with the situation, but nothing could be done about the bodies until after the judge looked at them the next day. We offered Father A a place to stay until morning, but he wanted to go back to his church. The villagers were all spending the night there. He didn't ask any of us to come with him, I guess because the inside of his car was covered with blood.

When we arrived in the village the next morning, the people wanted to show us the bodies. I took in the saddest scene I have ever encountered. It was a massacre of all the members of one household—eight bodies including one baby and a four-year old. The villagers told us stories about what they saw during the shooting. Many said they recognized Sri Lankan Navy men whom they had seen a number of times buying cigarettes in the shop, which was at the house where the massacre took place.

The judge arrived with an escort of navy and police forces. As soon as the villagers saw the armed forces coming, the tension was palpable. The women and children scurried back into the churchyard. The men clustered closer together on the street. I moved so I was standing between the cluster of men and the approaching armed forces. As the navy and police filed by, I just stood there, smiling and waving. Some of them smiled and waved back. That proved to be totally disarming and I felt the tension melt. In that moment, I knew in every cell of my body that I was safer unarmed than armed; no one was afraid of me.

The people in the village were in shock that morning and continue to be in fear. We have been providing our presence there almost full time since that morning. The people do their daily fishing, farming, and wood gathering activities during the days and then come back to the church for the nights. While foreigners are present, it is much less likely that any further harm will come to them.

A community meeting for the people to consider their next steps was held one evening. Some want to leave their homes because they do not feel safe. If they do that, they will become IDPs and suffer more difficulties (and likely some of the same sorts of dangers) wherever they go. Others do not want to leave their homes—they have lived on this beautiful island for generations. They can remember more peaceful times within the village when even though the war was ongoing, they were not the target of as much violence as they have become recently. They just want security. Unfortunately, one of the groups they fear is the navy, who is supposed to provide the security!

For these past few days, our nonpartisan unarmed presence has been providing the sense of security the villagers want. As the days have passed, we can see some relaxation in their fear and tension levels. Yesterday after providing 24-hour presence for several days, we thought it would be okay to leave during the day and to return before dark to spend the night. In the late afternoon as we drove back into the village, we saw beaming smiles of welcome and what appeared to be relief on their faces.

This morning, Father A requests us to continue with 24-hour presence again because he sensed much more tension yesterday when we had not been here. Thus, I stay today while my teammates go back to take care of things at the office. While I am here (even though it is only me), Father A says that he can see a big difference. I find it amazing (and hopeful) that just one unarmed outsider can make such a difference, and I think it provides a good model for the world that security can be provided without weapons. This experience reinforces my recognition that I feel safer because I don't have a weapon than I would feel if I had one.

May 25, 2006

We have gotten back into our more normal routines in and around the office this week. We spent about a week providing rotating 24-hour presence in Allaipiddy and in order for everyone to be at our team meetings during that time, we were holding the meetings at the church in Allaipiddy rather than in our usual location in our office/home.

Two families of witnesses testified in the local court about what they had seen the night of the massacre. These witnesses believe they are in extreme danger. We accompanied the family members to court the day of the testimony. Members of an organization providing legal support to the witnesses offered them a "safe" place to go after the court hearing, but the family members chose to stay in the church where they felt safe because we were there. At that point, we decided that at least one of us would remain awake at all times through the night and we took turns staying awake in three-hour shifts.

Then a mysterious message appeared on walls in the village posted by an unknown party that warned all the village people to leave the island; most of the people decided to go. They are now IDPs staying temporarily at two churches in Jaffna town and we are no longer needed in Allaipiddy twenty-four hours a day.

May 30, 2006

Anglican Bishop Duleep stopped in at our office one evening and we discussed with him what we have been doing—especially in Allaipiddy. An article in a Sri Lankan newspaper called The Daily Mirror (2006/05/27) says that after his visit here and to Trincomalee, Bishop Duleep said, "The situation in these areas is tense and dangerously volatile; various groups are engaged in a struggle for ideological, political and geographical space which invariably spills into the routine lives of civilians. Streets are deserted after 2 pm. and the people live in fear of each other."

In the article, Bishop Duleep describes the situation Tamil civilians are in feeling fear from all sides. They fear being suspected as LTTE sympathizers or as military informants. They fear the struggle for power between the LTTE and other armed Tamil groups most of who often are relations, neighbors, or associates. They fear for their adolescent children who may be conscripted by the LTTE or arrested by the Sri Lanka Armed Forces. Independent Tamil voices are reluctant to speak for fear of being caricatured as "the enemy." Duleep explains that the presence of an almost entirely non-Tamil security force creates a worrying polarization, especially in Jaffna where all civilians are Tamils and all Sri Lankan Armed Forces are non-Tamil.

Duleep speaks specifically of visiting Allaipiddy Island and seeing the tension, misery, and suffering that prevailed after the gruesome massacre of civilians. He goes on to tell about the Nonviolent Peaceforce: "The policy of this small team of foreign and local peace workers is to visibly stand by victims of violence, and needs commendation. All peace-loving people must do all they can," he says, "to appreciate and endorse such vulnerable groups whose mandate is to stand with the vulnerable, and whose only weapon is their moral strength to be able to do so."

The government is responsible for the care of IDPs; government officials want the Allaipiddy residents to go home now. The Jaffna District Government Agent (GA) asks us to return to the island with the people so that they will feel safe and be willing to return. He asks us to speak to the people at meetings that they organize at the two churches where the villagers are staying. We tell the villagers that we can be there full time for only a limited number of days and then we can come to visit them regularly, but we cannot provide them with 24-hour presence indefinitely. That isn't enough for them to feel safe enough to go back so most of the people decide to remain at the churches in town.

When I go to the two churches to say goodbye because I am leaving town now, the people from Allaipiddy ask me to come back to visit. I cannot promise that I will be back to Jaffna again, but I promise to visit them if I do return.

June 6, 2006

I am home and reflecting on my most recent experience in Sri Lanka. I realize that I love the work—especially this last time because it felt like we were really doing something that made a difference. I love TPNI—that is Third Party Nonviolent Intervention. My inner adolescent has a blast refuting Bush's created culture of fear and war on terror, and being in action helping to reduce the fears that might lead to increasing violence. I find that this work is a way to reclaim my aliveness from the hopelessness and numbness I otherwise feel about what my government is doing in the world in my name with my tax dollars.

However, at this point there is no more opportunity for short term work for me in NPSL. Before I left Sri Lanka this last time, the NPSL project director who has replaced William told me that he only wants me back if I will commit to stay for at least a year.

June 30, 2006

I just returned from guiding a women's wilderness trip. During my time in the wilderness, it came clear to me that I do want to go back to Sri Lanka and I will commit to stay for at least a year.

Amnesty International has sent out an e-mail appeal for support for that family I mentioned on March 29, when I included the father's letter. The boy was one of the five students killed in Trincomalee. A Magistrate's Court hearing into that killing was due to take place in Trinco town yesterday and the father was the only witness to come forward to testify for the prosecution. Amnesty International conveys that they believe threats allegedly made by the security forces to the father and one of his other sons are an attempt to force him and any other potential witnesses to withdraw from the case.

July 25, 2006
I have now committed to being in Sri Lanka from October 1st this year through all of 2007, with a leave already scheduled over New Year's to guide a women's vision quest.

August 7, 2006
In May, a hand grenade was thrown outside the office gate of the Mutur office and one of the team was injured. The international team members have not been staying in the Mutur office/ residence since then. Two of the local NPSL staff members are still in Mutur because that is where they live with their families.

Today, I receive an e-mail reporting on the current situation in Mutur from the NPSL project director. The LTTE blockaded irrigation water, which cut the water supply from people in government-controlled villages in the Trincomalee district. This set off a military confrontation. First, claiming they needed to clear the region before moving engineers in to repair the water tank, the military bombed LTTE targets. Then, ground troops of the Sri Lankan Army smashed the LTTE blockade. In retaliation, LTTE suicide bombers tried to sink a Sri Lankan

Members of the NPSL team

Army troop transport ship that had 850 military personnel aboard. The Army and the LTTE then battled with mortars and artillery overrunning several Eastern military camps, which took them to the town of Mutur where fierce fighting broke out for several days.

The LTTE managed to capture the town of Mutur after artillery destroyed many of the houses. No civilian areas were spared. The hospital and schools where civilians had sought refuge got hit, resulting in dozens of civilian deaths. The shelling and shooting between the LTTE and government continued while more than 20,000 Tamil and Muslim people fled to find safety in the jungle and other towns. Among the people who fled the town of Mutur were NPSL local staff members and their families, including children and infants.

Over the weekend, a short ceasefire allowed several NPSL trucks to conduct a search and rescue operation in convoy with other INGOs (International NGOs) and the International Committee of the Red Cross. One NPSL team brought one of the NPSL families to safety, but two of the children had gotten lost in the chaos. A day later, the second NPSL truck got stuck in a crowd throwing stones at the truck, which smashed the window and injured the hand of one of the field team members. By Sunday August 6, all NPSL staff and their families had been brought to safety where they received medical attention and assistance.

Although there are no official numbers yet, early reports indicate that over one hundred people were killed during the siege in Mutur. At the moment, many humanitarian agencies are trying to help the tens of thousands of people who are displaced in the town of Kantale. In the meantime, the LTTE has left Mutur town and returned to the positions it held at the time of the 2002 ceasefire. Approximately six thousand people remain in Mutur. Among those found dead are fourteen local staff people from the French non-profit organization Action Against Hunger, who had local but no international staff in their Mutur office at the time.

The project director's report includes a bit about other parts of Sri Lanka as well. The LTTE's regional political head has declared that "the ceasefire agreement has become null and void" and that "it is the government that has started the war." The Sri Lankan Monitoring Mission has also stated about both the Sri Lankan government and the LTTE, "In reality they more or less have terminated the ceasefire agreement in their actions."

Meanwhile, the Karuna Group (the split-away faction from LTTE in Batticaloa district) carried out a first suicide attack on the LTTE.

At this same time in Batticaloa, NPSL is supporting an initiative by fifty-five families whose children have been abducted. These family members signed and sent a petition to the highest authorities in Sri Lanka and internationally, raising attention to the loss of their children. This is a brave act on the parts of those families; they risk further danger having openly reported this loss.

October 2, 2006

I arrived in Colombo last night and I will be heading up to Trincomalee tomorrow to join my new field team, the Mutur team. As explained earlier, there are now two field teams in the Trincomalee district—one in Trinco town and the other is the Mutur team. The Mutur team has a residence/office in Mutur and we have one local field team member who still lives in Mutur with his family. Since the hand grenade incident in May, the international members of the team have not been staying there. Also, the other local field team member who was living in Mutur has moved and is staying with the rest of the Mutur team in Trinco since the events described on August 7.

October 6, 2006

I am very happy to be back in Sri Lanka. I realized after I met most of my new team (one teammate is on leave and will be back next week) that I had anxiety about how well (or not) my teammates get along and support each other. I am here with a sense of longevity in contrast with the short term stays the previous five times.

During those shorter stays, I found it fairly easy to accept and adapt to team dynamics as they were without getting caught up in them. Now, I am aware that how well we get along is essential in terms of our general well-being, our sense of security, and our ability to carry out our work. After having spent some time together, I am pleased. I hope that I continue to feel supported by my teammates and also find ways to make

Mutur office and residence

my best contributions to the team. Current members of the team include one woman each from Austria, Romania, and Mutur; one man each from Nepal, Rwanda, and Mutur; and myself.

We are currently staying at a run-down guesthouse on the beach north of the town of Trincomalee and I cannot imagine a better place for me to be. Our simple rooms all face the ocean and one of my greatest pleasures while I am in Sri Lanka is swimming in the warm blue sea. To be able to walk out my door and swim first thing in the morning as well as at the end of our workday is a total delight.

Though I love staying at the guest house at the beach, my teammates want to settle in a real house. We are seeking one or more temporary residences in Trinco town, because we expect it will be at least three more months before we feel ready to move back to Mutur. We will spend some of our time during the days in Mutur reconnecting with our contacts there and assessing the situation. We visited Mutur a couple of days ago; it was the first time the team had been there since early August.

October 13, 2006

Because of security concerns, our Jaffna team has been staying in Colombo since early August. I just read a BBC report from yesterday that there has been a lot of killing in Jaffna. Recently there was also a battle south of Trinco. Things have continued to be fairly calm here since I arrived. Our NP work in the Mutur area has included monitoring IDP camps and resuming our support of local Peace Committees.

We have found two temporary residences in the area of Trinco town for at least three months. The house in which I will be living is in this same compound as the guesthouse where we have been staying, so I will continue to be close to the beach.

October 17, 2006

One of our local staff members and I are now in the beach house. It is behind the guest house and thus does not have the view of the water. Our other house-mate-to-be is currently on leave.

One recent morning, I was awakened by the sound of a bomb blast off the coast where we live. It sounded like it was close by on land, but when we got out to the beach, we could still see fire and smoke on the horizon. A half hour later, I was swimming in that warm peaceful water—a surreal experience.

Another bomb was set off miles away the day before yesterday on one of the roads that comes into Trinco town. Almost a hundred navy personnel died and 150 were injured. A few civilian shopkeepers in the area of the bomb were also injured. One of our team was traveling back from Colombo and passed through the area just prior to the incident. Another team member from the Trinco town team got caught on the other side and had to stay overnight in a guesthouse there. Today a hartal has been called in Trinco. As I said earlier, a hartal is when everything shuts down in protest of the incident. We are working in our home office (which is the beach house).

One pleasure is swimming in the warm sea

© Rita Webb

I receive a text message that a navy camp in the south has been attacked and ongoing gunfire is continuing there. Although it is far away, it can still have rami-fications here. There are many internationals working here in the Trinco district in various agencies. We have set up a phone tree system, so whenever incidents occur that may contribute to further incidents, a text message is sent so everyone knows immediately what happened and where.

October 20, 2006

I read an inspiring e-mail message today about an interview with Elisabet Sahtouris, a scientist who has long been interested in the health of the planet. Sahtouris says that for too long Darwin's theory has been used to justify hunger, poverty, and the continual devastation of the planet; and that theory feeds a world view that emphasizes the separation between living things rather than the connection. In contrast, she states that increasingly, prominent scientists, philosophers, and spiritual leaders believe that nature is comprised of a refined network in which cooperation is key to survival and sustainable success.

Sahtouris believes evolution will create new human beings who do not exploit and dominate, but merge and evolve more harmoniously with their surrounding natural habitat. All healthy, living systems (including global human culture) organize and maintain themselves by the principle that individual and collective interests are equal; and in a mature system, every level expresses its self-interest, so that negotiations are constantly happening towards cooperation. She talks about a particular kind of bacteria as a metaphor for our current global economic system. These bacteria created devastating environmental and social

Mutur Peace Committee office

crises by pursuing economics based on invasions and exploitation; the very atmosphere they lived in became deadly to them, so they had to adapt or die. "They managed to solve every one of their problems by reorganizing their lifestyles from destructive competition into creative co-operation. . . These single-celled bacteria survived by merging into communities, so they could join forces."

Sahtouris believes that an inevitable evolutionary process of shifting from hostile competition to mature cooperation is happening now. Humans are being driven by evolution to form a cooperative global humanity in harmony with each other and with other species. Globalization is part of that evolution. Human empire-building has been a continual process of merging cultures and now, corporate cartels and mergers and a World Trade Organization can overrule national political laws and policies. However, monoculture is not a workable system. "It is time we learned to respect and cherish our human diversity as the creative source of potential harmonious complexity" (Sahtouris, 2006).

October 27, 2006

Because of team members on leave, yesterday was the first day the whole team has been together since I arrived. We were able to make decisions about team roles (to take care of the logistics of living and working together) and program areas (to carry out our work). In team roles, I am to be the point person for our monthly reports and the support person for accounting. In program, I am the point person for Peace Committees. The four other program areas include Human Rights, and work with each of three organizations with whom we have projects to implement: United Nations' High Commissioner for Refugees, UNICEF, and Christian Aid.

At the end of this one workday together yesterday, one teammate ended up in the hospital in need of an appendectomy; his operation was successful.

Tomorrow, two days of "peace talks" begin again. I hope these talks will help Sri Lanka come to peace with justice.

November 3, 2006

Unfortunately, no progress was made in the Peace Talks. Our housemate who just returned from leave is the only member currently on the Mutur team who was part of the earlier team; she is gradually introducing us to contacts with whom the previous team already had a relationship.

Monday we will be providing presence in the Sinhalese town called Seruvilla, a village on the way to Mutur, where three scary incidents have occurred on the last three Mondays—a missing person and two killings. Monday is market day, but because of the incidents Tamil people in the IDP camps are afraid to go to the market. A Sinhalese colleague of ours has requested our presence in and around the market, and along the route where the IDPs walk from the camps.

November 8, 2006

I cry this morning while swimming because I heard that an IDP camp near Valaichchenai was hit by a bomb yesterday. I just don't understand how or why anyone would bomb an IDP camp. Then I remember my visit to Iraq during the month prior to the start of Bush's 2003 bombing, when I saw the remains of the shelter that the USA had bombed during the first Gulf War a decade earlier. What can we do to shift powers that appear beyond our reach away from these atrocities of war and domination?

What am I doing here, really? We visit Muslims, Sinhalese, and Tamils and find that they are all loving, caring, peaceful people who just want to feel secure in their homes. Local peace workers who have worked to bring people from all three of these different groups into peaceful relationships with each other are discouraged because they cannot continue to do this while there are disappearances, killings, bombs, and shelling. Perhaps I am here to be with the reality of these atrocities of war as a part of my everyday life. Perhaps it is too easy for me to go into denial about these realities when I am home where this kind of violence is not so obvious.

November 18, 2006

Today I finalize the last-minute arrangements to fly home next week. Rita was initially invited and scheduled to do a speaking tour in the USA for NP in November and December. Because she so recently returned from her leave, and the tour dates are close to the dates I was planning to go on leave, a last-minute decision has been made that I will do the speaking tour instead of Rita. The tour includes presentations in Eugene OR, Seattle WA, Santa Rosa CA, Philadelphia PA, Boston MA, and Boulder CO. It is a happy coincidence that I'll be speaking in my home city of Santa Rosa as part of the tour!

I leave my field site the day after tomorrow, return home from the tour in early December, and then return to Sri Lanka January 12 after guiding a vision quest.

Vegetable vendor

December 23, 2006

I've been home from the speaking tour for several weeks now. I just read an interesting report from the Human Security Center at the University of British Columbia about worldwide trends of violence and war in recent years. The number of wars being fought around the world dropped significantly between 2002 and 2005. This decline is attributed in large part to an upsurge in international activism spearheaded by the UN that seeks to stop ongoing wars, help negotiate peace settlements, support post-conflict reconstruction, and prevent old wars from starting again. The fact that more wars now end in negotiated settlements than in victories is encouraging, but those wars that end through negotiation also last three times longer than those that end in victories and are nearly twice as likely to re-start within five years. Hmmm.

January 16, 2007

I've now returned to Sri Lanka after my journey to the USA for almost two months. After the speaking tour and through Christmas Day, I relished every moment of my time at home with family, my community, and other friends. Then I guided a wilderness trip. Returning from that trip I only had a week to prepare for being away from home for the rest of 2007. Now I am in Colombo and will be heading back to Trinco tomorrow.

January 24, 2007

The violent conflict here in Sri Lanka continues. A brother of one of our local staff was killed a couple of days ago. The man's wife had just given birth to their third baby that very day. We visited her home the next day as part of the traditional funeral rituals. A woman handed me the baby to hold while we sat beside the mother whose husband had just been killed. I don't think I have ever held a one-day old baby. The baby's mama had gone into silence and was refusing to talk. Sitting there with her baby in my arms, I gazed deeply into the mother's eyes and could only imagine the sorrow she must feel.

My adjustment back is proving to be difficult in other ways too. I'm feeling homesick. Part of my difficulty is that the two field teams in this district are being reconfigured. Two teams of five are going to become one team of seven and three of us will go to other field sites. We do not know who will go where yet.

February 2, 2007

We are continuing with our work: checking in with people in IDP camps and in the vulnerable communities where we have developed some relationships; encouraging connections; and providing accompaniment when asked by someone who feels safer doing their peace-related, community-building, or human rights work because we are with them.

I have not been able to swim since I returned from my leave because it is monsoon season and the sea is rough with a dangerous current.

February 17, 2007

Last Thursday/Friday, the International Governing Council for NP and some NP staff from various parts of the world were all in Colombo for an annual international meeting. Some field team members got a chance to spend time with them. I am thankful that I got to go. It was great to see folks whom I have not seen for several years and to meet face-to-face those with whom I have been in conference calls and e-mail conversations. I have served on a Rapid Response committee that has been discussing with the Program Department developing a team of trained reservists who could be on call for short-term work as needed. The committee consists of NP staff and volunteers from various parts of the world and meets via conference calls.

Monsoon season is over and the sea is calm again. I swam yesterday afternoon after coming home from Colombo and again this morning. I look forward to getting back into my usual morning exercise routine of swimming five laps (eighty strokes each way) out into the ocean and back. Also, the days are heating up.

We are still in limbo about teammates, but decisions are supposed to be made by March 1st.

February 21, 2007

The government official for the Mutur Division asked us to provide presence during an event called a "Go and See" visit. Now that the government has deemed the area safe for the IDPs to return, they are encouraging them to do that. Some forty men who are staying in IDP camps in our neighboring district visit their villages today to see their war damaged houses and gain a better sense of the situation, so that they can decide whether or not they feel ready to bring their families back. My teammate and I are with six IDPs from three different villages and a local government leader from one of the three villages in a van, and together we stop at each of the men's houses.

I feel sad as I watch the men's faces when they view their damaged and looted homes. In one home, the owner quickly walks through, retrieving important documents and two of the other men notice that we are walking over faded, scraped, water-stained photos scattered on the floor looking like trash. The two men carefully pick up and dust off some of the photos and place them on the counter. Before leaving the house, the owner picks up a couple of those rescued photos and puts them in his shirt pocket. My glimpse of that tender moment reminds me how nothing can be taken for granted when living in a war zone.

While we are in the van, I hear a precious story about a man in the IDP camp who had been separated from his wife for the past fifteen years. He had moved away from her back then. The man and wife re-united in the IDP camp and will be returning to his home together now.

March 8, 2007

Our team is set for now. All of us internationals on the Mutur team will continue on the new team together and we gain two other international field team members plus two local field officers from the Trinco team, which is otherwise disbanded. New teammates include women from Germany and the USA, plus a Sinhalese woman and a Muslim man from Trincomalee. I am feeling okay about the make-up of the new team, but now we have to cover all the work and area that both teams were covering prior to this. We'll just have to prioritize and do what we can do.

Because of the reduction in teammates, we have to give up the beach house. I am making arrangements to move alone into one of the smaller units back in the guesthouse that has the view of the water.

My housemate who is from Mutur has resigned and moved to Colombo to be with her family there. She and her family were among those who fled from Mutur on August 6. Her husband moved to Colombo at that point, but she stayed on to continue her job with NP as our interpreter. It is not unusual for people in Sri Lanka to live far away from their families in order to do their jobs.

While my other housemate is away on leave, I recognize that I am happy living alone, especially if I have a good space where I can be outside, which is the case here on the beach. I can maintain physical, psycho-emotional, and spiritual health in this situation and thus bring my full energy and contribution to my team and our work. This outdoor spaciousness is not available at either of our team houses that are in town on busy streets.

I have been continuing to work as committee chair of my first dissertation student while I have been here in Sri Lanka. She sends her work as an attachment to an e-mail message and I return it with my feedback in the same way. She has finally received approval from everyone on the committee after ten years of work and she is graduating in May, so I have decided to take another leave for most of the month of May and will be home to "hood" her at the graduation ceremony.

This opportunity for another long leave is possible because we receive and can accumulate a good number of leave days; and NP encourages us to give ourselves a real break from the stress of the work we do by getting away from the field site when we take leave time.

March 21, 2007

I am settling in to my new home facing the sea once more and loving it.

One focus of our work now is a new big IDP camp located between Mutur and Seruvilla. A large number of people who fled from their homes in the Mutur area settled in IDP camps in Batticaloa district and are now returning to Trinco district, but their villages have not been cleared of land mines so they cannot return to their homes yet. Instead, they must stay in this one newly built IDP camp facility that the government is calling a Welfare Center. It was set up for large numbers, but apparently is not ready for the numbers who have already come. One reason for the need to return is that there has been heavy shelling recently in Batticaloa district; more and more people from that area are fleeing their homes and also need space in the IDP camps that are located there.

Good cooperation and coordination among the international agencies in the area supports us all to best meet the needs of these IDPs who have just arrived and are facing difficult conditions. Security concerns are high and that is our niche. Our challenge is to figure out how best to support the people in ways other than providing 24-hour presence. This level of presence is not possible for our small field team when there are so many IDP camps needing attention.

March 29, 2007

I have the opportunity to be part of a small group organized by USAID to meet with a Foreign Affairs Officer from the US Department of State who is inquiring into human rights. It is a great risk for the local people who attend to speak up about human rights abuses, but my teammate who is also from the USA and I don't risk our lives when describing human rights concerns we have witnessed.

Some of my other teammates are attending an all-day training provided by one of our partner organizations for about forty members of the Peace Committees who are beginning to get active again in the Mutur Division. The Peace Committees are meant to provide a multi-ethnic venue to discuss community problems/issues with the hope of resolving them at the village level before they escalate further.

One of the benefits of the new team formation is that the Trinco team already had a cook who cooks wonderful lunches for us every day at minimal cost to each of us. All of us who are in the office on any particular day (both international and national staff member) are sharing a good meal together. Eating together holds and supports the spirit of a group as well as providing healthy nourishment for each of us on the physical level, so I am happy for this.

Two teammates—the other US American woman and the man from Nepal—

have informed us that they are leaving at the end of April, so the team composition continues to be shifting. As I said before, my home on the beach nurtures me and provides very important support for me to be able to flow with the challenges and changes.

April 3, 2007

We accompany another group of IDPs on a "Go and See" visit to their homes to see whether or not they feel safe to move back. The place we visit is a little island not far from Mutur town. The IDP camp where the people are living now is across the harbor, nearer to Trinco town. Everyone in the group travels across the harbor in small boat taxis. Two boats carry a total of about eighteen IDPs. A group of local government people come in a third boat with us. Army, navy, and police come in their own boat as does ICRC (the International Red Cross). I enjoy the informality of this excursion.

We walk together around the island and then settle under the shade of a big tree next to the school for a meeting. Rice and curry lunch comes in newspaper wrapped packets and we eat with our fingers (as the local people do at all meals). There are no trash cans anywhere, so we just throw the trash on the side of the road, which is normal here. Left-overs get consumed by dogs, goats, and crows.

April 25, 2007

The air temperature has gotten so hot that sitting under a fan feels like sitting in front of a heater. In the unit where I live now, my bedroom faces the sea and the sunrise and catches the sea breeze. I feel blessed to have this place to live.

May 6, 2007

I'm home in the USA on leave. A killing that occurred close to the airport in Sri Lanka caused many airlines to change their flight schedules, so my flight out of Sri Lanka was re-scheduled to leave fourteen hours earlier. My connecting flight was in Hong Kong; I spent eighteen hours there with accommodations provided by the airline.

June 2, 2007

My leave at home is over now. I arrived in Trinco yesterday minus one piece of luggage. The airline arranged for a local person to carry it all the way from the airport to Trinco and it arrives today in pretty good shape. That's impressive! I pity the driver who had to carry it, because it is difficult to get through checkpoints with someone else's luggage.

I met a Muslim man from a local organization called the Rural Development Foundation (RDF) on the ferry to Mutur before I went on leave. He was standing nearby when I was buying my ferry ticket and overhearing that I didn't have the appropriate change, he gave me some smaller bills in exchange for my bigger one. In our ensuing conversation, we found that there might be good ways NP Trinco and RDF could work together. One RDF project in the past was developing Rural Peace Councils that bring together a mixed ethnic group of local community leaders to: 1) help solve minor disputes, 2) plan events that bring the communities together, and 3) teach language classes (Tamil to Sinhalese children and Sinhalese to Tamil children). Many of these Rural Peace Councils had stopped functioning as the conflict got worse and some of the key participants moved out of the area. Out of this chance meeting on the ferry, the NP Trinco team began working in partnership with RDF to re-establish these councils. Today three of us from NP attend a meeting of thirty potential Peace Council members from seven different villages. They are gathered together to share ideas about activities, learn from each other about available resources, and express needs.

June 11, 2007

I've been back in the country for more than a week now. Because of more goings and comings, it is a new team again. Additional internationals in our office are a man from Ireland who is the new security officer for all of NPSL and a man from Egypt who was also on the Valaiaichenai team the last time I was there. We

© Emily Rosenberg

Boat taxis

now have seven local staff including two drivers, two field officers, two interpreters, and a housekeeper/cook. Three of the local staff are Tamil, two are Muslim, and two are Sinhalese.

Now, we are in a conference facility near Colombo for a three-day staff retreat. This was a much-needed event. We used to do retreats about four times a year, but this is the first one since last August. Yesterday, we talked

about our identity as NPSL: how it has changed as the situation has changed, how we describe ourselves, and how others perceive us. There was also a discussion and further instructions about measures for our own security. Because of some of our experiences in this pilot project—most notably the injury caused by the hand grenade in Mutur last year—NP hired a security officer who is making recommendations for changes in our practices that ensure greater security for ourselves. I find some of the changes limiting. I came into this work aware of and willing to take the potential risks of the job. I do not think we would have been able to provide protective presence the way we did in Allaipiddy where the massacre had occurred a year ago now that we are so concerned about our own security.

June 22, 2007

I read a New York Times front page article about the situation in Sri Lanka. I feel relieved that some of what I have seen happening here is being reported elsewhere in the world. Reading the story gives me an outsider's perspective and I cry some uncried tears, which I hadn't realized were there. I realize that some numbness has come over me because of seeing and hearing so many sad stories directly from the people experiencing them. Yet, life goes on and these resilient loving people still manage to smile.

I'm staying healthy, partially because of swimming every day and also drinking lots of water. The team is working well together. We enjoy being together, which makes such a big difference in our well-being and the work we can accomplish. We have a new teammate coming in a few days from Pakistan.

July 2, 2007

I think I am finally feeling more at home. I believe that I now know that I can take care of myself physically, mentally, and emotionally. I find myself taking time just to "be" during my time off in the evenings or on Sundays. It is too hot sometimes to feel like doing anything and I am drawn to just being fully present in this beautiful place where I live. I have often found that I would rather just be daydreaming than reading something that takes me away from where I am.

Yet the realities of war so close at hand are always in the background (if not in the foreground) of my awareness. Imminent death looms large, not so much for me but for all the local people around me whether Tamil, Sinhalese, or Muslim. What a gift these people give me every day just by being in my life. I can only hope that I am able to give something back to them by my presence here.

July 13, 2007

Last weekend, we had a staff beach party here at my house that included family members of our local staff. The party was great fun with an open fire barbecue, rice, and plenty of beer and sodas to drink. Then, some of us went swimming in the late afternoon and discovered that a bunch of little jelly fish (about the size of walnuts) were now in the water. Their stings were not so much painful as itchy, but since there were so many of them, it made for an unpleasant experience.

Three of us spent three nights in our office in Mutur last week. As I have said, this is the office that NP first set up here in the Trinco District, but after the hand grenade was thrown on the street in front last May, the team moved away. We have been visiting the office some of the days since I joined the team in October, but this was our first time staying overnight. One of those days in Mutur last week we drove out to an area where Swiss and Danish organizations are de-mining. Another day we provided presence for IDPs who were moving back to their village—the one on the island close to Mutur where we did the Go and See. These people have been displaced for almost a year. Most of them looked pretty happy to be moving back.

August 23, 2007

I've noticed a huge difference in the cost of health care here and at home. I had an infected mosquito bite that spread infection throughout my body. I saw a doctor, had a urine analysis, and got a topical ointment for a total cost of the equivalent of $5.10 (US). Then I went back a few days later to fill the prescription for the antibiotic that I initially hoped I would not have to take and that cost an additional $4.50. So the total was less than $10!

September 25, 2007

Our Sinhalese interpreter and I attend a village development committee meeting in a Trinco neighborhood that includes a majority of Sinhalese and some Muslim residents. This committee is made up of all women and is meant to help the five villages in the neighborhood make decisions and problem solve in the following areas: health, agriculture, community service, religious programs, cultural activities, self-employment, and women's development. About ninety women fill the room.

A body of officers and a subcommittee of seven plan the agendas and have been functioning for a short while with all Sinhalese members. The decision is made at this meeting to reselect these organizing members. I am interested to see how they go about coming to consensus, as much as I can understand due to the language barrier. Seven women are nominated by group members for the subcommittee and then everyone in the room is asked for agreement. When some disagree, they do not have to indicate with whom they disagreed, but a new panel of seven is nominated. Some of the same women who were in the initial group are re-nominated and some members are different than those nominated in the first round. I witness a lively and loud discussion with some anger expressed. Finally, the local government authority for this division (a Sinhalese woman) stands up and points to seven women for the subcommittee and everyone accepts her nomination/appointment, which now includes several Muslim women.

On our way back to the office, our interpreter explains to me how decisions are made at this local community level. The members strive for everyone to be in agreement, but if they can't come to that kind of (consensus) agreement, the local government official will make the final decision based on what she has heard during the discussion.

October 15, 2007

I had to go to Colombo last week to get a visa for India. My brother and sister-in-law are coming to Sri Lanka when my contract ends at the end of December. We will travel together in Sri Lanka for a week and then go to India for two weeks.

I traveled the full day trip back from Colombo with a driver who did not speak much English. The van began having a noticeable mechanical problem when we were in the middle of "the jungle" within 2½ hours of Trinco. We were out of range for a cell phone signal. He stopped to look at the engine, then began driving quite slowly checking regularly for a cell signal. On the side of the road, there happened to be a flatbed truck with two guys working on the engine. The driver pulled over. One of the "mechanics" stopped what he was doing and came to work on our van. He first tried a giant leaf, then a piece of paper rolled into a funnel shape, and finally a plastic bag to squirt oil up from underneath the van. He ended up with black oil coating his arm up to his armpit by the time our vehicle was ready to continue the journey. I guess we had run out of oil. No one spoke much English, so I just had to infer what was happening. I didn't see any money exchanged between the driver and the mechanic. It seems it is simply a matter that this was a job that had to be done and the mechanic was able to do it, so he did.

November 7, 2007
We have scheduled a three-day staff training workshop away from the field site for both national and international staff of the Trinco team to do some staff development together. I have had a lot to do with initiating and forwarding this team retreat and with planning the content and format.

November 16, 2007
The man from RDF whom I met on the ferry to Mutur (see 6/2/07) was brutally killed on Saturday by an "unknown group" in his home district north of Trinco. His service work was supportive to many people and his death is one of many that are a tragic loss to the people of Sri Lanka. I remember when we attended that meeting that formally brought our two organizations together, he introduced the Nonviolent Peaceforce to the thirty Rural Peace Council leaders with the story of our chance meeting on the ferry. Aside from the meetings we organized for the two organizations, we also had visited with each other a number of times when again, we found ourselves on the same ferry to Mutur. Every time I saw him, his enthusiasm for and commitment to his work and all the people with whom he worked was apparent. He was an energetic forty-year-old Muslim man. In the current situation, he might as easily have been Tamil or Sinhalese because all the local people here are at risk.

In all the time that I have been here, I have spent too many sorrowful moments being with people as they grieve the loss of loved ones who have been killed. I am painfully aware that people here live daily in fear for their lives and the lives of their loved ones. This is the first time when someone with whom I have had an ongoing relationship has been killed as part of this war. As one of my teammates said, "It brings the whole tragedy of the situation ever closer to us."

November 27, 2007
We just returned from the four-day team retreat for staff development. All but one (our field officer who lives in Mutur) of the members of our team were there,

including program and support staff, so there were six national staff and five international staff. First, we had a day long workshop with an outside teacher on both how to be a good interpreter and how to work with interpreters.

Next, we had a day with an outside facilitator helping to surface some of how we do what we do. This was especially timely since several of us internationals who have been here for months and years will be leaving the project within the next few months; it's good to capture what we have learned so that as we turn over our work to new international team members, we can learn from what others have learned prior and grow as a team.

I facilitated the final afternoon on "What Internationals Might Never Know Otherwise" intended for us internationals to learn from our national staff how best (or better) to behave in culturally appropriate ways. I thought this was important because I had noticed in a report written by an NP International Governing Council member from India who had carried out an evaluation of the national staff's experiences working for NPSL that we internationals were still committing some cultural offenses without realizing it. I designed the activities for this part based on two assumptions: 1) that internationals might feel shame, guilt, or regret once we learn what something we did means to local people; and 2) that national staff may hesitate to say something that might cause uncomfortable feelings. The activity helped to surface some new learning, but I think there is a lot more that we internationals don't know that we don't know about culture in Sri Lanka that the national staff still did not share.

December 7, 2007

My time remaining now seems way too short. I mention this to my German teammate, Kati, who has become my good friend here. Kati has been here in Trinco two years and will be leaving Sri Lanka in February; she agrees that it probably doesn't matter when we actually do leave, it will seem too soon.

I get a message from Human Rights First today. They are proud of their success with getting some of the potential presidential candidates for the 2008 elections in the USA to take a stand against torture. That's good news, but I find it pretty absurd that it is even a question. I am ashamed to be a US citizen much of the time these days.

December 18, 2007

Three new international teammates arrived in Trinco yesterday: a man from Portugal, a woman from Japan, and a woman from Egypt. I am preparing to leave the field team; my last day to work is December 27. I will go to meet my brother and sister-in-law at the airport in the middle of the night on the 28th-29th and bring them back to Trinco. I am having a beach party on December 30 for them to meet all my field teammates and their families. We will celebrate New Year's here in Trinco. Then the three of us will travel to Kandy, a touristy place in the center (higher elevation and cooler) of Sri Lanka. After they have a week in Sri Lanka, we will go on to India for a couple of weeks. I can't believe that this fifteen-month commitment is already coming to an end!

December 25, 2007

It's Christmas today. The sea gives me a wonderful gift. It has been so rough with high waves and strong current that I haven't ventured forth to swim my laps for nearly a month. I really was not expecting to be able to do so again before leaving the country. But today it is calm enough to swim. I am painfully aware that the moments I have left here are all so very precious.

December 30, 2007

I introduce my brother and sister-in-law to the international members of my field team and the families of the local field teammates at my beach party today. I give each of the local staff a parting gift from among the special altar pieces that I had brought from home.

January 1, 2008

Today I leave Trinco with my brother and sister-in-law. Though it is difficult to leave, I'm feeling complete for now. I promise the national staff that I will see them again; I will come back to visit even if I don't come back to work. Our local field officer gives me a wonderful altar piece that I treasure—Muslim hands in prayer. These hands are not like Christian hands in prayer; they are cupped upwards as if to catch the power of spirit from the sky. He translates the Arabic words written on the piece, "Pray for you."

During this last fifteen months in Trinco, I have never again gotten to see Father A whom I had gotten to know in Allaip-iddy. We reconnected last April by e-mail and spoke on the phone every so often. In recent calls I told him that I would be leaving the country and I thought he understood. But I guess he thought I was just going

NPSL peacekeeper observing funeral

to India for a few weeks, and then returning to continue to live in Sri Lanka. We talk on the phone for the last time today when I'm in my hotel room in Kandy. He finally understands that I'm leaving with no plans to return, and he tells me that it will be a sad New Year for him.

January 8, 2008

There is a news report (Swamy, 2008) that the Sri Lankan government has finally officially withdrawn from the ceasefire agreement. They have militarily driven the LTTE out of the Eastern province (including Batticaloa, Valaichchenai, Trinco, and Mutur) and are beginning to focus on doing the same in the North (including Jaffna). Karuna, the military commander who split off the faction in the East, is now in custody in Britain.

End of January, 2008

Often in this work, we don't get to hear what happens later for the people we support through moments of their lives. Yet, I do have an end to one story that has been part of this journey. The Trinco team continued to provide a protective presence at the doctor's house—the one who had testified in court regarding the killing of his son (see 3/29/06 and 6/30/06). We also made several trips accompanying him and various family members at different times to Colombo as arrangements were made until they finally did manage to get out of the country on asylum. After I had left the team, Kati provided that final accompaniment when the family members (father, wife, and the two other sons) were on their way to a safer home out of the country.

7

Iran

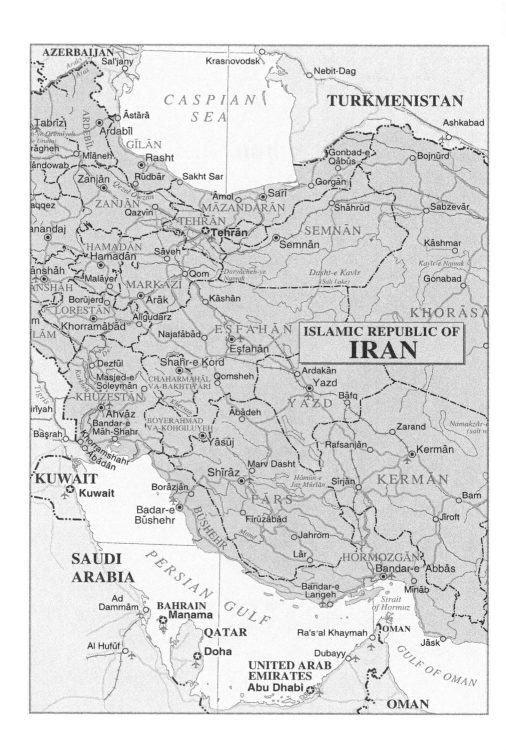

ONCE HOME FROM MY FIFTEEN MONTHS in Sri Lanka, I gradually re-adjust to life in cold and rainy Northern California. I begin to settle into routines. I start teaching a research proposal development course and I am looking forward to co-guiding vision quests in upcoming months.

My current sense of my spiritual practice includes loving through just being in my relationships. My inner guidance reaffirms: *You are spot on your path. You are learning about love and loving, and making your contribution.*

I continue to ask myself questions. Where are the war, abuse, and torture in me? For what am I responsible? Where can I focus energy in order to shift such realities in my world? And I get an answer: *Just keep being all that you are in every moment, fully present.* I recognize a need to manifest my spiritual path through loving, giving, and caring.

On March 19, I get arrested in San Francisco for civil disobedience (CD) while honoring the five-year anniversary of the bombing of Iraq. It is fun to do CD. I want people to know the pleasure of this act, so more will want to do it. My inner adolescent has a blast. It's like being subversive or "naughty," but getting to feel totally righteous about it. Depending on the action, there is always some risk involved, but I feel as though doing CD is much healthier or safer than not doing it . . . until the unhealthy and destructive system changes.

I stand on the corner of Montgomery and Market with a sign that says *no blood for oil.* Many people take my picture, including a woman from the San Francisco Examiner, and I get interviewed by two radio stations. Later, three of my fellow community members hear the bit of my interview that was broadcast on National Public Radio. The action is a "die in" to represent all the Iraqis and US military who have been killed in the Iraq occupation. Beginning at noon, those of us who are risking arrest make our way through the line of police and lay down in the middle of the intersection as if dead. The first few to cross the police line carry a cardboard coffin covered with a flag and flowers, which they place in the center. The police lining the intersection allow us to remain there for longer than I expect and we watch the sun break through the San Francisco fog while we are lying in the street.

The police who arrest us are polite and gentle. I have a great time talking with one of my two arresting officers. He asks my favored candidate in the upcoming primary and we talk about our work. I even describe the work I do on peace teams and how we are able to provide a sense of security without weapons. As part of the procedures of this arrest, I get my picture taken with him. I know it is going to be a great picture and I really want to see it, but it's a Polaroid camera and the photo takes too long to develop. The policewoman who escorts me to the vehicle is in a hurry and takes me away before the picture appears. The police hold us in a pen for several hours and that isn't much fun. As the sun gets lower in the sky, I'm glad I have a warm jacket. One woman in the pen reflects on how great it was to lie down in the middle of the intersection. She says, "You know, that's a view of San Francisco you'd never get otherwise." I receive a citation with a court date. Although it is a day when I have plans to be out of town, a lawyer's guild will represent us in court and most likely the charges will be dropped.

Thus far in my experiences of participating in CD, I have never been held for more than a few hours, but the possibility of getting locked up for longer is one of the risks involved. Another risk is that I might get caught in a violent confrontation; not all police are so kind. Yet, I enjoy interacting with the officers as human beings who are simply doing their job, just like I'm simply doing my job as a citizen in a democracy.

Several days after the arrest, I am feeling melancholy again. I'm feeling the mundaneness and day-to-day grind of my life at home, not nearly as exciting as living in Sri Lanka. I'm glad I have good work to do here; however I'm especially missing some of the local people I got to know in Sri Lanka.

Spring 2008

In April, I am in base camp as a guide while the participants are out spending three days and nights of solo time in the desert. I lie awake one night, a cold wind blowing, and think briefly about the book that one of my professors from my PhD program is encouraging me to write (this book). I want to inspire people to be with their fears and follow their hearts anyway. At the same time, I recognize that I also want to be with my own fear and follow my heart into unfamiliar and unknown territories of love and loving.

I continue to be aware of my let-down feeling of being home rather than in Sri Lanka, and how I'm trying to feel my way along my path to find what I'm supposed to be doing now. I notice that it is particularly difficult when people ask if/when I'm going back to Sri Lanka and I don't have a definite answer. Again, I recognize the feeling of glamour that came with my work in Sri Lanka that's missing in my everyday life at home.

Summer 2008

George W. Bush has been talking about a need to invade Iran based on a fear that they are developing nuclear weapons. In early July, I have a telephone interview to join a citizen diplomacy trip to Iran with an organization called Global Exchange. I am accepted and will be going for two and a half weeks in October. Citizen diplomacy offers opportunities for citizens of two countries whose governments are in conflict to meet and get to know each other as individuals. The idea is to have experiences with each other and develop understandings that can overcome fears and prejudices.

On the first of August, I receive the information to begin preparations to go to Iran. The information includes a significant list of suggested readings. Because sharing what I learn from my experience there is an important component of citizen diplomacy, part of my purpose for going is to develop a presentation about my experience that will teach other US citizens what I learn about Iran and Iranians and support them in also overcoming fears and prejudices that are often perpetrated by the media. I have an intention to do more in the way of presentations when I return this time than I have for previous trips. In the past I accepted when invited to make a presentation, but I wasn't proactively reaching out to create opportunities. I send a message to my e-mail list suggesting that my readers consider organizing an opportunity for me to present after I return. One friend enthusiastically responds immediately, ready to schedule three events where she lives on the California/Oregon border.

I don't particularly like to give presentations in front of groups, but I feel ready to push that edge a bit. With the preparatory reading about the situation in Iran and the information I gather through my experiences there, I plan to develop an engaging presentation that does more than "preach to the choir." I am interested in inspiring people to take some sort of action. I'm thinking in terms of classrooms, house parties, and kitchen table discussions over tea, as well as more public presentations promoted through organizations. A theme that I want to communicate is the importance of being with fear and not letting it stop us from doing what our hearts yearn for us to do.

I sign up to go on a vision quest as a participant (rather than a guide) in September. Following that trip, I will have only four days before my departure to Iran.

My ideas for how to approach this book project are becoming clearer. I finally begin writing in the last week of August.

Since I have an Israeli stamp in my passport and the temporary one that I obtained to go to Iraq expired after two years, I have to acquire a new passport before I can apply for my visa to enter Iran. For several days after I do apply for my visa, I am concerned that my application might not get accepted. Only seven out of nine in the first batch of visas sent by Global Exchange for this delegation were accepted and the Iranian embassy did not give reasons for denying the two. I am relieved when I do receive my visa.

September 2008

I do my vision quest as a participant. This one goes out for four days fasting alone in the desert. The idea is to remove all distractions from our lives, so we are really there with ourselves reflected back to us from the natural world of the desert. On the trip, I "get" that I need to be more generous of myself by being more visible— that the more I show up, the more I give. I am also reminded that it is time for women to reclaim our power and that power is the power of love. I see how that was true in my way of being while I was in Palestine, Iraq, and Sri Lanka—not only providing a presence, but providing a loving presence. Love is a powerful force that goes a long way. I reflect on one of the Muslim men on the Trinco team when I was working in Sri Lanka. I recognize how his open-heartedness had provided the glue that held the team together because he was open-hearted to everyone—the Sinhalese, Tamils, and internationals as well as the Muslims on the team and in the community. That loving way of being seems to be part of the conditioning of Muslim culture. I so hope that US citizens learn something of that.

Home from the wilderness, I write a history timeline of Iran (Persia), synthesizing the notes from the various articles and books that I have been reading. Here is a brief summary of some of the significant points with regard to the US relationship with Iran in the most recent sixty years.

In 1951, Iran held its first democratic election and Mohammed Mossadegh became the prime minister. He was very popular, supported by the secular and the religious, and considered a beloved national hero. Among other things, he nationalized oil in order to keep the profits in the country. The US and UK didn't like that because up until that time, Western oil consortiums had benefited from importing vast stores of oil and returning to Iran only a slim share of the profits. The CIA carried out a coup in 1953. In four days, they managed to remove Mossadegh from the country and place the previous shah Reza Pahlevi back into power. "The shah" remained in power for many years and was a cruel dictator. Among other things he maintained the SAVAK, a secret police trained by the US who committed horrendous abuses on the people of Iran.

In 1979, the Islamic Revolution began with the capture of hostages at the US Embassy. The revolution led to a new government called the Islamic Republic of Iran under the supreme leader Ayatollah Khomeini.

Ruins at Persepolis

In January of 1981, the day of Ronald Reagan's inauguration, the US hostages were released. In signing the Algiers Accords, the US pledged to never again attempt to overthrow the Iranian government.

The Iran/Iraq War began in 1980 and extended to 1988. During the war, Iran had the older weapons that the US had supplied during the time of the shah and at this point the US was supplying Iraq with more modern weapons. Iraq's Saddam Hussein unleashed chemical weapons on Iran while the world watched and the US continued to assist Iraq. Iran's strength at that time was that it had the largest population in the area. Many of the poorer Iranian people—who received better services under the Islamic Republic than under the shah—chose to serve their country as martyrs. These martyrs often marched unarmed ahead of the trained military in order to clear the mine fields.

Iranian Peace Laureate Shirin Ebadi (2006) in her memoir describes those times:

> How to begin describing the gradual infusion of martyrdom into our lives? How to convey the slow process by which everything—public spaces, rituals, newspapers, televisions—became dominated by death, mourning, and grief? At the time, it didn't feel alien or excessive, this engorged enthusiasm for martyrdom and the aesthetics of death.

In the end, the Iran/Iraq war cost both sides about $500 billion; killed 450,000 and wounded 600,000 more; produced 2.3 million refugees; and the US and European companies who sold arms were the only ones to benefit.

In more recent years, the George W. Bush Administration has been engaging in a systematic campaign to convince US citizens that the Islamic Republic of Iran poses an imminent threat to the USA. This campaign includes accusations about Iran's nuclear program when neither the International Atomic Energy Agency nor the US's 2007 National Intelligence Estimate have found evidence of Iran developing nuclear weapons in at least the last five years. Iran has signed the Non-Proliferation Treaty; its program to develop nuclear power is legal and in compliance with that treaty. Furthermore, Iran has not invaded another country in more than one-hundred years.

Women shopping

Many people believe that a preventative strike initiated by the USA would be a serious mistake and could give the Iranian government an excuse to invoke Article 10 of the Non-Proliferation Treaty, which gives the country a right to withdraw from the agreement in the face of imminent threat.

Also, an attack from outside the country is likely to thwart progressive movements within Iran. For example, last year two female women's rights activists in Iran were released from prison. One of the women said in an interview: "In the past two years, women's issues have become much more widely discussed throughout society. It is well on its way and will continue unless something unusual happens, like war, to stop the progression" (Keshavarz, 2008).

October 13, 2008

After our arrival in Iran, the Global Exchange delegation spends two days in Tehran and then flies to Yazd. We're engaging in tourist activities and talking

© Ghazal Arabi

Hussein Nuri painting

to Iranians as much as possible. Despite the history I reviewed above that would give Iranians good reasons to dislike us, most of the Iranians we meet say they love the USA and the American people. They just don't like our government. Many Iranians have family members living in the USA, people who came during the brutal time of the shah. When we meet Iranians, we are careful not to ask them their feelings about their own government. Answering such questions could put them in jeopardy.

While visiting the Museum of Contemporary Art, two of us meet a man in a wheelchair, Hussein Nuri and his wife, Nadia Maftuni, who are both artists. They tell us that he was injured during the time of the shah, losing the use of both his arms and legs. Later, by going to his website I learn that he was actually injured by the SAVAK when he was in high school because he had produced a play about human rights. He also lost two brothers as martyrs in the Iran/Iraq War. Now because he cannot use his hands, he paints by holding the brush in his teeth. A couple of years ago when I was in Sri Lanka, I heard about a Danish man who drew a political cartoon that was very derogatory toward Muslim people. At that time, Iranians protested at the Danish Embassy. Nuri attended the demonstration in his wheel chair with his paint brush and canvas. He was painting a beautiful rendition of the Christian Mother Mary and later gifted it to Denmark to represent the honoring of all people of all religions. Despite these good reasons to dislike the USA, Nuri and Nadia gift us with a packet of postcards depicting their paintings and ask us to tell the people in the USA that they love us.

Later this same day, we hear the same, "I love Americans" from a young Iranian soldier. Iranians are required to serve eighteen months in the military.

At the bazaar in Yazd, we watch a man working on metal coating copper trays with tin. He has three boys working with him—orphans from Afghanistan whom he and his sister have taken into their homes. The two adults are trying to get the boys enrolled in school. In the meantime, he's teaching them his trade.

October 16, 2008

We are in Shiraz for a couple of days. Among other things, we visit a theological school where young men study to become clerics. We meet with one of the officials at the school (an *imam*). He also says, "We love Americans. We don't like

President Bush." The *imam* voluntarily shares with us that he is hopeful about our upcoming election in November as well as the upcoming election in Iran in June.

Today, we visit the ancient city of Persepolis, the center of the Persian Empire during the reign of Cyrus the Great and until Alexander the Great destroyed it. Many pictures portrayed on the walls of the ruins of Persepolis picture the diversity of people who were part of the Persian Empire, all bearing gifts. No pictures of weapons of any kind are portrayed here. Cyrus was known to be one of the first human rights leaders in the history of the world.

October 19, 2008

Now we are in Isfahan, a beautiful city with parks extending for miles along the river that goes through the middle of the city. This was a stopping place along the Silk Road in ancient times. Families now make use of any public green space all over Iran for picnics: breakfast, lunch, and dinner. Sometimes they'll put up a tent and spend the whole day. We see families even picnicking on the side of a street where there is a strip of grass.

I am aware that Iran is quite a vibrant country. In all of the cities that we have visited, the streets have been full of men and women, and commerce seems to be thriving. Even after dark, the streets are lively with both men and women.

I have also been impressed with some ancient technology we have seen. First are the wind towers used for air conditioning. Wind comes in from any direction at the top of the tower and flows through a net of wet straw like a swamp cooler and then into the building.

The icehouse is another example of ancient technology. This is a tall, cone-shaped thick-walled structure. During the winter, the people would add layers of water to the huge bowl shape dug beneath the structure. As one layer froze, they added another layer of water. Then ice was available once the warm season came. Sometimes they still had ice as late as August.

A canal system distributes the water from the mountains into the urban areas,

Wind towers

which are often in the middle of the desert. Our guide tells us that the total length of the canals in Iran (above and below ground) extends twice the distance to the moon and back.

2009

I always go through anxiety before a presentation and I often notice myself thinking as I drive to do one about Iran that I don't want to do any more after this one. Then I get feedback indicating that the presentation really does change people's perceptions, so as long as I keep receiving invitations I continue to present.

Many of the same activities and themes continue in my life through 2009: teaching graduate students, guiding vision quest experiences, participating in my intentional community, following my spiritual path, singing in a community choir. President Obama is inaugurated into office and his inability to accomplish what progressives had hoped is discouraging. Among other things, he increases our troops in Afghanistan.

President Ahmadinejad is re-elected in Iran in June. That is a surprise and a disappointment. Many Iranian people there believe the election was not legitimate and engage in (mostly) nonviolent mass protests. Perhaps we in the USA can be inspired by those actions. I wonder why we didn't show up in mass protest during the George W. Bush elections in both 2000 and

Icehouse

2004, which also appeared illegitimate to many of us.

In December, I once again receive an e-mail with this inspiring reminder written seven years ago by Clarissa Pinkola Estes, which I pass on as a holiday message to everyone on my list serve.

> Ours is not the task of fixing the entire world all at once, but of stretching out to mend the part of the world that is within our reach. Any small, calm thing that one soul can do to help another soul, to assist some portion of this poor suffering world, will help immensely. It is not given to us to know which acts or by whom will cause the critical mass to tip toward an enduring good. What is needed for dramatic change is an accumulation of acts, adding, adding to, adding more, continuing. We know that it does not take everyone on Earth to bring justice and peace, but only a small, determined group who will not give up during the first, second, or hundredth gale.

8

Afghanistan

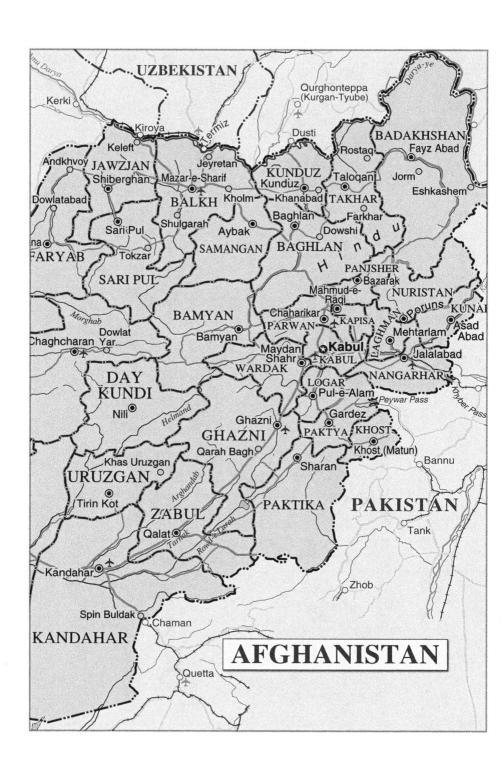

January 2010

RABIA ROBERTS E-MAILS A SURPRISING PERSPECTIVE on the US presence in Afghanistan. I have known Rabia for many years as a peace activist whose views I respect and appreciate. She had been in Iraq for months with the Iraq Peace Team at the time I was there for two weeks. Following are excerpts from her recent letter about Afghanistan. It leaves me with questions and a desire to go to Afghanistan to see for myself.

> Most of my liberal friends are discouraged about Afghanistan. They are convinced the Afghans don't want us there, that the military is not capable of doing anything right, and that we have to admit the Taliban are the default leaders of so backward and misogynist a country.
>
> To summarize the role the US has played, we armed and supported the most fundamentalist Mujahedeen warlords to fight the Soviets for ten years, then walked away in 1989 when the Soviets left. Without reconstruction and even a modicum of international security, the Mujahedeen then fought among themselves for power, throwing the country into five more years of a terrible civil war that ended when the Taliban entered Kabul. The people of Afghanistan will tell you the Taliban rule was "a living horror, a blanket of fear." In 2002, after bombing the country and chasing the Taliban into Pakistan, we turned our misguided attention to Iraq and once again abandoned the people of Afghanistan, leaving them undefended against the returning Taliban, growing corruption of the government, and the build-up of a criminal drug economy.
>
> Each time we have ignored our role in helping the Afghans help themselves rebuild, the situation has returned worse than it was before. We need to leave behind some stability and security and a workable process—a process of development in which we partner with all Afghans and with the international community for the well-being of Afghanistan, the region, and ultimately for all of us.
>
> This will be tough to measure for a while—this is why hope and commitment are so important. There are many different voices in Afghanistan and even more in the US media telling us what the Afghans want. When I was in Kabul in October with a peace delegation, I was surprised to hear that most men and women I spoke with felt it was premature for the international troops to leave. Their country is under attack. They need and want protection until the Afghan army and national police force are able to do it.

Recent research confirms that despite eight years of misguided military policy the Afghans still support an international military presence. Last month in a new survey conducted by ABC news, the BBC, and Germany's ARD, approximately 70% of Afghans said they support the presence of international forces in their country and 61% are in favor of the US military build-up of 37,000 reinforcements. This survey was nationwide, including both rural and urban areas. Furthermore, Afghans today are generally more optimistic than they were a year ago. 70% think their country is headed in the right direction—that is up 30% from last year. 61% of the Afghans surveyed expect the next generation will have a better life. This too is an improvement over past surveys. The people of Afghanistan clearly see the Taliban as the source of their problems, not the solution.

We hear that Afghanistan is a place of chronic abuse of women, medieval tribal codes, terrorist bombings, kidnappings, increased drug use, etc.; it is true that these kinds of things are happening. Yet when we pay heed to the progressive voices in Kabul, we can clearly see that one of our most essential roles is to protect the breathing space of Afghans working for a future where the violent, criminal, repressive, and woman-hating ideology of the Taliban no longer has a foothold.

Afghans will tell you about the first public demonstration for women's rights last spring on the streets of Kabul. This was unheard of in previous regimes. There are a great many people working very hard to bring changes to the lives of the Afghan people throughout the country. They all need security to continue. We cannot expect to see the results of this work right away. We would have seen more, more quickly, if we had provided the physical security and economic development needed between 2002 and 2008. We did not.

February 2010

It doesn't look like there will be an opportunity to go back to Sri Lanka to work on short-term assignment, and since I promised the local people in my final field site (Trincomalee) that I would come back for a visit if I didn't come to work, I'm fulfilling my promise now. Kati (my German friend and teammate on the Trinco team) has been living in a spiritual community called Auroville in India since she left Sri Lanka. Kati and I decide to meet in Sri Lanka and stay together at the beach guest house where I stayed when we worked in Trinco. We are there for a little more than a week, and then we travel to Auroville together.

We have a wonderful visit with our local field teammates. The Trinco office of NPSL is closed now and the local staff members there were offered jobs with

NPSL in other field sites in Sri Lanka. Almost all of them come back to Trinco to see us during our visit. In general, it seems that everyone is feeling better now that the Sinhalese government has killed the military leader of the LTTE and taken full control of the country ending the war. They have less fear, more freedom of movement, and a sense of hope. Tourism has increased in the North and East— more tourists from within the country (Sinhalese people traveling into these parts of their country where they didn't feel safe to travel in the past) as well as more international tourists. Yet, the Sinhalese tourists bring their own businesses, so their tourism is not benefiting the Tamil and Muslim people who live here. I fear that land disputes will soon become more evident in the Tamil areas of the North and East.

March 2010

I receive another e-mail from Rabia Elizabeth Roberts with her thoughts about Afghanistan. Here are excerpts.

> This is another post in a discussion about peace making and the role of the military in today's world. I am using questions sent to me by friends in the peace movement questioning my publicly stated belief that US troops are necessary in Afghanistan at this time—a change for me from forty-five years of protesting all war. Politically, there is no global unanimity about what constitutes a situation or government that is so corrupt or abusive of its people that outside intervention is warranted. Furthermore, despite a growing global consciousness, nations still act from self-interest and can't be trusted to make unbiased decisions about the legitimacy of other governments.
>
> But there is a deeper question: How shall the world community take care of itself? Where is the moral high ground? Was it correct to let the people of Rwanda and Burundi drown in genocidal chaos? Can we ignore what is happening in the Republic of Congo? What if China attacks Taiwan—should the US honor its treaty and retaliate?
>
> The situation in Afghanistan and our response to it is an opportunity for us all to learn how to build better national and international security. And it is an opportunity to show the Muslim world we are committed to their right to human dignity. It is an opportunity to help both the US Congress and citizens view security through a much broader lens—one that includes wide scale development, reconstruction, and nation building as the basis for a new definition of human security. And it is an opportunity for the peace movement to complement its idealized vision of a world without war with pragmatic strategies for achieving less violence on the ground.

We are seeing, repeatedly, that the violent terrorism, drug and human trafficking, absolute poverty, ethnic conflict and genocide that are developing in the 40-50 "failed states" around the globe are genuine security risks in our interdependent world. We cannot pretend we are safe or thriving in the midst of such misery.

I think we do need a global police. It is what the UN has been trying to do. But the US cannot withdraw all its troops and bases until regional alliances and the UN are up to the job—this may be a fifty-year-long effort in consciousness raising. At this time in history, human security requires functioning states and sovereign states require military power. At present the conversation about how to achieve this is much too narrow in Congress, in the media, in the military, and among those of us in the peace movement. The single-minded focus on withdrawing troops from Afghanistan can obscure the broader, more difficult and ultimately more important issues.

Summer/Fall 2010

I still don't know where I stand with regard to Afghanistan. I find myself rather lost in a maze of many issues, trying to decide where to focus my personal resources.

I join the Climate Ride. It is a five-day-long 300 mile bicycle ride from Fortuna (near Eureka, CA) to San Francisco. The purpose is to raise money for three green organizations in the USA and to raise awareness about climate change. I'm also doing it because I think it will be fun. I spend much time training in order to get into physical shape and I also raise more than the required $2,400. I borrow a bicycle, and feel blessed to have several bicycling friends who coach me in a training program. It feels great to be getting out and exercising so much.

Winter 2010-11

Fr. Louie Vitale is an activist with whom I've crossed paths once in a while. He is once again serving time in prison for civil disobedience. I send him a card in December and I enjoy the personal note I receive from him in February while he is still in prison. He says, "It goes well here. I am happy to be back at Lompoc—I was here last November '09 to May '10, so I have many friends and had a great welcoming." I smile, thinking that some people can create community anywhere.

March 3, 2011

I just bought my tickets to go to Afghanistan from March 16 to April 4. Kathy Kelly—one of my personal heroines whom I met in Iraq with the organization that was then called Voices in the Wilderness—sent me an e-mail invitation to join a delegation to Kabul because I'm one of the people she knew had "experience in nonviolent direct-action projects that involve risk." I have been hoping for such an opportunity ever since I received that first letter from Rabia. I want to see for myself how it is for the people in Afghanistan with the presence of US forces in their country.

Kathy's organization is now called Voices for Creative Nonviolence (Voices). During three delegations to Afghanistan between May and December of 2010, activists from Voices and several other organizations have been building relationships with a group called the Afghan Youth Peace Volunteers (AYPV). AYPV has now asked for Voices' participation in a series of actions in Kabul highlighting and supporting non-military solutions to the conflict in Afghanistan.

The AYPV youth are coordinated by Hakim, a medical doctor from Singapore who has lived in the circumstances of poverty and violence in Afghanistan for eight years. During his first two years, Hakim lived among Afghan refugees on the border with Pakistan learning the Dari language. He then accompanied the Afghan refugees back to their home in the Bamyan province and has now lived there for six years.

Kathy and the earlier delegations have also grown to know Dr Ramazon Bashardost, a populist leader who came in third in the last presidential election and is a former Minister of Planning. He is now again a Member of Parliament and advocates for the government sharing resources fairly with the common people.

Kathy expects that we will have opportunities for mutually creative exchanges with the Afghan youth who are our hosts; with Hakim, their coordinator; and with Dr Bashardost. I have a great deal to learn, especially from these young people whose families have been living with war for three decades.

In the following rendition of my experiences in Afghanistan, I try to bring to life the complexity of the situation and the varying perspectives that I hear from people I meet. I also try to capture some of the possible leverage points that emerge in our "mutually creative exchanges" in hopes that maybe something will eventually crystalize that can support a better quality of life for the common people of Afghanistan.

March 18, 2011

Six of eighteen delegation members arrive in Kabul on the same flight from Dubai. Hakim meets us at the airport in a van and drives us to the office of a local organization called Open Society. Some of us will be staying in this office because our hosts think it is safer than staying in an international hotel. On the way, Hakim tells us that in a report written on March 15, the International Red Cross said that security here is worse now than ten years ago and that life is untenable due to the surge in Taliban attacks and "accidental" NATO strikes. NATO (North Atlantic Treaty Organization) is the alliance of countries from North America and Europe who are committed to fulfilling the goals of the North Atlantic Treaty that was signed in 1949. Two children were just killed by NATO led forces while working

Young people's demonstration

© Hakim

on the irrigation in their family's fields. Hakim says that civilian casualties are under-reported because it is impossible to tell the difference between Taliban and civilians.

During our first group meeting with AYPV and Open Society, we learn some safety precautions. These young people face fear for their lives every day, and they are especially concerned about us since we are their guests. We should not be in a big group of foreigners while outside. We should stay away from foreigner-frequented places and avoid doing anything that gains attention. We should walk confidently, but not arrogantly. They even give us some pointers on what to do if abducted: try to get away, be alert about details of people and places, don't panic, be personal so they see your humanity (but as a female with male abductors, we have to be careful about that). Ugh! This is frightening to me because I don't tend to notice details about people's appearances, and I have no sense of direction when I travel without a map. Furthermore, I have no idea how to show my humanity to a strange man of this culture without him interpreting it as a "come-on."

Tree planting

© John Volkening

We learn that "peace" is a bad word here for various reasons; to many it means support for the Taliban. Afghans have learned not to trust each other because of so much violence and corruption. In every Afghan family, someone has been killed. The AYPV are working on how to build trust and restore hope. They believe that nonviolence is worth pursuing even if they won't see the results in their lifetimes. 60% of the population of Afghanistan is under the age of twenty-five.

Hakim has been working with the AYPV for four years. They are attempting to attract youth from mixed ethnic groups. Currently members are Hazara and Tajik. The boys we meet are ages forteen through twenty. Girls are involved back home, but for cultural reasons, they were unable to travel the ten-hour-long drive from Bamyan to Kabul.

AYPV sewed leather cell phone pouches with the word PEACE and gave them to the children in a Pashtun orphanage in Kabul. Pashtun is the ethnic group from which emerged the Taliban, so there is much prejudice against Pashtun people among the other ethnic groups. Yesterday, forty young people—AYPV, Open Society, and others—marched in the streets of Kabul wearing sky blue scarves. They chose the color of the sky because there is one sky over all people. They did not want our participation as internationals in this outdoor demonstration because of security concerns. It was dangerous enough for them to be doing it without us.

Open Society is a group of young adults in Kabul who are working on democracy and human rights through cultural activities such as photography, film making, art, and music. Their aim is to encourage Afghans to overcome fear and speak up. The director Zahra thanks us for coming to "this exceptionally dangerous country." She says that all the revolutions here have been violent, so when the people think of change it is scary.

March 19, 2011

Today, we join the youth for a tree planting ceremony at a local school. When we first arrive at the school we meet 21-year-old Lena who is one of the teachers. She tells us that she has seen the children becoming more hopeful in recent years. They don't talk as much about guns and war as they did in the past. When asked, both Lena and the school principal agree that if the US troops were to leave, there is a better chance for peace. They say that peace has to come from within the country. Instead of spending money on the military, we could better be spending money on education, "training good Afghan teachers who will teach the students not to be corrupt."

During the ceremony, the principal announces that they are naming the garden where we are planting trees the Friendship Garden in honor of our presence here.

I overhear one Afghan man expressing to Kathy a positive perspective on the presence of US/NATO forces. He claims that the US bombs are necessary for security. He wants the international troops to continue providing security against insurgents from within and invaders from other countries in the region, to give Afghan people time and space to develop a just system that would provide a foundation for peace from within the country.

We participate in a candlelight vigil in the late afternoon in memory of all people who have been killed in wars. The youth specifically name nine children who were killed by US/NATO forces while gathering firewood March 1 and the two who were killed while checking the irrigation in their fields March 15.

March 20, 2011

The AYPV activity today is a Global Days of Listening Skype phone call. It is a regular opportunity for people all over the world to ask questions and listen to the perspectives of these Afghan youth who are committed to building nonviolent solutions within their country. The boys speak and understand English at varying levels, so Hakim translates.

One caller asks what she can do to help bring hope to the youth. Abdulai (age fifteen) requests her to stay in touch with them (AYPV). Ghulamai (age fourteen) responds that it brings hope when he knows that we're raising the voice of the common Afghan people in our home countries. Faiz (age twenty) says that he discovers hope when he sees "volunteers come to visit for no good reason except to encourage us."

During the call, Abdulai states that it takes patience for change to come; that people need to rise up together and it is a challenge to bring together the differing perspectives. There needs to be a change in the entire system of power in Afghanistan. "As it is, even an angel would become corrupted." Abdulai also claims, "Global systems do not support human nature" and he talks to a caller about the importance of the human heart.

Mohammad Jan (age twenty) says, "Yes there is hope, but it is not immediate. We need to build more friends and break down barriers person by person." He also expresses that one of the most positive things in the past few years for him has been recognizing strength in his friends: "Seeing the strength in each other has brought hope." Mohammad Jan is Tajik while the others in the group are Hazara.

One of our delegation members talks about how every week for fifteen years now his group has demonstrated in front of a weapons manufacturer in his hometown even when they haven't seen any results. The boys are touched by that because it resonates with their experiences of continuing to do their work without obvious results. Ali (age sixteen) feels tired of trying for nonviolence in Afghanistan, but sees that he has no choice but to recognize that even if it may not happen in his lifetime, it is still worth doing.

Ghulamai says that financial support is best when given directly to the people because there is so much corruption in the system.

A man on the phone asks what to say in the USA when people ask about the split in Afghan opinions about the US presence. Khamad (age twenty) responds that it is out of fear that some Afghans want the US and NATO forces to stay, but that many others are against the presence of foreign troops.

A girl in New York calls. She had communicated with Abdulai through email after she saw the YouTube in which Abdulai said, "I wish to find some love and truth." In her first e-mail she told Abdulai that it was the first time she had seen a common Afghan person. The two of them have been in e-mail communication since then and this was the first time they have spoken on the phone.

The youth emphasize that the media all over the world are not covering what ordinary people of Afghanistan want, and ask that we help spread the word. These interactions with friends around the world offer mutual encouragement. Progress is slow. "The only thing that is fast here is corruption," says Ali.

We learn that 70% of Afghans have psychological problems and there are many suicides due to depression. 40% are unemployed, and 60% are below the poverty line.

March 21, 2011

Today is New Year's Day here. Bazir, one of the Open Society members guides us among the crowds of people who are walking through the streets of Kabul to the mosque. Other Open Society folks are also keeping a watchful eye on all of us. Police are present. They stop and search some people. They are also controlling how many people enter the mosque at any one time. Bazir has a press pass, so we are allowed easy passage in and we get to go up on a roof with all the journalists where we have a clear view of the event. Masses of people are still arriving. Many are inside and around the mosque, and many others have climbed up on the hillside to watch the festivities from above.

A flagpole is raised and the way that the flag unfurls is an omen about the year to come. As far as I can understand, the coming year will be okay—not great, but not too bad either. As part of the ceremony, people push and pull in order to get to the flagpole to kiss it. That activity seems to go on all day. I assume that sometime

New Year's celebration

© Paki Wieland

Viewing celebration from hillside

© Steve Clemens

Delegation and guards at celebration

© Patrick Kennelly

today all who want to kiss the pole will get through the mosque gate and eventually work their way to it.

Hakim gathers our international delegation, AYPV, Open Society, and other friends on the mosque roof for a picture. Some members of the group hold their hands out gesturing the peace sign. I notice some of the police and guards watching and scowling and I think about peace being considered a bad word. After the photo, I ask Hakim if it would be okay to ask for a picture with some of them. He translates for me. Some of the youth and other members of the delegation join me in a picture with some of the guards and soon many such pictures are being taken.

A TV reporter asks two of us for an interview. Hakim translates. I get to say why I came to Afghanistan—I came because I wanted to hear from the people how they feel about the US presence here.

Back at Open Society, we meet with a lawyer from the US who is part of the Tribal Liaison Organization. He works with issues in the detention system. Since there is no process to determine who is a combatant and who is a civilian, many innocent people are detained; they often get stuck in the system where their families cannot find them. The way people are treated here can be worse than Guantanamo because they are further away from scrutiny and the officers can claim that they cannot apply certain conventions because it's a war zone. The lawyer thinks that a quick draw down of US troops would be destructive. He states that urban areas are now secured to the extent that "people can have some life."

We meet with the AYPV and learn more of their stories and their activities designed to overcome distrust person by person. Some of these activities have led to successful media coverage and people express appreciation. In 2009, AYPV built a Peace Park in Bamyan and put up a tent. They wrote a letter to President Obama asking for troops to be removed responsibly as soon as possible. They held vigil in the tent, planning to stay until Obama got their message. After seven days of vigil, a US ambassador came all the way from Kabul and spoke with them. He promised to deliver their letter to President Obama.

Abdulai and Khamad are brothers; their father was killed by Taliban eleven years ago. They had to escape through the snow in the mountains. Khamad carried Abdulai. Khamad now struggles with depression. He says that he lost his mind as a result of that killing and that it is time for Afghans to stop killing one another.

Faiz lost both his parents to illness at a young age and then one brother was dragged out of the room and shot during the war.

Ali had two uncles who were killed in the war. When he was young, all the news on the radio was about killing; it's encouraging to him to hear and think about peace with the Afghan Youth Peace Volunteers.

March 22, 2011

Today, we meet with several members of the Transitional Justice Coordinating Group (TJCG). Transitional justice comes into play after a change in government where human rights were violated. This organization is a coalition advocating for the victims of past conflict. We learn that an action plan for peace, justice, and reconciliation had been developed, but it expired in 2009, largely unimplemented. We also learn that an amnesty law in 2001 forgave all war crimes; now the war lords whom the people know to have committed dreadful crimes on humanity have been re-armed in the role of "local police" and many are in parliament.

Liah, a woman who is part of the TJCG, wants the US/NATO forces to remain; she believes that the majority of Afghans hold this opinion. She states that the international forces are here by Afghan request. A spirited argument ensues and much of what is said does not get translated. I notice that youth and adults, men and women, foreigners and Afghans are all speaking up freely and being heard in this discussion. I muse that those of us from the USA are arguing against the US presence in Afghanistan and many of the Afghans are arguing in favor of it. Fayyaz, an older gentleman who is a friend of AYPV and has been involved with us ever since we arrived, is sitting next to me and is getting more and more agitated as the discussion develops. Hearing some of what is said, I realize that the pain and suffering of the Afghan people in the hands of the Taliban is greater and deeper than I could ever imagine.

Since we have been invited to dinner at the home of a member of the TJCG, we have to end the animated discussion. One of the TJCG people offers a conclusion: "In the long term, we want no international forces in Afghanistan, but we need a credible government without criminals and strong security forces of our own before we are ready for the international forces to leave. We need human rights defined and not compromised. We need a credible government elected by the people and then the international forces can go and we can run our country."

As we leave, Liah invites us to come to her office for more discussion tomorrow. During dinner, we sit on cushions on the floor in an elegant hall. A musician plays a traditional stringed instrument and sings while we drink tea. Then large rolls of plastic are spread on the floor at our feet and rice, chicken, beef, and vegetables are served.

March 23, 2011

We learn today that Fayyaz had spoken angrily to the boys over dinner last night, even saying to Abdulai that he wished the Taliban had killed him when they killed his father. We ask the boys how they feel about this comment. They say they recognize the depth of experience, suffering, and trauma Fayyaz had received in the hands of the Taliban. As far as I could tell, the boys did not take his comments personally.

Hakim explains that the narrative that the current government leaders give creates a dominant sense of fear that paralyzes public opinion, so the presence of US/NATO seems like a reasonable alternative. The boys speak in favor of gradual responsible withdrawal, not a sudden withdrawal that would leave the country in

© Paki Wieland

Guards on roof

chaos, and they believe in the possibility that the Taliban will negotiate with the people if all the international forces leave the country.

We walk in small groups to Liah's office. She and a few men from her office are present. Liah begins by saying that the youths' opinions are naïve because they haven't lived through the experiences that the adults had with the Taliban. She states that especially women are better off now than in the years under the Taliban.

Abdulai points out that last year (post-Taliban) 2,300 women and girls committed suicide. Abdulai also explains that his father was killed by Taliban and that now he needs to choose his own way forward. If he were to take revenge, the Taliban would likely kill the rest of his family.

I ask Liah and the men from her office how they feel about drones. One of the men says that drones are a good way to target insurgents. He goes on to say that if the US and NATO were not maintaining security, we would not be able to talk like this and dialogue would not be possible among the factions. I recognize truth in his words because of my experience in both Iraq and Iran—due to the governments that were in power while I was in those countries, people were unable to reveal their feelings about what was happening politically.

Kathy points out that those in the USA who are benefiting financially from keeping the war going are much wealthier than any of the war lords here. Liah says that people of Afghanistan do understand that the US and NATO are not necessarily here for the good of the Afghans, but for their own interests to remove the safe havens for al-Qaida; but she believes that for Afghans the US/NATO are the best of two evils. She points out that Afghans also feel threatened by other countries in the region such as Pakistan and India.

We return to Open Society and meet with an agronomist who works with the Ministry of Agriculture; "one ministry that is not corrupt," he says. He believes, "The best resource is the people themselves" and reflects that the re-election of Karzai was corrupt. "Paying money is how democracy is working in this country." He also claims, "Peace and security can't be imported into a country. It develops as people become aware, understand, and become confident that their voices count."

Many delegation members leave today. Now, we are shifting into a different mode with a smaller delegation. I'm feeling overwhelmed with all the perspectives and confused about what messages to bring home. The youth who are following a Gandhian path represent those who feel ready for the US/NATO troops to leave sooner rather than later. After thirty years of violent occupation and conflict affected by outside interventions, they want Afghans to be left alone to sort it out for themselves. They are in favor of developing relationships among the ethnic groups and are even hopeful for the possibility that negotiations could take place with the Taliban if the outside influences leave.

For others, it is definitely a better situation here now than under the Taliban. The suffering and trauma experienced at that time leads to fears of what might happen if the US/NATO troops leave. All the systems are corrupt and people can't trust each other. Eventually they want the international troops to leave, but they need a credible government without criminals, and strong security before they feel ready for the foreign troops to leave. Even though they recognize that the USA is here for its own interests, they feel they are better off with its presence than not. In contrast with what they've had before, they are even willing to put up with drone attacks and the killing of children for now.

We on the delegation are appalled by atrocities such as drones and civilian deaths, and furthermore fear that the USA will never leave Afghanistan and will repeat the situation that we have created in Iraq.

Hakim describes a vision for what could happen when the US/NATO troops leave. Transitional security could be provided by the UN for two to three years followed by freer and fairer elections. War lords and other war criminals could be brought to international courts. Reparations must be made, but not excessive punishment. Finally, he asks us to imagine Afghanistan, Pakistan, and India like the EU (European Union).

March 24, 2011

Zahra, the director of Open Society, is feeling discouraged today about the possibility of change in Afghanistan and what she can do to support it. She says, "In Afghanistan, I can't find my identity." Then she lights up while talking about cultural work as a potential way to make a difference. Zahra's

Highway through village

© Peggy Gish

sister who is a film maker tells us that she would be a physicist if she lived in a developed country, but living here she is compelled to make films because that is her contribution to work toward change.

I gain a clearer understanding of the Mujahedeen and the ethnic groups. The Mujahedeen were the war lords of the various ethnic tribes who joined together to fight against the Soviets. Once the Soviets (and the USA) left, the

Meeting at Open Society office

© Steve Clemens

Mujahedeen with their tribes fought among themselves to determine who would gain control over which areas. The Taliban emerged and took power. Pakistan Taliban worked with the Afghan Taliban, who are almost all Pashtun. Pashtun are now 40% of the population. Other main ethnic groups are Hazara (20%), Tajik (about 8%), and Uzbek (less than 8%).

Most of the AYPV travel home to Bamyan today. Four of us from the delegation get a chance to go out of the city for a day trip into the province of Panjshir. The teacher we met last week, Lena, and her brother go with us. We go with Afghan Logistics, a company that caters to tourists and is known for not having had any abductions occur on their tours. I thoroughly enjoy getting out of the city and into the country. There is a river flowing through granite as we climb further into the mountains and it looks a lot like the eastern side of the Sierra Nevada Mountains in California.

Traveling through Kabul, we pass an intersection where a big crowd of day workers are waiting for work. Lena says that when someone comes looking for workers, the workers mob the vehicle. We also pass an IDP camp. The people there are very poor and there is no organization supplying rations, so if a man does not get day work, his family goes hungry that day.

In the villages, I notice that hearts are used to decorate many of the vehicles. We see leeks and grapes growing in fields, and go through a village where trees, flowers, and other live plants are sold. Wild pistachio trees grow along the river.

Back in Kabul talking with Hakim, I learn that USAID, an aid organization funded by the US government, has bought many of the TV stations in Afghanistan, and that forty-nine countries with confusing agendas are present here. He predicts that if things continue the way they are, the divisions among the ethnic groups will just get worse. He suggests that internationals keep listening to the ordinary people and make sure those voices are heard and their needs are met. He also wants to portray the Taliban in a human way.

Bazir tells us the story of his abduction by the Taliban and his captivity for ten days in 2004. He notes that kidnapping here is for prisoner exchange, but when the abductors see that there is no possibility of exchange, they might kill their captives. Bazir and a colleague were kidnapped and taken by three Talibs from mountain to mountain where they slept in caves each night. The Talibs taught them lessons in the Quran and the ways of the Taliban.

At one point, two of the three Talibs went to town and the one who had stayed behind started having bad stomach pains. The two captives helped him by starting a fire and putting heated stones on his belly. Then that Talib felt indebted to the two of them. After nine days, the Taliban realized there was no possibility of prisoner exchange so they planned to kill the two captives. The one they had nursed warned them, but he said that he couldn't do anything else to help.

That evening, the captors were having a little party celebrating some Taliban victory that had occurred, and they weren't paying close attention; Bazir and the film director sneaked away into the woods. They were crossing a river, and managed to get their bodies under water enough so they were not easily seen when Taliban pursuers shot multiple shots all around them. Finally, they got away; the Talibs expected them to go toward the lights of the nearby town, but instead they went the other direction.

Once they were free and safe, Bazir's fellow captive went to Australia on political asylum, but Bazir insisted on staying in Afghanistan to do his work to help his people. He has been unable to consider producing a film about the experience because it is still painful to tell the story, but he notes the humanity of the Taliban who had captured them. "They taught us lessons and did not hurt us."

March 25, 2011

Najiv, a journalist friend of Hakim's, comes this morning. He is an open-minded Hazara and speaks the languages of both the Pashtun and Hazara people. He believes that Afghanistan is entering a new phase. There are some places such as the Bamyan, Panjshir, and Kabul provinces that are ready to take over their own security from the NATO forces.

Shafik arrives. He is another broad-minded journalist and a friend of Najiv's. He is Pashtun and speaks a bit of Dari (the language of the Hazara people). Hakim, Najiv, and Shafik discuss possible ways out of the difficult situation in Afghanistan. They are "thinking out loud" about the Afghan people's concerns and what they want.

Shafik points out that for every civilian killed by the US/NATO forces or the Karzai government, more people will join the cause of the Taliban with intention for revenge. He thinks that if the international forces pull out, the people will work it out street by street. He states that 90% of the people are against the Taliban and will never allow them to rise up again. Najiv believes that even in the south, the people have seen what the Taliban have done and do not favor them, but there is likelihood of civil war due to interference from Iran and Pakistan. He thinks that life for the people in Kabul appears more orderly and better economically with the presence of US/NATO, but in the rural areas people are not in favor of US/NATO presence.

Najiv claims that the international peace movement's message just to end the war and bring the troops home is not enough. Afghans need more than that; the USA needs to address what happens after withdrawal. Afghans need to hear that the international peace movement is not just against the killings by US/NATO, but also against the killings by the Taliban and the war lords.

Najiv remembers when his family made one trip back into Afghanistan while they were living as refugees in Iran during the time of the civil war following the Soviet withdrawal. He recalls horrific scenes of bodies all along the route with no one to claim or bury them. Memories are etched into the minds of all Afghans who were alive at that time. Shafik says that things he's seen cannot be described, such as unburied bodies eaten by dogs. In Islam, "jihad" is a holy word, but now people hate the word because so much killing has happened for the sake of that word. Relative to all this, what the people are experiencing under US/NATO presence is better.

In the afternoon, we visit an orphanage called Mahboba's Promise. The orphanage was started by Mahboba, an Afghan woman who lives in Australia. We meet with her brother Sadik who is the director. The orphanage has a program to support widows by providing food rations and sewing lessons for possible livelihood. A permaculture garden provides the widows the opportunity to learn gardening skills that they can apply back in their homes and supplies good food for the orphanage.

About the US/NATO presence in Afghanistan, Sadik's perspective is, "Nine years have passed and we haven't seen any improvement, so get rid of them." He thinks they need to have Afghans who are Muslims in office and that democracy will work if they follow Islamic law.

© Peggy Gish

Mahboba's Promise orphanage

Kathy and I go to the Internet café this evening. It is crowded with students who are hoping to get their college placement exam results. They had taken the exams in October. The only way that the results are accessible is over the Internet, so students who don't have access to the Internet cannot get their results. Also, because of corruption, students who are well-qualified but poor often do not even get placed. The sister of Khamad and Abdulai was the first person in her village to go to higher education. She had hoped for a better placement, but had at least gotten into a teacher's college in Bamyan. Mohammad Jan learns today that he is accepted into a technical school, which is also less than what he wanted; he is also the first in his family to qualify anywhere.

March 26, 2011

We get to meet with Dr Ramazon Bashardost today. Kathy had talked about him in one of her first e-mail messages when we were planning this trip. Dr Bashardost meets with us in a lot where he has pitched a tent. The guard at the gate is unarmed. Dr Bashardost has another office in Kabul, but he meets with many people at his tent as a symbol of his solidarity with the common people. Hakim says that some people think that Afghans won't be ready for Dr Bashardost's ideas for one-hundred years. I like that he is standing up against the culture of fear that the government is promoting by using a tent for an office and having an unarmed guard at the gate.

Linda with Dr Bashardost

Two young women arrive and meet with Dr Bashardost as we wait. He listens, makes notes, and gives them his business card. He tells us that students have to pay money to get accepted into the schools that they want. These two girls had just told him that many good students had been told they didn't pass the exams and yet some of those who passed were known to be poor students. He responded to the girls that he would make a call to the Minister of Education.

Further about corruption, Dr Bashardost tells us that judges in court openly ask for money, so when ordinary people have problems with others they are more likely to go to a Talib because he doesn't ask for money. Dr Basherdost notes that US money supports war lords in their rich lifestyles. He says, "We see on TV former war lords known to have tortured and killed people are now in top positions in government cabinet, parliament, and the supreme court." He believes that the war is actually strengthening the Taliban. It is not a situation between good and bad, but a situation between bad and worse. He thinks that if the international community would refuse to accept fraud in elections, things would change. He also explains to us that the Taliban won't negotiate with the international community because they never negotiate with the killers of family members. He thinks the best solution for peace with justice in Afghanistan is for the UN Security Council to organize a court against corruption and against everyone who has killed an ordinary person. He emphasizes, "We must find solutions for the everyday problems of the Afghan people."

Dr Bashardost's perception of foreigners is that "most people care but don't know how to help. A lot of people don't know the situation in Afghanistan." He points out that politicians who visit have a very different experience than what we have had, because when they come they are among the rich war lords.

March 27, 2011

I learn that in Pashto (the language of the Pashtun people), when one asks about feelings the words translate as, "What does your heart say?"

We visit the International Legal Foundation. We first meet with an Afghan who says that it is most important to allow those prisoners who are under US jurisdiction to be transferred into the hands of the Afghan government. The US forces will be slowly moving out by 2014 and the prisoners need to be held closer to home. A couple of months ago, a detainee died in Guantanamo and when his body was returned to his village, the people were angry that he died outside the country. Being inside one's own country is more humane for family and friends.

The Afghan who speaks to us at first has to leave, and the one international who works for this organization talks further with us. He is from Iran but has been living in Texas most recently and has been here in Kabul only five months. He says the US spends a lot of money on justice reform and things are getting better. He's hopeful that perhaps the war lords who have been in power with the US presence and now have plenty of money may just pull out when the US leaves.

March 28, 2011

Kate, a trial lawyer from the US who has focused on human rights, arrives today. With regard to Afghanistan, she has faith that "somewhere somehow, there's a button to push that can alleviate the confusion the world is in right now." Hakim mentions that Dr Bashardost has said that he would stand by the people if they rise up against civilian killings, so Kate decides to focus her human rights expertise on the possibility of supporting the people to rise against civilian killings committed by the USA.

March 29, 2011

Najiv and Shafik come again. Kathy, Hakim, Kate, and I join them for a sort of brainstorming discussion about next steps to support a better situation for the common people of Afghanistan. Shafik states that the media here have served to further divide the people. Najiv notes that Wikileaks have revealed 92,000 secret documents from Afghanistan. Kate asks, "If a foreigner were to make those Wikileaks available to the world, would that be a good idea?" Najiv answers, "Yes."

Najiv says that because of the tribal mentality of looking up to leaders, the people don't think independently. We consider the recent Arab Spring uprising in Egypt and recognize that the people must have prepared for thirty years prior to that moment of uprising. "Here, over the past thirty years, the people have seen only war and bloodshed. It will take a long time before people here will start speaking up."

Hakim says, "So we must start now."

Hakim points out that what is common to the current global movements in places like Egypt, Libya, and Wisconsin is the need for livelihood. Najiv agrees that the "right to bread" can reach across divisions. "We need to have joint actions with a clear message."

Mountain village in Panjshir

© Peggy Gish

We have had an Afghan driver who has been with us since the first day. He has to go back to his province to be with his family now. He left a note, which Hakim translated for us:

> Dear Kathy and Friends,
>
> Welcome to the "destroyed" country of Afghanistan. I hope this has been a memorable journey. You are brave and kind in coming to a dangerous place. Your coming has given our hearts hope, like the spring flowers giving us life with their colors. We don't feel alone with your friendship. Don't forget us. We hope that you have happy days and we wish for peace in the world.
>
> Your friend, Mohammad

In an impromptu thinking-out-loud-together conversation in the Open Society office, Kathy summarizes an article that she read that concludes that with unity of purpose, the international community has helped resolve other conflicts in the world that seemed intractable. Hakim thinks that a negotiated political settlement is needed now that would bring the war crimes on all sides to justice. Zahra points out some of the complexities:

> Yes, negotiation, but it is important who is negotiating. Including the Taliban is a problem. The people will not accept the Taliban in government. Negotiators of the past have not represented the people. War lords have been involved and they are known by the people to have killed, so neither Taliban nor other war lords should be part. There are many foreign people here now and the ordinary people don't trust them. How do we get the ordinary people to arise? Maybe start with one message that all war crimes must be brought to justice, even though realistically it may take a long time.

Another Open Society member says that he knows a commoner who published a list of war criminals that included everyone in the current government. He had to run away to Pakistan the day after the list was published.

Hakim concludes, "Focusing on the small actions as we have been doing is encouraging to people. Vision needs to develop from the Afghan people. The message needs to be simple. Numbers will gradually grow."

March 30, 2011

We attend the National Victims Conference offered by the Transitional Justice group. We listen to a panel of internationals talking about challenges that face victims after a war and strategies to address them. Here are some of the relevant viewpoints I hear expressed:

- You can't have peace if the truth hasn't been told, nor if people haven't been held accountable.
- We need to take some small steps in Afghanistan before addressing the big problem of impunity.
- Memorialization has two purposes. One is for family. The other is politically to remember what happened so it doesn't happen again.
- Victims need to be involved in negotiations.
- The people who committed crimes need to be excluded from government.
- There needs to be a focus on long-term needs of victims including psycho-social support and property restitutions.

Questions are also raised. Who would be the parties to sign a peace agreement in Afghanistan? How do we find truth with all the complexities here? Who owns the truth?

We bring Kate to meet Dr Bashardost. They are both lawyers; I learn from their discussion that there is no international court that can look at the issues in Afghanistan. The International Court is only for cases that are country against country, which isn't so in Afghanistan currently, and the International Council of Justice is advisory only.

March 31, 2011

We participate in a discussion in a class at the American University in Afghanistan. The teacher is from the USA and is a friend of one of the delegation members. I'm assuming that these Afghan students are from fairly well-off families because it is a private school that would cost more than many of the common people could afford. Hakim and Mohammad Jan present about the AYPV, and Zahra presents about Open Society. The presentations are in Dari so I don't understand exactly what is said, but some of the students use English in their responses, and Hakim writes on the board in English, so that helps.

About fifty students (five of them girls) engage in a lively discussion. I gain a better understanding of the bad feelings about the use of the word "peace," because the word has meant imperialist forces and multi-national organizations taking money and controlling the people's lives. One student expresses the sentiment that he would rather live under tyranny than under that.

When Hakim asks who thinks peace is impossible in Afghanistan, eight students raise their hands. One responds: "Peace is only possible if the US, China,

Pakistan, and others come to agreement and that's not going to happen." Hakim captures on the board a list of reasons the students give why peace is difficult:

- Not everyone wants true peace
- Divisions—intolerance, ethnic, gender, and religious discrimination
- Regional and foreign interference
- History
- Illiteracy, lack of education
- National and international development strategies
- No vision
- Lack of political and economic independence
- Lack of awareness
- Weak government/leadership

One student suggests getting rid of the war lords. Another says that the war lords are the real Afghans. Another believes a good strategy would be to make military service compulsory and thus "take the young people from the war lords."

One says, "We have now practiced democracy for almost ten years and we have almost a failed state. We don't need democracy any more. We should have a dictator. That helps to bring identity, then revolution, and at least we know who the enemy is."

Another student claims we need to build trust among the international community, Afghans, and the government. Still another says, "What does peace benefit in Afghanistan? Generally, people will make do with what we have."

April 1, 2011

I hear today that the life expectancy here has recently gone down from age forty-five to forty-two. Hakim says that the pain that the Afghan people have suffered at the hands of the Taliban is so great that we cannot address any of the other pains until we have processed that. Kathy refers to the truth and reconciliation process in South Africa—how it was very difficult for families to forgive at first, but later they came around. Hakim thinks the students yesterday were paralyzed by fear, hate, and anger; and that they need clarity of vision. I say that the vision needs to include what responsible withdrawal would be. Hakim reiterates what he heard Najiv say, that it would be good to have some UN peacekeepers with Muslim background.

We go to another university and meet with two Afghan professors, one a political scientist and the other a sociologist. A third Afghan professor joins us part way through the conversation, but does not speak at all until the end.

The political scientist states that peace in Afghanistan depends on several things. "First, is strengthening the government, because Afghanistan is a weak state. The government needs to build the state, build the army, and eradicate corruption." Second, they need to strengthen the process of democracy—elections and political parties. Third, they need to work on their relationship with Pakistan.

The sociologist thinks that Afghanistan can build economy, education, and improvement of life at the same time as focusing on security. He says in the short term, they have to improve their military forces. In the long term, other aspects are important. He thinks that in place of spending so much money on US troops, we could use it to strengthen the Afghan Army and put some into education. If we can improve the situation for Afghans, they may not need to turn to war lords. The key to making peace is improving civil society.

I ask whether there have been studies in either of their fields about the use of fear to stay in power, but they don't seem to understand my question. I also ask how long is the "short term." The political scientist declares that the needed change will take a long time. He says that short term is 1-5 years and in that time, the Taliban and Al Qaeda should be removed from the country and the government should be able to get strong enough. Finally, I ask about drones and he believes that they are a necessary strategy for targeting centers of Taliban power along the border.

The professor who came in late finally speaks, saying that there is a need to change a mindset that is corrupted. The USA has focused resources to strengthen military presence in geographic areas that are insecure, but we should build on areas of Afghanistan that are secure, like Bamyan. He believes that the USA could bring peace and security to Afghanistan in three months by changing the hearts and minds of the people, and suggests that we invest in schools, hospitals, and development in the provinces that are safe. Finally, he points out another mistake of the USA: that we did not use power and force to deal with the war lords and criminals. Instead, we have put war lords in the cabinet and other government positions.

April 2, 2011

An attack on a UN office last night killed some internationals. This attack was a response to the burning of the Quran that took place in the USA. We decide to stay inside all day. I spend part of my day—when we have electricity—reading a student paper. I fly out tomorrow.

April 24, 2011

I've been home from Afghanistan three weeks now. I took seventy-seven pages of notes and have thousands of photos taken by other delegates. The task of making sense of it all feels like a research project. My first presentation will be to the local Veterans for Peace on May 9, so I have to have something ready to present by then.

August 19, 2011

I've given my presentation six times and had two radio interviews about my trip to Afghanistan. My intention for the presentation is to bring my experience with the ordinary people to life in order to inspire my audiences to want to find ways to make a difference in support of the people of Afghanistan. I develop the sense of complexity of the situation throughout the hour-long presentation and offer three statements or conclusions at the end: 1. no more civilian deaths; 2. responsible withdrawal (whatever that means); and most importantly 3. stay in touch with the AYPVs because doing so provides them with encouragement. I ask someone to take a digital photo of each group to whom I present. I also distribute 3x5 cards and invite participants to write messages to the AYPVs. I send the picture and messages to them and hope that these little efforts support them in their big work.

In response to one of those e-mails, Mohammad Jan writes: "Linda Jan, please thank all your friends who wrote lines of encouragement to us." "Jan" is a term of endearment.

Faiz writes: "Bamyan is very green and beautiful now. I go fishing sometimes. Though you are not with me, I feel you are with me. You are in my heart. Be well!"

Final Thoughts

This story of the decade of my life that began September 11, 2001 is complete with my trip to Afghanistan in 2011. Afghanistan was the first country the United States bombed in retaliation for the terrorist attack now commonly known as 9/11, so concluding with my trip there brings my story full circle. However, a year following my trip to Afghanistan, Kathy Kelly calls in late January to ask if I can go to Bahrain for the February 14th anniversary of their Arab Spring uprising. The Bahraini government (a monarchy supported by the United States) and police have been brutally suppressing the people who have been protesting for their democratic rights all year. A human rights leader there is asking foreigners to come witness at this time of the one-year anniversary; the Bahrainis expect that the police will increase the brutality on that day. Kathy's call comes two weeks before the trip, and I realize that similar calls may come at any time. This work may never end, but this memoir has to end at some point. To honor the Bahrain trip and the need to end this memoir, I am including a section about my experience in Bahrain here as part of my Final Thoughts.

After the story of my trip to Bahrain, I identify resources that have supported me in following this path of my heart since September 11, 2001. These resources include my spiritual practices, some particular attitudes, and some strategies. Then I close with some final reflections about this whole journey: What does it all mean, anyway?

Bahrain

I get a call from Kathy Kelly mid-day on January 29, 2012 inviting me to join a delegation to Bahrain. She and Medea Benjamin of Global Exchange had received a request from Nabeel, a human rights leader there requesting a delegation of as many as possible:

> On the 14th of February, thousands of Bahraini people will celebrate the first anniversary of our peaceful uprising. We would expect the regime to be so aggressive and therefore we would like to invite you to come and stay with us as an international observer in Bahrain for a week or two.

Nabeel cautions that they are turning human rights activists and journalists back at the Bahraini airport because they don't want the world to know what is happening. He recommends that we look like rich tourists and preferably arrive in couples because journalists generally travel single. Kathy sends me a link to a very disturbing video called "Bahrain: Shouting in the Dark," which shows the brutal treatment of the protesters and the arrests of the medical practitioners who treated the injured a year ago.

I check my calendar and note that I can get away for a couple of weeks, then watch the beginning of the video and see how horribly the authorities have been treating their own people. I send an email to Kathy: "I want to hear what you all hope we can do by going. Is there a reason to believe that we would be safer than the protesters?" She responds:

> Nabeel is completely convinced that our presence will be protective for people in the villages. I don't think we'd have any particular protection at a big demonstration. My hope is that we could offer some protection and lift the curtain, along the lines of "where you stand determines what you see." I think the US gov't didn't want to "see" the terrible and brutal repression that Bahraini and Saudi authorities inflicted on civilians there.

I feel fear and I'm in resistance, but by the end of the day I have bought my ticket. Later a friend asks why I do this kind of thing. I respond, "Because I can, due to the circumstances of my life, and this is what I was trained to do by the Nonviolent Peaceforce."

I will be meeting another traveler named Brian at the airport in Washington DC. We will enter the country together as a couple. I borrow a classy blouse and vest from a member of my community—my rich tourist costume.

Nabeel had also contacted several people who have been part of the International Solidarity Movement (ISM) in Palestine and one of them is the first to attempt to get into Bahrain. The authorities at the airport do an Internet search and turn him away. Brian and I decide to apply for our visas online rather than waiting to do so when we arrive at the Bahraini airport. We both get our visas and are informed that this does not guarantee entry into the country, but Kathy is not issued her visa online and decides not to risk flying all the way there just to be refused entry. We agree not to make any public announcements about what we are doing until we get into the country.

Bahraini activist and Linda

© Paki Wieland

At the airport in Bahrain, Brian and I are told to sit aside and the officials take our passports into the other room for about twenty minutes. They return and ask us a few questions about our plans while we're in Bahrain. Brian has made a reservation at a five-star hotel. I let him do the talking. I'm prepared with an answer if they should ask why I'm staying a week longer than he is, but they don't ask. They hand us back our passports and wish us a good stay. We have a cab take us to a less expensive hotel where we spend the night.

A young Bahraini activist meets us at a coffee shop the next morning. She gives us mobile phones and takes us to the communication center in the middle of a shopping mall to activate the phones. There she happens to see one of the doctors who was arrested for treating protesters in the initial uprising a year ago. We learn from him that many of those doctors and nurses are still detained now.

We go to Nabeel's house. Paki, a woman who was a teammate in Afghanistan, is already here. I get to stay in a room with her right here in Nabeel's compound. Upon seeing his home, it is immediately clear that Nabeel's family is well off and I don't hesitate to allow all of my expenses (mostly meals) to be covered by them. He has a fondness for rabbits, which are penned at night but hopping all over the compound during the day. Nabeel's wife has an extra laptop that she offers me to use while I'm here. Wireless is available in the house, so I am able to keep up on my email correspondence.

Four ISM activists arrive at the house. They have set up a website called "Witness Bahrain," and have already started making contacts with international media. We are not keeping our plans secret any longer even though there are more delegation members still to arrive in Bahrain.

We prepare to attend a peaceful demonstration. Nabeel hands out gas masks and goggles for us to use and extras to pass out to other protesters in case of tear gas. After lunch at a home in the neighborhood where the demonstration will take place, we walk in small groups to the gathering place.

Nabeel leads the march toward the forbidden site of the Pearl Roundabout, where the uprising took place last year. Soon we are met with tear gas and sound bombs. This is the first time I've experienced tear gas. We run; some of the gas gets into my gas mask and stings my nose and eyes.

While running down one of the alleys, I am forced against the wall. A policeman has grabbed a Bahraini protester behind me. I stay close to the scuffle and mentally prepare myself for third party nonviolent intervention. One of the ISM women is videotaping. She gets into an argument with one of the police. Next to me, Paki has started a friendly conversation with a young policeman. Many of the police are foreigners (mostly from Saudi Arabia), but this one is a pro-government Bahraini. He asks us what we are doing here and Paki says that we are tourists and that we are curious why they are treating the peaceful protesters this way. He encourages us to see other parts of Bahrain. Paki ends up taking his phone number. Two of the ISM women who are confrontational to the authorities get arrested and later deported. The police are videotaping throughout the protest.

Back at Nabeel's house I send an email to my list, my first communication letting the people in my life know that I have come to Bahrain and why. I provide a bit of context: The US has an important base here, has been selling arms and tear gas to the government, and has been ignoring the government's human rights abuses. The people have been feeling very alone and feel relieved that we are here.

We don't want any more of us to be deported before February 14, so the next day we keep a low profile. We stay inside Nabeel's house much of the day; in the evening, we split up to attend separate protests in various villages around the city. As she drives to our destination, the woman who is my Bahraini partner tells me that it's safe to get into a car with other women if we should get separated. We sit out at the end of a street that the residents have blocked. In order to keep the police from moving freely through the neighborhood, they have blocked off many of the streets and it is like a maze driving through the neighborhood. They have distributed maps to all the residents so they can find their way through. Tonight, the authorities never come to this protest. My street buddy seems disappointed, but I feel relieved.

Teargassing the protesters

A huge permitted protest with more than ten thousand people is planned on February 13. Many protesters are planning to break off from the large group, which is on the legal route, to march toward the Pearl Roundabout again—an act of civil disobedience. Nabeel wants to keep the internationals separated so that if some get arrested, it won't be all of us.

I am with a young Bahraini man who is a photographer and we split off with the group that is marching illegally toward the Pearl Roundabout. Soon, the riot police start shooting tear gas and protesters are running. I think that I am keeping my eye on my street buddy while he is taking a photo, but then all of a sudden I realize that the one I was watching is not him and I don't see him anywhere around me. I turn to join those who are rushing the other direction, but I am still looking for my partner. Another local man whom I don't know notices me and encourages me to run. He flags down a car of young women who have one seat available and he quickly pushes me inside. The women don't speak English. They drive me back to the street that is part of the permitted route. It seems safe here so I get out of the car.

I am lucky to find Paki and the Bahraini man who is her street buddy. We watch as the police fire canister after canister of tear gas into the crowd that still remains at the intersection where we had made the turn off the legal route. So now they are gassing the area that had been permitted. They are using tear gas as punishment. The tear gas comes from the USA, and everyone here knows that because the canisters are clearly labeled.

The riot police come in our direction, still hurling tear gas. Again, two locals in a car—strangers to the local man who is with us—invite all three of us into their back seat and drive us to safety. Others in our group of foreign witnesses are also picked up by locals. In one car, locals actually get out in order to make room for my teammates to get into the car and out of danger quickly.

The experience of getting separated from my street buddy scared me. In the evening, I'm thinking that I may not be up for being on the street the next day and I consider staying back to do the job of relaying reports from the street to the media. However, in the morning of February 14, we decide that all of us will be together and visible thus being more obvious, but also risking arrest and deporta-

Protesters running

tion. Since we'll stay together, I decide that I am comfortable with joining the action on the streets. We also decide no one needs to stay behind to do media work.

Together, we local and international activists drive in several cars that are all supposed to be following Nabeel. I am in a vehicle with Brian, Paki, and two local young men. We see police road blocks and dozens of brand new armored personnel vehicles lined up all around the city to keep people from entering from the villages.

We are on the freeway and many people are honking the rhythm (beeep, beeep, beep beep) that means "Down with the king," and giving us peace signs. Suddenly we notice tear gas in the air over the freeway behind us. We had gotten ahead of Nabeel and that is where he decided to get out of his car and start the protest march. We start calling our teammates. I get through to one and she tells me she is arrested. Brian gets through to others who tell him where they are at a coffee shop. The local activist who is driving our car gets going back the other direction, but the freeway exits are blocked. Finally, he decides we will get out of the car on the freeway and he turns the car over to his buddy who was riding in the passenger seat. We walk down from the freeway to the street below and head in the direction of the coffee shop a few blocks away where we hope to meet our teammates. A police vehicle stops us and asks for our passports; we are arrested and we didn't even make it to a protest.

Six of us have been detained: the three of us who were together in our car, and three others who were present at the protest with Nabeel. We wait in a comfortable room with couches, overstuffed chairs, and a wide-screen TV; and chat with female police officers who sit with us while other authorities check our identities in another room. The authorities take us into another room one at a time and tell us why they are canceling our visas. When they accuse me of being involved in an illegal protest, I can't argue; I know they had filmed us that first day. They offer to put us on a flight to London and then from there to our various destinations. The two women who had been arrested and deported that first day had been resistant throughout their arrest and they had been handcuffed behind their backs for the whole seven-hour flight to London—unable to eat, drink water, or go to the toilet. I am worried about being handcuffed like that, so I ask about it and they reassure me that as long as we cooperate they will not have to handcuff us.

I am disappointed to have cut my trip so short and also relieved to be home. That was my scariest adventure yet, and I'm glad that I went. Eleven internationals had gotten into Bahrain in time for February 14 and three others were turned away at the airport. All eleven of us were deported within a week. Nabeel and the other Bahrainis we met felt that our presence did make a difference in terms of how much brutality they faced. We also managed to get media coverage that brought international attention to the situation there. It felt like a success.

Resources

My goal for this writing is to inspire readers to find the courage to listen to their hearts and embark on their own paths. Upon reflection, I identify the resources that support me in following my path and I share them here hoping they might be helpful to others. These resources include my spiritual practices, some particular attitudes, and some strategies.

I recognize that there are many spiritual paths and different practices to pursue for finding and following a spiritual path. For me, the vision quest type experience is a spiritual practice that supports the process of listening for, hearing, and following my inner guidance. Certainly, time alone—be it in prayer, meditation, or walking in nature (to name a few potential practices)—gives the opportunity for that subtle voice within to emerge. My experience is that the inner voice will remain hidden unless invited and encouraged. Besides a vision quest, the spiritual practices I employ during these years in this story include: meditation, free writing, shamanic journeying or self-guided visualization, time in nature, and journaling.

I also identify attitudes of patience, openness, willingness, and trust as particularly helpful. Patience is probably my biggest challenge. Once I see clearly what is needed, I have difficulty understanding how it is that others don't necessarily see it the same way. Furthermore, once I see what needs to be done, I want it to happen now. I feel a sense of urgency about the problems that exist in the world. Yet, I have found that each action happens in its own timing, and though I may be able to influence the timing, I certainly cannot control it.

Openness and willingness are similar and related to each other. I have to be open to hearing the guidance from within and I have to be willing to carry it out. Sometimes that guidance shows up in the form of desire and then an opportunity presents itself in its own timing. After I decide to take advantage of the opportunity, I live with that decision and trust what happens. Some challenges may emerge and I face them. For example, I feel the desire to join Iraq Peace Team. When a trip becomes available during a period that is open on my calendar, I do not hesitate to apply. A challenge emerges—a need to get a new passport in time to join the delegation—and I say to myself, "Well, if I am able to get the passport, I guess that means I am meant to go." In this way, I sometimes get a clear sign externally that leaves me without doubt. Such certainty can be helpful in getting through all the other challenges that might emerge. Being willing to be with, fully embrace, and learn from whatever fears emerge is important also (more on that under strategies below).

The final attitude that seems essential is trust. I have to trust the inner "knowing" or guidance. I have to trust myself to be able to handle whatever situations arise as I follow through on the guidance I have received. I have to trust the organization and the people whom I have joined in the endeavor. And in the end, I have to trust that someone in the world is a little better off due to my activity, even when it isn't obvious that it has made a difference.

Some strategies I identify as helpful in my process are internal strategies such as intention, acceptance, and embracing fears. Further strategies have to do with gaining the support of others.

In my experience, intention is a powerful inner tool. Once I am clear about an intention, then much of the support that I need in order to carry it out begins to "magically" appear. Perhaps that support was already there anyway, but it becomes apparent to me once I have set the intention and so I can access it because of the intention. For whatever reason, it works and what's important is to know about and use the power of intention as a strategy.

A second internal strategy is reducing the "shoulds" in my inner dialogue. Another way of describing this is acceptance—acceptance of whatever is. I accept that this is the situation in the world and that prevents me from going into denial about it. I accept how I feel about the situation in the world and that moves me to need/want to get into some sort of action. Then I accept what emerges that I want to do in relation to what is happening and how I feel about it. I don't see my inner guidance as a "should," but as a calling. The source of a "should" is outside of myself even if I hear it as a voice within. Initially that "should" probably came from a parent, teacher, minister, society, or other authority. A calling comes from within me and is true to my spirit. If I hear myself saying "I should" about anything, I let that be a flag that I may be expecting something of myself that is not true to my spirit.

A final internal strategy is embracing my fears. As I mention in my story, witnessing many participants go through the vision quest while supporting them in facing their "real" fears has helped me to know how to support myself through facing my own "real" fears. I have learned that sometimes fear is important in order to guide me away from real danger, but more often than not fear is imaginary, very susceptible to suggestion, and easily blown out of proportion. I believe fear stops us from doing what we really want to or need to be doing.

I'm not saying to deny fear. I don't believe we can ever do away with it, but I think embracing our fears allows us to learn from them and not be controlled by them. If I recognize a fear, then I can get into relationship with it, and even ask what it has to teach me or what it is wanting of me. I can think about what I will do if that which I fear were actually to occur. When I deny fear, then it is less accessible and thus has more control over me. I am more likely to perceive it as the voice of reality.

Finally, I have several strategies for gaining support of others. I have found that many people believe in the work that I am doing, but their life circumstances are such that they cannot do something similar themselves and they are happy to support me in some way. So it is a matter of getting clear about what I want and then asking for it. Sometimes asking for help is as simple as informing the people in my life about what I am doing and being open to their contributions. The support that Michelle gives me both in my preparation and during the time I am in Israel/Palestine is invaluable. Thinking out loud with her in preparation helps me think what other help I need and whom to ask. Having her at home staying in touch with me on a daily basis while I am away and then communicating with everyone else at home is comparable to an umbilical cord to me. My energy is drained when for part of a day I think that connection isn't there, and I find I can't be fully present until that connection is restored.

Another way to tap into support from others is through support groups. The Living with War support group is helpful in that it keeps the awareness of the US actions in the world in the foreground of my thoughts, so that I don't go into denial about these atrocities and get distracted by "business as usual." My whole community at home supports me in that first trip to Israel/Palestine by sending me off with good thoughts, poems, and a necklace full of blessings.

So What Does It All Mean, Anyway?

The world situation continues to be discouraging. For two and a half years after my trip to Iran I wait and find myself wondering where I next need to focus my time, energy, and resources. With President Obama in office, my inner knowing seems less clear. I finally receive the opportunity to go to Afghanistan and that gives me direction for another period. For a while I think I'm finished with this kind of work. The Occupy Movement takes off in the USA and I am happy to have that happening in my home town. Then I'm faced with the possibility of going to Bahrain and find that I can't refuse. This is my work. I must go because I can.

My experiences have brought me to a deeper and more complex understanding of war, peace, and justice. I evolved from an avid peace activist to a place where I am not ready to promote immediate withdrawal of troops from Afghanistan. I am now sitting with the question about responsible withdrawal. A bigger question is: What are ways of being in relationships with each other within nations and among nations that promote peace and justice for all peoples? Truth and reconciliation, restorative justice, listening to really gain understanding of "the other," and opening my heart in each and every one of my relationships are a few answers.

The vision that draws me forth is a vision of a healthy planet, with sustainable resources; and a world at peace because we all have what we need and no one takes more than needed for him/her at the expense of others. This is a vision that I do believe is possible, and similar to the Afghan Youth Peace Volunteers, I don't expect to see it become reality in my lifetime. Even so, I want to live my life in support of bringing that vision forth in whatever ways I can.

I believe all of us have unique gifts to give, the giving of which brings happiness to ourselves and also contributes to others. The powers of domination in our society thrive by keeping us small and afraid, preventing us from finding and acting on our gifts. It takes listening to the guidance from within us, and willingness to face the unknown and trust whatever chaos may result in the process.

What I found that I have to contribute is an open heart, deep caring, and love for others. I believe that caring and love is present in each of us and we all have that to give, if nothing else.

I want to leave the reader with one final message—to be, be you, and don't let fear get in your way.

Acknowledgments

MY FIRST ACKNOWLEDGMENT MUST GO TO Liz Campbell who encouraged and supported me to begin writing this memoir and continued to provide that encouragement throughout the six years it took to see the writing to completion and begin the publishing process.

I also wish to thank the readers who each went through all or part of the first draft providing essential feedback that helped create a much more reader-friendly version than I could have produced alone: Arlene Houghton, Kay Lambert, Donna Wojtkowski, Carroll Hirsch, Judy Helfand, Joan Linney, Paul Loper, Kati Hoetger, and Angie Sartor. Further for the refinement she provided, I thank Elizabeth Kasl who read the entire second draft. I so appreciate her acute and highly valuable feedback, which she gives in some sort of magical way that encourages me to keep writing. Finally, additional acknowledgment goes to Carroll Hirsch, who read the entire document two more times—once to do copy editing and then once more to provide the final final feedback.

I acknowledge graphic artist Gabriel Graubner and the crew from Cune Press for the beautiful formatting of the book. Also other delegates on each of the trips provided the photos, and children in Palestine provided some drawings. The maps used in this book are based on United Nations maps, so I thank the UN for their use.

Above are the acknowledgments that are due for the actual writing and publishing process, and there are many more acknowledgments due for those who supported me through the experiences that made a memoir worth writing. I must begin with Michelle Crawford who encouraged me to take that first giant scary step of traveling to Israel/Palestine. Next are all the members of Monan's Rill, the intentional community where I live, who gave me their blessings to leave my responsibilities to the community behind for long periods of time, and took care of my house when I was away. My brother Dale Sartor, sister-in-law Judy Winzeler, and niece Angie Sartor also gave their blessings and pretty well kept their fears to themselves so as not to hinder me from doing this that my heart was insisting that I do. Finally, I want to thank all the people that I met along the way who despite my unconsciousness and ignorance of their cultural ways welcomed me with hospitality and grace.

There are also the growing number of people who are on my e-mail listserve. Beginning on my first trip, I started sending regular e-mails to the list. My intention was to reassure everyone that I was safe and the e-mails also gave readers a glimpse of what I was experiencing. The regular e-mails provided the primary data for this memoir. The interest of and replies from the people on the list also provide support to me to continue to do this challenging work.

Notes

1. I want to acknowledge that this book I wrote was before another US citizen named Rachel Corrie was killed in Palestine in 2003 by an Israeli bulldozer driver when she was participating with ISM. Thus that sense of safety that I felt then was illusionary and if her death had already occurred I probably would not have been as bold as I was.
2. Looking back nearly twenty years later, I want to note that she never again works on the needlepoint project.
3. In retrospect, I think this is the most heart-breaking experience for me in Iraq.
4. I go numb and can't even listen to him. I get much of this description later from a report written by my teammate who is a doctor and was able to more fully comprehend what he was saying.

References

Andrews, Ted (1997). *Animal-speak: The spiritual and magical powers of creatures great and small.* St. Paul, MN: Llewellyn Publications.

Ebadi, Shirin with Azadeh Moaveni (2006). *Iran awakening: A memoir of revolution and hope.* New York: Random House, Inc.

Gibran, Kahlil (1968). *The Prophet.* New York: Alfred A Knopf.

Keshavarz, Hahid (January 1, 2008). Interview with Jelve Javaheri: From a reading group to the Campaign for One Million Signatures. *Payvand News.*

Macy, Joanna (1983). *Despair and personal power in the nuclear age.* Philadelphia: New Society Publishers.

Sams, Jamie and David Carson (1988). *Medicine cards: The discovery of power through the ways of animals.* New York: St. Martin's Press.

Sahtouris, Elisabet (2006). Think global, act natural. *Odewire.* Retrieved from http://odewire.com/?s=Sahtouris&sa=Go

Sartor, Linda and Molly Young Brown (2004). *Consensus in the classroom: Fostering a lively learning community.* Mt. Shasta, CA: Psychosynthesis Press.

Storm, Hyemeyohsts (1972). *Seven arrows.* New York: Ballantine Books. pp. 68-85.

Swamy, M.R. Narayan (January 8, 2008). Sri Lanka crisis set to worsen. Al Jazeera.

Further Reading

The Passionate Spies: How Gertrude Bell, St John Philby, and Lawrence of Arabia Ignited the Arab Revolt by John Harte, 2022.

Coming Back to Life: The Updated Guide to the Work That Reconnects by Joanna Macy and Molly Young Brown, 2014.

Dissent: Voices of Conscience by Colonel (Ret) Ann Wright and Susan Dixon, 2008.

Music Has No Boundaries: Bob Marley and the Beatles + Call-in Radio = A Bridge Over Troubled Waters in Israel / Palestine by Raf Gangat, 2022.

Stage Warriors: Women on the Front Lines of Dangerous Drama by Sarah Imes, 2016

Muslims, Arabs & Arab Americans by Nawar Shora, 2022.

The Nonviolence Handbook: A Guide to Practical Action by Michael N. Nagler, 2014.

Apartheid Is a Crime by Mats Svensson 2021.

Waging Peace: Global Adventures of a Lifelong Activist by David Hartsough, 2014.

Credits

Maps

On behalf of the Secretary of the United Nations Publications Board it is our pleasure to grant you permission to reproduce the following UN maps in the forthcoming publication by Linda Sartor entitled: *Turning Fear Into Power: How I Confronted the War on Terror.*

Israel, Map No. 3584 Rev. 2, January 2004
Bahrain, Map No. 3868 Rev. 2, January 2004
Iraq, Map No. 3835 Rev. 5, March 2011
Sri Lanka, Map No. 4172 Rev. 3, March 2008
Afghanistan, Map No. 3958 Rev. 7, June 2011
Iran, Map No. 3891 Rev. 1, January 2004

The above maps are based on UN maps. Our thanks to the UN.

Photos

Note credits are beside each photo. The following key will decipher acronyms used in photo credits:

NP – Nonviolent Peaceforce
NPSL – Nonviolent Peaceforce Sri Lanka
UN – United Nations

Front Cover Photo Credit: On the highway between Kabul and Panjshir one passes Soviet tanks abandoned by the side of the road. This photo was taken March 24, 2011 by Peggy Gish. Back Cover Photo Credit: Linda Sartor by Ken Saltzberg. Uncredited photos from Sri Lanka are by NPSL Teammates. Photos from Palestine by Mats Svensson from his book *Apartheid Is a Crime* (Cune 2021).

Photos from Palestine

Photos by Mat Svensson from *Apartheid Is a Crime* (Cune 2021)

Index

Cune Press

Cune Press was founded in 1994 to publish thoughtful writing of public importance. Our name is derived from "cuneiform." (In Latin *cuni* means "wedge.")

In the ancient Near East the development of cuneiform script—simpler and more adaptable than hieroglyphics—enabled a large class of merchants and landowners to become literate. Clay tablets inscribed with wedge-shaped stylus marks made possible a broad inter-meshing of individual efforts in trade and commerce.

Cuneiform enabled scholarship to exist, art to flower, and created what historians define as the world's first civilization. When the Phoenicians developed their sound-based alphabet, they expressed it in cuneiform.

The idea of Cune Press is the democratization of learning, the faith that rarefied ideas—pulled from dusty pedestals and displayed in the streets—can transform the lives of ordinary people. And it is the conviction that ordinary people, trusted with the most precious gifts of civilization, will give our culture elasticity and depth—a necessity if we are to survive in a time of rapid change.

 Aswat: Voices from a Small Planet (a series from Cune Press)

Looking Both Ways	Pauline Kaldas
Stage Warriors	Sarah Imes Borden
Stories My Father Told Me	Helen Zughaib & Elia Zughaib
Girl Fighters	Carolyn Han

 Syria Crossroads (a series from Cune Press)

Leaving Syria	Bill Dienst & Madi Williamson
Visit the Old City of Aleppo	Khaldoun Fansa
The Dusk Visitor	Musa Al-Halool
Steel & Silk	Sami Moubayed
The Passionate Spies	John Harte
The Road from Damascus	Scott C. Davis
A Pen of Damascus Steel	Ali Ferzat
White Carnations	Musa Rahum Abbas

 Bridge Between the Cultures (a series from Cune Press)

Empower a Refugee	Patricia Martin Holt
Confessions of a Knight Errant	Gretchen McCullough
Nietzsche Awakens!	Farid Younes
Muslims, Arabs & Arab Americans	Nawar Shora
Apartheid Is a Crime	Mats Svensson
Kivu: Journeys in Eastern Congo	Frederic Hunter
Arab Boy Delivered	Paul A. Zarou
The Wealthiest Woman in Afghanistan	Sanaullah Momand
Music Has No Boundaries	Raf Gangat

Cune Cune Press: www.cunepress.com

LINDA SARTOR IN AFGHANISTAN. © Asif

Linda Sartor is a peace/justice activist and an educator based in Northern California. She has been arrested a number of times when protesting atrocities committed by the US, as she says, "in my name with my tax money." She cites, in particular, the development and testing of nuclear weapons and the use of drones for military purposes.

After she saw the US military response to 9/11, she realized that for her participating in protest marches and teaching peace classes in the public schools weren't enough. She was shocked, tormented, and her heart led her to travel to Afghanistan and five other war-torn places described in this book.

During her more regular life, Linda lives in an intentional community, teaches research courses in a master's-in-leadership program, guides vision quest wilderness trips with a non-profit organization, and is the volunteer coordinator for the Peace and Justice Center of Sonoma County.

CPSIA information can be obtained
at www.ICGtesting.com
Printed in the USA
JSHW040708110822
29010JS00007B/4